AF269642

# Nightmare in the Pacific

## The World War II Saga
## of Artie Shaw and His Navy Band

Michael Doyle

University of North Texas Press
Denton, Texas

Permissions:
University of North Texas Press
1155 Union Circle #311336
Denton, TX  76203-5017

The paper used in this book meets the minimum requirements of the
American National Standard for Permanence of Paper for Printed Library
Materials, z39.48.1984. Binding materials have been chosen for durability.

Library of Congress Cataloging-in-Publication Data

Names: Doyle, Michael, 1956- author.
Title: Nightmare in the Pacific : the World War II saga of Artie Shaw and
   his navy band / Michael Doyle.
Description: Denton, Texas : University of North Texas Press, [2024] |
   Includes bibliographical references and index.
Identifiers: LCCN 2024042370 (print) | LCCN 2024042371 (ebook) |
   ISBN 9781574419467 (cloth) | ISBN 9781574419566 (ebook)
Subjects: LCSH: Shaw, Artie, 1910-2004--Performances--Pacific Area. |
   Shaw, Artie, 1910-2004--Health. | United States. Navy--Bandmasters--
   Biography. | United States. Navy Band 501--History. | World War,
   1939-1945--Music and the war. | World War, 1939-1945--Campaigns--
   Pacific Area. | BISAC: MUSIC / Individual Composer & Musician |
   HISTORY / Wars & Conflicts / World War II / Pacific Theater | LCGFT:
   Biographies.
Classification: LCC ML419.S52 D69 2024  (print) | LCC ML419.S52
   (ebook) | DDC 781.65092/21823 [B]--dc23/eng/20240913
LC record available at https://lccn.loc.gov/2024042370
LC ebook record available at https://lccn.loc.gov/2024042371

The electronic edition of this book was made possible by the support of the
Vick Family Foundation.
Typeset by vPrompt eServices.

To Mom and Dad:

Joy Fairchild Doyle and William Curtis Doyle.

She dug Preservation Hall jazz. He served in the
United States Navy.

They made lovely music, together.

# Contents

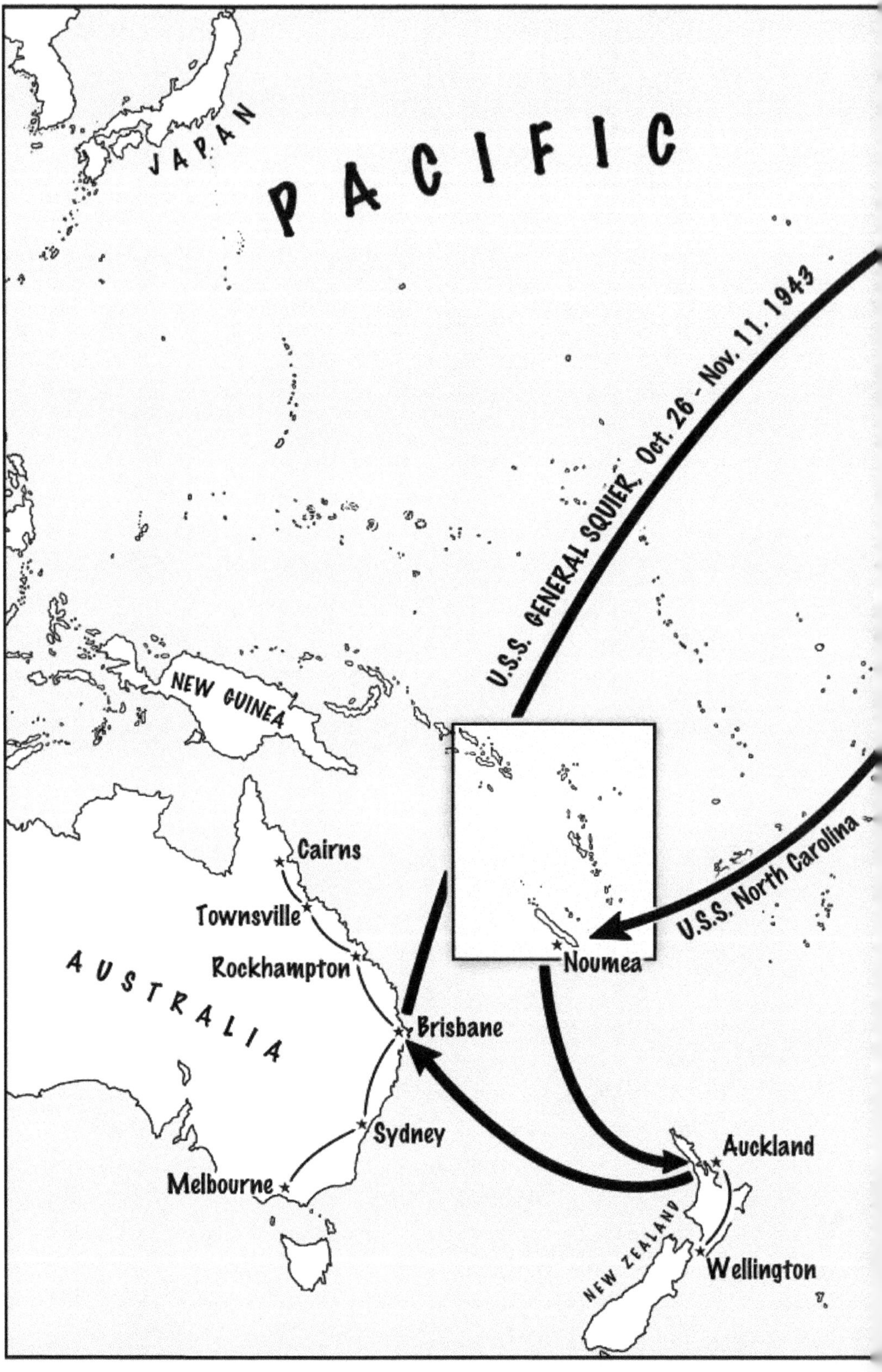

JAPAN
PACIFIC
NEW GUINEA
AUSTRALIA
U.S.S. GENERAL SQUIER, Oct. 26 - Nov. 11, 1943
U.S.S. North Carolina
Cairns
Townsville
Rockhampton
Brisbane
Noumea
Sydney
Melbourne
Auckland
NEW ZEALAND
Wellington

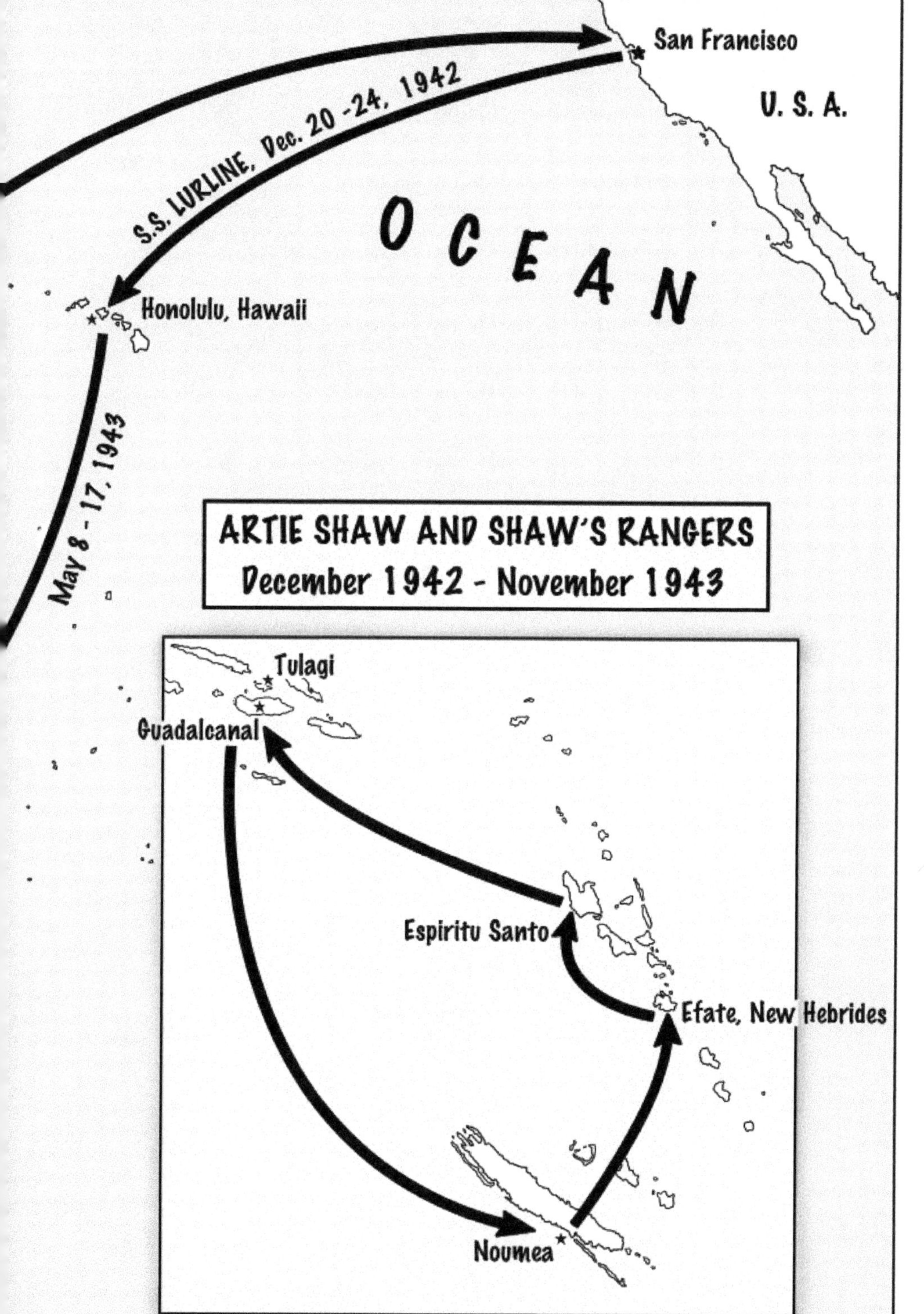
San Francisco
U. S. A.
S.S. LURLINE, Dec. 20 -24, 1942
OCEAN
Honolulu, Hawaii
May 8 - 17, 1943
ARTIE SHAW AND SHAW'S RANGERS
December 1942 - November 1943
Tulagi
Guadalcanal
Espiritu Santo
Efate, New Hebrides
Noumea
Rhys Davies

# Introduction

Artie Shaw split yet again somewhere in the South Pacific.

It may have been Guadalcanal that finally sent him. The air raid sirens there beat the bandleader like an untuned drum. He was only on that fetid island for a week, but it didn't take much to set him off. Shaw was tightly wound long before he came under fire in the navy. Throughout his long and extraordinary life, he would frequently take off at a moment's notice, leaving behind wives, orchestras, and his own troubled past. He would, in his time, abandon religion, music, children, and a dying man struck in a New York City crosswalk.

But first and foremost, Artie Shaw made music like no other. He was, critic Max Harrison observed, "a surpassingly brilliant clarinetist with a particularly beautiful tone and extraordinary control of the top register."[1] Artie wrote, selected, arranged, and performed songs that made people happy and moved them on the dance floor. Commercially, he was as successful as they got. Boosted by his rendition of a Cole Porter song enigmatically entitled "Begin the Beguine," Shaw's band was voted the nation's best in the 1938 *DownBeat* magazine reader's poll. The next year Shaw told reporters he anticipated his net income would be "in the neighborhood of a quarter-of-a-million dollars."[2] Several months before the United States entered World War II, *DownBeat* had touted the "$1,000,000 Talent in Shaw Band" and proclaimed that once it got underway, it "should shape up as the greatest dance combination ever assembled."[3]

Beyond popularity and riches, Artie Shaw sought perfection. He pursued beauty, artistic and otherwise, and more than once attained it. Some thought him a cold and calculating SOB, but in his fierce drive toward his goals, he showed both grit and integrity. As a prewar civilian bandleader, Shaw canceled in the South rather than abide by a contract that required him to seat the Black trumpet player Hot Lips Page at least fifteen feet from the other band members.[4]

And when his country went to war, Artie Shaw went along with it. Maladies, real or concocted, could have exempted him from service. Instead, he donned a well-tailored uniform and did his part. Given a green light by navy leaders, Shaw recruited musicians from among the nation's top bands. They formed a unit designated in official circles as Navy Band 501 but known popularly as Shaw's Rangers. They were a World War II military outfit unlike any other.

Island-hopping across the immense Pacific theater, Artie Shaw's Navy Band lightened the hearts and lifted the spirits of tens of thousands of soldiers, sailors, and civilians. They performed on aircraft carriers, battleships, and any other fighting vessel that would have them. They set up on makeshift stages in airplane hangars and jungle clearings. They lent atmosphere to evening soirees and honored bedside requests in hospitals. They bounced about in bombers, PT boats, army transport planes and mine-laden ships. They spread the gospel of American jazz and influenced a new generation of musicians in Australia and New Zealand. They traveled an estimated sixty-eight thousand miles, carrying a torch the entire way. "It was a different kind of audience," Artie recalled later. "You're playing for kids who were out there, and you were kind of representing a piece of Americana for them out on these desolate islands."[5]

The musicians were awarded no Purple Hearts, but some came home wounded nonetheless. Trumpet player Max Kaminsky would wake up screaming for months. Drummer Dave Tough pickled himself in alcohol.

Some bandmates came to blows; some came to loathe Shaw so much that they half joked about chipping in to pay off whoever would shove him overboard. Artie himself ended his navy service with a medical discharge after a nervous breakdown. "You were playing in these horrible places," Artie recounted. "After a while that got to be a bit much. I mean, I couldn't handle it."[6]

Artie Shaw left much unsaid about his World War II navy service. Some of what he did say was exaggerated, misremembered, or polished into convenient anecdotage fit for a press release. Following his return to civilian life, his management company's flacks declared that "instead of worrying about the world situation or the lack of new ideas in music, Artie spent his time ducking the bombs that fell from Japanese planes." In the South Pacific, the flacks added, "Shaw underwent many attacks, often during a performance."[7]

Artie recognized the hype for what it was, saying that "I don't know the publicity man's Artie Shaw very well. He's a stranger to me, but he does have his uses."[8] Reporters, too, amplified the drama for the sake of a better read. Upon Artie's death one obituary writer would assert that the musician had led his navy band to the South Pacific where "it remained, almost constantly under fire, for eighteen months."[9] Band members offered similarly fanciful accounts of combat and close calls. Kaminsky and Tough, shortly after they left the navy in 1944, regaled civilians with a colorful yarn of how they came close to sinking a Japanese submarine while manning a 40 mm gun aboard a transport ship. "My fingers were itching," Tough recounted. "We were right on top of the Jap. We couldn't have missed."[10]

Artie all but ignored his nearly two-year long navy service in his eccentric 1952 autobiography, *The Trouble with Cinderella: An Outline of Identity*. In the entire 394-page book, he allotted only about 3 pages to the war. The omission, while a biographical shame, may itself have spoken volumes about the experience. "It was a disastrous time. It was a nightmare in my life," Artie said decades later in a 1994 radio interview. "I don't even like to think back on it."[11]

Artie knew all about nightmares. As a child he suffered from them and from assorted "night terrors," a navy doctor later reported. As an up-and-coming bandleader, Artie would conjure an eerie theme song and call it "Nightmare." Even as a high-flying star, Artie kept running as if hounded by night specters. "His life has been characterized by anxiety, strong drives for achievement, insecurity and restless impulsiveness," one navy doctor would report.[12]

The chronic fearfulness did not necessarily hold him back; in some ways it probably drove him upward and onward. On the very day that the Japanese attacked Pearl Harbor, December 7, 1941, Artie impulsively told his band they were all done; it was time to serve. His actual enlistment would take longer than he would later admit, and when he finally did join, he pulled strings so he could recruit a navy band to match any of his million-dollar civilian outfits. He reeled in the subtle and self-destructive drummer Dave Tough. Claude Thornhill, another gifted and complicated man, joined on piano. He lured Max Kaminsky, another former bandmate who ranked fourteenth among all trumpet players in the 1941 *DownBeat* reader's poll. Number fifteen on the trumpet list was John Best, whom Artie was also recruited despite some complicated history between them.[13] He snagged saxophone player Sam Donahue, an up-and-coming bandleader in his own right.

When fully arrayed, Artie's navy band was a powerhouse outfit armed with trumpets, trombones, saxophones, bass, drum, piano, guitar and Artie's clarinet. In San Francisco and Hawaii, Shaw drilled his recruits into musical shape. Finally, in May of 1943, Shaw's Rangers set out on a battleship for the front.

"Practically every type of conveyance was used to carry the band to outlying bases," a navy writer reported in 1945. "Ships, trains, planes, trucks and even oxen carts were used to transport three tons of band properties."[14] The band members liked to say they had been hauled around by every type of warcraft except a submarine. "I think they had that in mind once, but the bass wouldn't slide in, or something," Kaminsky would later say, his tongue, probably, in cheek.[15]

Sometimes squeezing several shows into a single day, Shaw and his men performed well over 150 times throughout the Pacific theater. When it was done, Artie spoke of his service with the stoicism of a combat veteran. "Scared? You bet," he told a *Metronome* magazine reporter. "You just quake and wonder if it's you or the next guy who got hit. You take your battle station and you do your job."[16]

Guadalcanal was the worst. It left its mark, though Artie's band spent barely a week on the island that navy historian Samuel Eliot Morrison pungently observed offered "no natural resources but mud, coconuts and malarial mosquitos."[17] Ground combat had ceased by the time the navy band arrived in July 1943, but the Japanese had not forgotten about the US troops on the island. They sent their regards nightly.

Shaken awake by the evening air raid sirens, Shaw's Rangers would stumble from their tents to their foxholes and huddle there until the all-clear came. They heard explosions and wondered if their own number was up. Artie spoke of being bombed or torpedoed seventeen times during his Pacific tour, a curiously specific detail that drew some skeptical questions, as did some of the more gee-whiz accounts of his band's wartime service.

"He's one of the greatest clarinet players in the world, his band is made up of fine musicians [and] the music they gave out was enjoyed by all who heard," one soldier wrote to *DownBeat* in 1944. "But what hardships did they endure? Being transported by the Navy's finest ships? Making jumps in big Army transport planes?"[18]

The question is as valid now as it was in 1944: What hardships did Shaw's Rangers endure? Put more broadly, what did they go through? What *was* Artie Shaw's World War II navy experience? Complicating the search for an answer is the apparent elusiveness of diaries, correspondence, or key unit records. Artie's complete navy personnel file was apparently among millions lost in a catastrophic 1973 fire at the National Personnel Records Center in St. Louis. His medical file survived, though, shedding light on how he fared under the wartime pressures. Other archived navy documents, contemporary newspaper and periodical accounts, court records, a thoroughgoing band history compiled by Harold S. Kaye, and the assembled papers of public men flesh out more of the story.

Shaw himself endorsed several competing accounts of his navy service, including a specific and defining episode in which he suffered a nervous breakdown. The different versions of this dramatic episode have in common a build-up of pressures that culminated in Artie splitting the scene, just walking away without knowing or caring where he was bound. The basic outline of his nervous breakdown story goes something like this:

Exhausted after one too many air raids, Artie one day took off somewhere in the Pacific, destination unknown. An officer in a jeep saw him wandering.

"He says, 'where [are] you headed, sailor?'" Shaw recalled. He told the officer he didn't know. "He just said, 'get in.' And I started to cry."[19]

The exact timing, scope, and location of Artie's breakdown and walk-off remain ambiguous. That Artie suffered was, however, beyond dispute. One navy doctor who examined him toward the end of the band's Pacific tour recognized right away what he was dealing with. "He presented a typical picture of acute anxiety; he was excitable and depressed," the navy doctor would later report. "He showed many signs of emotional instability. He was suffering from insomnia, loss of appetite and appeared to be under tremendous tension, overcome with countless fears and worries."[20]

At some point following this sobering assessment, Navy Band 501's wartime tour was deemed over. The outfit returned from Australia to the United States, where Artie and two other wrung-out musicians were cut loose from the service. Later, under new leadership, the navy band Artie had organized would take England by storm and achieve at last its full potential.

Artie would go on innovating right up until his abrupt 1954 retirement from the music business at the age of 44. He would spend the next half century pursuing perfection in far-flung fields like competitive target shooting. He would sit for interviews, and he would, when asked, spin a few wartime snippets that never quite did justice to the story of Artie Shaw and his Navy Band 501.

"Oh, that was a saga," Shaw said. "A ridiculous saga."[21]

# Chapter 1

# "All Worked Up Inside"

Artie Shaw would not stand still.

He slipped from one identity to another. Circumcised under the name Avraham Ben-Yitzhak Arshawsky, he was called Arthur by his mother. As a young musician, he tried "Art" on for size. Finally, at the reported insistence of his record company, he became Artie.[1] Raised Jewish, he identified himself as Protestant on a navy medical form.[2] At the time of his enlistment in 1942, Artie was on his fourth marriage. He still had four more to go. He lived in a constant state of churn. "He has, in the past, frequently left good positions and contracts because he was 'all worked up inside' and 'wanted to get away from it all,'" a navy doctor would recount.[3]

Artie dropped out of high school to play music. He left music to write. He skipped town when disciplined by an early boss, later recalling that "by the time I stopped running, I had covered quite a distance."[4] Another night, when Artie belonged to a midwestern-based band, he recounted that "suddenly and impulsively, I decided that I had to get away from Cleveland, right then and there, if only for a few hours." He drove some forty miles through a blizzard to Akron, of all places. There, the restless fugitive sat in the Mayflower Hotel lobby and did nothing at all. Several years later, having reached celebrity status, Artie bugged out yet again.[5] "I decided abruptly [and, as it turned out, prematurely] to make a complete break and go off to try to live my life along new and entirely different lines," Artie said, in a statement that was true more than once.[6]

Artie's abrupt departures became as much a part of his reputation as his intellectual bite and his musical flair. Songwriter Sammy Cahn was one of many whose friendship with Artie eventually dissolved as if splashed by acid, but prior to their split he came to recognize Artie's MO. Cahn recalled that Artie would abruptly "decide he didn't want to perform any more, he wasn't feeling well."[7] The canny bandleader, Cahn said, would then eventually agree to resume playing in exchange for the right to sit out every other set. The negotiating ploy worked precisely because everyone knew Artie was prepared to bail. In 1939 a dance promoter sued him for upward of $10,000 after Artie led his entire band in walking off the stage midshow.[8]

"The fact that Shaw had at least eight different bands between 1936 and 1955 . . . is symptomatic of both his searching and his confusion, and ultimately of his inability to find what he was looking for," jazz scholar Gunther Schuller observed.[9] Assessing him in 1944, a three-member navy medical board would note that back in 1939, "at the height of success in the popular music field, he impulsively gave up his orchestra and went to Mexico, sacrificing contracts worth half-a-million dollars."[10]

Toward his fans, Artie had mixed emotions. He split from them too, even as he craved acclaim. Fame was not simply bestowed upon him; it was something he chased after and seized with both hands. Of all the Artie Shaw young-man-in-a-hurry episodes, the most perfectly framed was his oft-told account of the time early in his career when he and a friend were walking in New York City's Central Park. It was dusk, or perhaps a bit later. Together the two young strivers saw the lights gleam from the apartments of the Upper West Side's toniest domiciles. "One of these days," Artie recalled vowing, "every one of those people up there, behind every one of those windows, is going to know my name."[11]

He attained his goal, though that did not quench his thirst. The fans bought his records, packed his dance halls, voted him number one. They paid for his fancy cars and his sharply tailored suits. They screamed his name and warmed his bed. But Artie aspired to be more than just commercially successful. He was not a hack but an artist, and so the same fans that cheered him eventually repulsed him as they craved more of what he had already moved beyond. Altogether, Broadway gossip columnist Louis Sobel wrote in September 1942, Artie was an "impetuous gentleman who juggled his crown with utter disdain, abdicating every other fortnight."[12]

Even the bandleader's navy enlistment entailed an abrupt withdrawal, a walking away from the stage and into his nation's service. At least, that's the way Artie would later cast it.

On Sunday, December 7, 1941, Artie's latest civilian outfit was on the last afternoon of a four-day run at the Metropolitan Theater in Providence, Rhode Island. Artie had rolled out this configuration earlier in the year. It included a large string section, some seasoned stage veterans like sax man Les Robinson and a 23-year-old singer formerly with the Glenn Miller Orchestra, Paula Kelly. It was a mark of how far Artie had come that he now employed as his road manager a man, Austin Wylie, in whose Cleveland orchestra he had once played. Between his live shows, his record sales, and his occasional movie appearances, Artie was reportedly earning upward of $250,000 a year. A *Billboard* survey of college students in 1941 placed his orchestra among the nation's top favorites. Even some of the critics who had typecast him as an arrogant SOB applauded his stage presence that was on display in an early October 1941 appearance at The Palace in his old Cleveland stomping grounds. "Forgetting the maestro's high-hatted appearance two years ago," *Variety* reported, Cleveland fans saw an Artie who was "more affable and displaying more naturalness than he ever did before."[13]

In the run-up to the Providence show, Artie had led his troupe through the familiar but still grueling circuit of one-night gigs that could run musicians ragged. In October their unrelenting itinerary took them from the Collinsville Park Ballroom in Illinois to Memorial Hall in Joplin, Missouri; the Pla-Mor Ballroom in Lincoln, Nebraska; the Surf Ballroom in Clear Lake, Iowa; and the Prom Ballroom in St. Paul, Minnesota. In Oklahoma City the band made an October 18 appearance at the Municipal Auditorium, where it was reported that six hundred seats had been "reserved for colored fans." The Oklahoma City show was a homecoming for a 33-year-old Black trumpet player in the band named Oran Thaddeus "Hot Lips" Page, and it was also another illustration of Artie's progressive instincts. Oklahoma City's *Black Dispatch* newspaper noted approvingly the bandleader's "liberal attitude" and his readiness to "jam with sepia cats at any time."[14]

Back on the East Coast after their midwestern grind, Artie and his band faced a full house at the Metropolitan in Providence for the December 7 afternoon show. Artie's band that day was part of a broader revue that included comedic interludes, jugglers and dancers. "I went back in the wings while a dance act went on," Artie recalled four decades later. "The stagehands' radio was on, and we were hearing a hysterical announcer talking about the [Japanese] having bombed Pearl Harbor."

CBS radio broke into its broadcast of a New York Philharmonic Orchestra performance to report the attack at about 2:35 p.m. EST. The Mutual Broadcasting System reported it at about the same time. Backstage at the Metropolitan, there was much Artie didn't yet understand. Pearl Harbor, he thought, sounded like a sleepy isle somewhere out in the South Pacific.

"I had to go back out on stage. Just before I went out, I got a note from the manager: 'Please announce that all military personnel are to report to their bases immediately,'" Artie recalled. "So I went out onstage and did that, and about three-quarters of the house got empty." Seeing the young men depart for war triggered a kneejerk response. Artie turned to alto saxophone player Les Robinson, who was in the first row. "I said, 'Les, pass the word, two weeks' notice,'" Artie recalled. "Total impulse."[15]

Robinson had a comfortable relationship with Artie. They had played together between 1937 and 1939, with Robinson handling the lead sax duties on the smash hit "Begin the Beguine." He had rejoined Artie's reformed orchestra again earlier in 1941. Decades later, Robinson echoed Artie's recollection of the December 7, 1941, show with the bandleader breaking the news just as the band was about to swing into "Stardust."

"Artie turned to me, and said, 'give the band two weeks' notice,'" Robinson recounted, "and I turned around and [said] 'two weeks, we're out of here.' So he broke the band up.'"[16]

As he would periodically later recall it, Artie then wasted no more time on peacetime frivolities. "Three weeks later," Artie told radio interviewer Terry Gross, "I was . . . enlisting in the navy. I just felt that there was no place for me as a civilian. Had to be part of it."[17]

# Chapter 2

# Taking Off

The only son of Harold and Sarah Arshawsky was born May 23, 1910. Harold, a native of Russia, and Sarah, born in Austria, had been married the year before. They called their child Arthur, the father garbling the name in what the embittered son would recall as a guttural Yiddish accent. Harold failed sequentially on New York City's Lower East Side as a portrait photographer and as a tailor, with his beleaguered wife, Sarah, the seamstress. When all else failed, the family retreated to New Haven, Connecticut, where they might start over. In New Haven, Artie wrote, "I learned what it means to be a Jew." And not in a good way.[1]

His new classmates, Artie would recall, threw slurs as if they were dirt clods when they heard his alien last name. Rather than fight outright, Artie said he "drew into a little shell, a coat of armor of outer toughness, inside which I tried to conceal my feelings."[2] At the age of 13, he found his weapon at a theater on New Haven's Church Street. A band was playing, and a saxophone player decked out in a natty blue-and-white striped blazer preened by the footlights near where young Artie sat, agog. The saxophonist played a tune called "Dreamy Melody" on his shiny gold instrument.

"Well, sir," Artie wrote. "That did it."[3]

He wanted that shine.

"Suddenly it popped into my addled head that if I could manage to get hold of one of those complicated-looking gadgets and learn to play the thing, I too could be doing what this lucky fellow was doing. At the time, it seemed to be the ideal version of any Good Life I could imagine," Artie wrote.[4]

With the money Artie earned from a deli job, he bought a used saxophone for forty dollars and began practicing until his mouth bled.[5] While his rival, Benny Goodman, born a year earlier, was receiving paternal encouragement for his own developing musical interests out in Illinois, Artie received either indifference or grief from his own father right up until the time Harold Arshawsky split for the West Coast when Artie was about 14.

"Just got up and left," Artie said. "No more money. No more nothin'."[6]

Fatherless, for all intents and purposes, Artie kept practicing like he was possessed. By the time he was hired in 1925 at the age of 15 to play alto saxophone in the New Haven–based Johnny Cavallaro Orchestra, he had begun calling himself the less ethnic-sounding Art Shaw. "That's right," Artie acknowledged, "I was ashamed of my name."[7] He would later further revise his first name to Artie at the suggestion of a record company executive who, the story goes, thought that Art Shaw, when said fast, sounded like a sneeze. By the age of 16, the young man left school to play music full-time.

Artie passed through several bands and plenty of hard times, later telling a reporter that in Kentucky he had once slept in a park, washed his clothes in a fountain, and gone without food two days running. In Florida, Artie recounted, he once came to the small dance hall "straight from the beach and played in a bathing suit."[8] Starting in 1926 the teenager played in several Cleveland-based bands, first in one led by violin-playing Joe Cantor and then in Austin Wylie's outfit. Wylie oversaw a peppy and well-regarded orchestra that toured regionally in addition to holding down a regular gig at the Golden Pheasant, a Chinese-American restaurant with a capacious dance floor. His orchestra members decked out in bow ties, Wylie gained a following for what one enthusiast called an "ultra-modern way of arranging and playing the latest popular musical hits."[9]

In Cleveland Artie honed his skills as both player and arranger. Laboriously, he would spread pieces of paper around his cramped apartment's floor. Armed with a pencil and eraser, the teenager would jot notes first on one page and then another, doggedly moving onward until he had gone so far that he had forgotten his beginning. He would also absorb the lessons offered by the likes of Fletcher Henderson, a Black piano-playing bandleader and arranger with a knack for finding young talent, and Paul Whiteman, a three-hundred-pound showman who brought with him the astonishing young cornet player Bix Beiderbecke.[10]

Finally, Artie also found a peer he could talk to.

Claude Thornhill was about two years older than Artie, born in Indiana in 1908 to a coal-miner father and a church-organ-playing mother who believed fervently in her one and only son's great potential. Artie would describe the family as "American Gothic," without elaborating other than to recount that upon his death, Claude's overbearing mother supposedly said, "I miss my Claudie, he brung us fame."[11]

Claude had perfect pitch and an imperfectly recollected personal history. Profiles written once he hit the big time routinely stated that Claude had studied at the Cincinnati Conservatory of Music and the Curtis Conservatory of Music in Philadelphia. A reporter for *Coda* magazine looked into the matter and determined there were no records of Claude attending either conservatory. His navy enlistment form lists his education as being limited to three years of high school.[12] Claude, like Artie, learned his music on the job. He went from playing the calliope on an Ohio River showboat as a teenager to spots in his first big bands, starting with Barney Zeeman's Kentucky Kernels. In time Claude would leave behind the corny alliterations and join the higher-minded likes of Benny Goodman. He also took to arranging.[13]

Claude was playing with a traveling band in the summer of 1929 when he heard Austin Wylie's orchestra work out on one of Artie's arrangements. He thought it excellent, and he told Artie so. Gratified, Artie asked his new acquaintance to play some piano. It was then Artie's turn to be impressed.

The two young men ended up talking all night. "He must have been pretty bottled up too, at the time, for he seemed to need the talk as much as I did," Artie recounted, "We parted at daylight. Although I had only known him for one night, I felt far closer to him than anyone I had ever known in my life before."[14]

Artie managed to get Claude hired as an arranger and second pianist for the Austin Wylie outfit, and they eventually shared a small apartment in Cleveland's Winton Hotel, conveniently close to the Golden Pheasant. Theirs was a meeting of minds that would finally crack in wartime.

Artie escaped the Midwest after he entered, on a whim, a nationwide contest to affix a title to a novelty foxtrot-style song touting the glories of aviation. Artie did not win the national song title contest; that honor went, inexplicably, to the author of "Big Boy Jess of the Western Air Express." But along with a handful of other finalists who had produced the likes of "Sky Cruisin's my Choosin'" and "Goodbye Train Folks, Hello Plane Folks," Artie was a regional winner for his title of "Song of the Skies" and the 150-word essay that accompanied it. That earned him a trip to the West Coast in September of 1929.[15]

Southern California was a revelation, with its blue skies and movie star allure. Musically, Artie took note of an orchestra called Irving Aaronson and His Commanders. Artie didn't think much of the group's stage antics at the Roosevelt Hotel's Blossom Room, but he also noticed how Hollywood's luminaries welcomed Aaronson and his crew of merrymakers. Years later he would recall how he "stared down glassy-eyed at such mythological folk as Jean Harlow, Joan Crawford, Charlie Chaplin, Richard Barthelmess, William Powell."[16] Two of Artie's friends from the New Haven days were among those making merry, and they urged him to consider joining the Commanders on an upcoming tour. The group's stage presentation wasn't really Artie's style, but the schlock reliably sold out the room. Though embarrassed by the group's horseplay, he was encouraged by his girlfriend at the time, Betty Goldstein, to seize the moment.[17] "I felt I would blow my top if I didn't get out of the rut I was in," Artie explained.[18]

With Artie as a member, Irving Aaronson and His Commanders hit Chicago in the sweltering summer of 1930. In late August Artie was informed first that his father had been hospitalized in Los Angeles, and then, in a follow-up telegram, that he had died on August 30. The father was 50 years old at the time of his death, a divorced tailor lodging along with one other boarder and a young family of four.

Artie's first reaction shocked the bandmates who brought him the telegram. He "laughed and laughed," Artie later wrote, until tears came to his eyes. His bandmates were aghast, wondering what kind of cold-hearted creature would laugh at the news of his own father's death. Once alone, Artie said his mind ran wild. He had once hated his father, the loser who had abandoned his family, but the rage became tempered by something close to pity. Above all, Artie recalled, "there was a sense of something lacking in me, a feeling of guilt at not feeling more."[19]

From Chicago the Commanders moved on to New York City. The orchestra opened at the Beacon Theater on October 10. Five days later, Artie's single-minded drive to the top brought disaster.

# Chapter 3

# Young Man in a Hurry

Artie was in love.

Betty Goldstein, his girlfriend, was from the small city of Conneaut, Ohio, about sixty-five miles northeast of Cleveland. Her father, Max, was a grocer and first-generation American whose father had emigrated from Russia. Betty was a knockout—a combination, Artie would later write, "of Eve, Lilith, Delilah, and Helen of Troy." Her eyes, he recalled, "were as blue as a cornflower, but with depths and shadings that no cornflower on earth has, or could ever have." Her hair was "the color a field of new wheat might have if it were powdered with pale gold-dust." In other words, Artie said, she was "breath-takingly, magically, deliciously, ravishingly lovely."[1]

They had met in Ohio when Betty was 16 and Art was 17. She followed him to New York City when Irving Aaronson and the Commanders went there for the October 1930 run of shows. Betty took a room at the Hotel Marseille, at 103rd Street and Broadway, while Art listed his residence as 2482 Grand Concourse in the Bronx.[2]

On Wednesday, October 15, the couple was about ten blocks from Betty's hotel in a car still affixed with its red six-number Ohio license plates. At the intersection of Broadway and 91st Street, their car hit a pedestrian. Artie was driving, and he didn't stick around. "The car sped from the scene, according to police, who obtained its number from bystanders," the *New York Times* reported.[3]

The injuries proved fatal for the pedestrian, a single, 60-year-old Baltimore native named in initial newspaper accounts as George Woods. He had reportedly been working as a chef aboard a Sag Harbor–based yacht. In his pocket police reported finding a letter indicating he had just inherited $9,000. He was transported about ten blocks to what was commonly known as the Reconstruction Hospital, a bluntly named facility that specialized in the treatment of industrial accidents and disease. There, the unfortunate pedestrian was pronounced dead.

Two hours after the accident, police discovered Artie's car on Columbus Avenue and Patrolman Edward Garvey arrested both Artie—identified as Arthur in newspaper accounts—and Betty on suspicion of homicide. They were each released on a $1,000 bond while police tried to sort things out. An October 24 date was set for the couple to be brought before Magistrate Alexander Brough, a veteran of more than fifteen years on the bench who oversaw what reporters called Homicide Court.[4]

Artie was 20 years old, a musical backbencher of no real repute, and the brief accounts of the hit-and-run incident were buried deep inside several New York City newspapers. The articles were also inaccurate. The official death notice subsequently identified the victim as George W. Wood, not Woods, and he had led quite a life before Artie's apparent negligence cut it short. A member of a large family, Wood worked in jobs variously described in census records and city directories as "ship steward" and "mariner." He had sailed several times around the world as a civilian, and during World War I he had served first aboard a Canadian destroyer and then as a crewman on the USS *Piqua*, a converted yacht that battled German submarines off the French coast in 1918. "As Sherman said, 'war is hell,'" Wood wrote an acquaintance in April 1918."[5]

Both of his parents had died years before, making the source of the reported inheritance check found in his pocket one of the many mysteries fogging the incident. Wood left behind three sisters and two brothers, all single and, according to the 1930 Census records, all living together in Baltimore.

Artie maintained he didn't stop after the accident because he thought he had hit a traffic stanchion. Several decades later he insisted that Wood had "stepped off a curb in such a way that it was utterly impossible to avoid hitting him. Anyone who happened to be driving in that place and at that time would have hit him. It just happened to be me."[6] The statement that Wood had "stepped off a curb in such a way" all but conceded that Artie had known from the start that he had hit a man and not, as he initially told police, a stanchion. Jazz writer Gene Lees, who had extended conversations with Artie half a century later, recounted that Artie acknowledged he was "speeding in his car down Broadway" when the accident occurred. This would have been in character for a man who drove his whole life like a young man in a hurry.[7] Speed limits were for others, cars were for passing, and reckless abandon got him where he needed to be. As he put it later in life, "I was nobody from nowhere, and I had to elbow people aside to get anywhere."[8]

Artie's devil-may-care driving prompted white-knuckled recollections, including one from his second son. Jonathan Shaw recounted holding on for dear life as their car "careens along the blurry white lines at ninety miles per hour, and suddenly I feel like a helpless little kid again sitting on Mr. Magoo's Wild Ride at Disneyland. I look around and realize there's nothing to do but pray." Artie was 92 years old at the time.[9]

Following the alleged hit-and-run, the subsequent "legalities and litigations," as Artie called them, dragged on. Criminal charges were eventually dropped, but individuals that Artie described in his autobiography as the "plaintiffs"—presumably Wood's surviving siblings—filed what he described as an $80,000 civil lawsuit. Because Artie was still a minor, the lawsuit reportedly also named his mother, Sarah Arshawsky, as a defendant. This would eventually lead, he wrote, to a bankruptcy filing. Even more than two decades later, Artie acknowledged that writing about the incident stirred "a strong emotional involvement and a set of painful sense-memories."[10]

The relationship with Betty did not survive. She ended up moving back to Ohio, where in March 1935 she would marry and settle into a private life.[11]

Artie, stuck in the city while the hit-and-run matters dragged on, lived for a time with his mother in what he described as "a cubbyhole of a flat way out on the Grand Concourse, where she took in a little sewing to keep us in groceries."[12] He was pretty much a lost soul. His biographer Tom Nolan recounted that Artie "slunk around the city at night on his own, riding the subway for hours and falling asleep until the car reached the end of the line, then making the return trip."[13]

The young musician kept his ears open, though, and in time he made his way to Harlem. There, one night he found himself outside a basement joint on 133rd Street named the Catagonia Club but known popularly as Pod's and Jerry's. The place typically opened at midnight and offered red-and-white checkered tables where customers could sit and order pig's feet, rice, and chicken and listen to what was really happening. Standing outside, Artie heard some wild piano playing by a man he came to know as the derby hat–wearing, cigar-smoking stride piano ace named Willie "The Lion" Smith. Artie described the moment much later in his lightly fictionalized short story "Snow White in Harlem, 1930." "My God! What in the world was that?" Artie's short-story alter ego thought. "He had never heard anything like it. Whoever the hell it was playing the piano in there, the son-of-a-bitch had to be some kind of a real wild man."[14]

Born in 1893, Smith had reportedly earned his leonine nickname while serving during World War I with the 15th Infantry Regiment and the Army's 350th Field Artillery Band. After the war he had toured the country before returning to Harlem, where he established himself as a flamboyant showman with a quick temper and no patience for fools.[15] Artie earned his regard, and Willie the Lion subsequently welcomed him into his den and escorted him around the city's subterranean jazz scene. Artie described Willie as his "open sesame" into this new world.[16]

Artie eventually secured his musician's union card and began making connections, picking up work here with the Dorsey Brothers for a weekend college gig and there with the Red Nichols group for a hotel gig. In August of 1931 he found some security with a seat in the CBS radio orchestra. For a 21-year-old musician, this was a significant accomplishment, and a sign of both his talent and his rigorous practice regime.

In 1933, at the age of 23, Artie walked away from music with the purchase of twenty-five rural acres near Erwinna, Pennsylvania. He intended to write a novel. He plugged away—typing like mad, selling firewood for extra cash, and entertaining the occasional visitors—until he returned to music as a sideman in early 1934. The upwardly striving high-school dropout stretched himself thin, taking courses at Columbia University while building his reputation as a creative sideman. He played with any number of bands and seemed a constant presence in recording studios. He really began standing out when, for a May 24, 1936, swing music show at the Imperial Theater in the heart of New York City's theater district, he composed a three-minute-and-forty-nine second work for string quartet, clarinet, and rhythm section called "Interlude in B-flat."[17]

Short as it was, the piece was acclaimed for its musicality as well as its novelty. It earned the young composer invitations to lead his own band and record. On August 21, 1936, the up-and-comer appeared at the Hotel Lexington, located at 48th Street and Lexington Avenue, under the name "Art Shaw and his Orchestra." They were playing in the hotel's Silver Grill, an oval-shaped room with good acoustics and its tables arrayed on several tiers.

"Shaw, a clean-cut looking chap, presents a pleasing, reserved front," critic George T. Simon wrote in *Metronome*, adding that "he quite obviously knows what dancers want." Simon gave Artie's band a grade of an A-minus, with the prescient observation that "it's going to be interesting to hear how this outfit will sound in about a half-year from now."[18]

For a show at New York City's Silver Grill, to be broadcast over CBS radio, Artie was pressed to quickly compose an introductory number, a theme with which the band would be identified. Benny Goodman invited the audience in with "Let's Dance," saxophonist Charlie Barnet had "Cherokee," and Count Basie came on to "One O'clock Jump," among others. Now, Artie needed his own signature piece. He summoned from somewhere deep inside an eerie two-minute-and-fifty-second revelation that he would call "Nightmare." In the library of big band theme songs, there's nothing else quite like it.

"I wrote it because I felt it had an odd sound that might attract people's attention," Artie told an interviewer decades later. "People were being besieged by bands in those days. Every time you turned on the radio after 9 or 10 p.m., all you got was bands playing remote broadcasts. I figured that when I came in it might as well be with something that caught people's attention."[19]

That it did. Artie wrote out the first sixteen bars of the piece; the rest, he recalled, was improvised up until the finale reprised the first eight bars. The tune was open-ended, so an orchestra could squeeze it or stretch it, depending on time constraints. By Artie's account, the day after he composed it, "When somebody asked me for a title, 'Nightmare' sounded right." Tony Pastor, a singer and tenor saxophonist who performed with the Shaw band in 1936 and 1937, said he was the one who thought of the name after hearing Artie play the piece at 4:00 a.m. the morning of its conception.

It was about this same time that Artie, by his later recollection, received an early and disquieting lesson in the bottom line of popular music. A venue manager berated him for delusionally thinking his job was to play music. "If you want to take your pants down on that goddamn bandstand every night and take a crap up there, and if people will pay to come here and see you do it, I'll pay you to take a crap up there every night," Artie quoted the venue manager as saying.[20] Set straight, Artie and his band hung in at the Lexington for six weeks before moving on to a succession of colleges and other venues before he finally disbanded his outfit in early 1937. Advertisements still billed him as "Art Shaw and his Orchestra" until in the late summer and early fall of 1938 Victor Records began using the name "Artie Shaw" on the records he was making for its Bluebird label.

The name change did nothing to relieve the pressure on Artie as he juggled myriad payroll, lodging, transportation, and personnel obligations. He argued with agents, musicians, and bookers, dickered with dance hall managers, and stayed awake night after sleepless night. The race to the top was a marathon punctuated by the nightly ballroom sprints. The June 22, 1938, issue of *Variety* itemized one illustrative itinerary that started June 25 at the Philmont Country Club in Philadelphia. The band then traveled 140 miles to Norwalk, Connecticut, followed by a 360-mile haul to Johnstown, Pennsylvania. From there it was another 215 miles to Parkersburg, West Virginia, and then 276 miles to Charlestown, West Virginia before the band hit the final 172-mile stretch, concluding July 2 at the popular Sunnybrook Park in Pottstown, Pennsylvania.

"I was a wild man, a crazy man," Artie recalled, adding that "it was one big, long battle, one big, long rat race, with me as the head rat. And talk about tension! It was about this time I began to develop a little thing called migraine."[21]

He dosed himself first with aspirin and then, when that no longer sufficed, with codeine-loaded Empirin. The underlying stresses, though, remained untouched. If anything, they became more intense. Goodman, whose musical rivalry with Shaw was both real and overhyped by reporters, had seized attention on the night of January 16, 1938, when he led the first jazz concert at New York City's venerable Carnegie Hall. It was a gutsy play, introducing swing into the hallowed halls of the philharmonic; famously, trumpet player Harry James quipped that it made him feel like a whore in church. But boosted by the imprimatur of impresario Sol Hurok, the concert sold out all 2,760 seats in the hall and the atmosphere was charged as Goodman kicked the show off with "Don't Be That Way." He then offered up a jazz smorgasbord that included ballads, small ensemble pieces, a jam session, and an overview of what the program billed as "Twenty Years of Jazz."

Though the audience cheered the performers on for two encores following the concluding "Sing, Sing, Sing," some music critics shrugged. The Yale-educated critic Miles Kastendieck summed up swing the next day as either "savage music" or "by its very nature formless," and he quoted an unnamed Carnegie Hall usher as saying the jazz was "all right for the evening, but give me the symphony orchestras for a longer period of time."[22]

Artie rebounded when he came upon a song from a floundering Cole Porter musical comedy called "Jubilee." He was intrigued by what he called "a kind of Latin beat" to the song, called "Begin the Beguine." In the summer of 1938, Artie worked up an arrangement with Jerry Gray, a man who played a key role in Artie's rising reputation. Born Generoso Graziano, Gray first teamed up with Artie as a violin player when he was 20. It was at Artie's suggestion that he changed his name to escape any perceived ethnic taint, and it was with Artie that he developed into a fine arranger. He would later end up leaving Artie and joining Glenn Miller.[23] Dennis Spragg, author of the definitive biography of Miller's military service, observed that Gray's success with Miller contributed to Artie's harsh put-downs of the trombone-playing bandleader. But before their relationship frayed, Artie Shaw and Jerry Gray made some magic together.

The piece that Gray and Artie worked up and recorded on July 24, 1938, at the storied Victor Studio on East 24th Street in New York City was initially shrugged off as a throwaway. It was the B-side to the presumed front-runner, a little number with vocals by singer Tony Pastor called "Indian Love Song."[24] "I had no idea it was going to zoom," Artie recalled, adding that it was "the other side of a record that we thought was going to be the big one."[25]

Suddenly, it seemed, Artie was famous. Photographers and autograph hunters dogged him. Minions met his every demand. *Life* magazine devoted a three-page spread in its January 23, 1939, issue to the musician that it proclaimed as the newly crowned king of swing. Frenzy, not music, seemed the point, with photos showing jitterbuggers dancing atop tables at the Hotel Lincoln. At a subsequent show, dozens of hopped-up kids jumped the stage at New York City's Paramount Theater and began jitterbugging in such an undulating mass that Pastor couldn't make his way to the microphone to sing.[26] The next month, at a popular Pittsburgh venue called Willows, *Variety* reported that "the swing-slammers were going through the eenie-meenie-minie-mo of ecstasy, rocking the balcony and yelling so wildly Shaw's announcements as M.C. couldn't be heard."[27]

The pressure took a toll. In April of 1939, rumors were flying around the entertainment world about Artie's condition, with columnist Karl Krug declaring midmonth that "Swing Master Artie Shaw's nervous breakdown will have him bedded in his Manhattan home for three months."[28] Krug added that this would cause Artie to miss a string of dates at the Palomar Ballroom in Los Angeles. Other reporters insisted that the buzz about Artie's ill health was all wrong and that the six-week run set to start April 19 was still on.

The place had quite a daunting legacy to live up to. Back in August of 1935, Benny Goodman and his orchestra had landed at the Palomar following what seemed to be a disappointing cross-country tour. They were surprised by exuberant crowds that had been primed by his "Let's Dance" radio performances, sponsored by the National Biscuit Company's Ritz Crackers. The Palomar audience really let loose once Goodwin uncorked the hottest arrangements in his music library, and the cheers followed him back to New York. Historian David W. Stowe called this the "conventional account" of the beginning of the swing era, and though he noted the era's origins went well beyond a single show, it was a fact that the Palomar had a history that might daunt any striving young musician, especially one who, like Artie, was making his first appearance at the storied venue.[29]

As he took the stage, Artie was feeling under the weather. He had recently been treated with a potent medication for strep, but he would not give himself a moment's rest. Artie's body could not match his willpower, and he collapsed. He was out cold for five days, his condition cloaked in a secrecy that was shadowed by columnist Walter Winchell's April 24 report that his condition was "grave."[30] "I was plenty frightened when they stretched me out on an operating table and began pumping other people's bloods into my veins," Artie admitted, adding that while "a number of magazine and radio polls had elected me King of Swing, the bugs inside of me had no respect for royalty."[31]

His band continued at the Palomar Ballroom without him until Artie returned to the stage weeks later with a new piece sardonically entitled "One Foot in the Groove." He also unburdened himself about all the hubbub when he talked with his characteristic candor to *New York Post* "Reporter at the Play" columnist Michael Mok in September 1939. "I'm interested in making music," Artie told the columnist. "Autograph hunters? To hell with them! My advisers tell me . . . that these people made you. I tell them if I was made by a bunch of morons, that's just too bad."[32]

"Before . . . when we were not in demand, we had time to rehearse, prepare things, create nice effects," Artie told Mok. "But they won't let you stay at the top. They won't give you a chance to breathe. . . . And I don't like the crowds," Artie added. "I'm not interested in giving the people what they want. I'm interested in making music."[33]

This did not play well.

Having a reputation as being aloof and intellectual was one thing. With Artie it was all part of the package, but he seemed to carry it too far.

Advertising agency representatives in late September summoned Tom Rockwell, head of Artie's booking agency, General Amusement Corporation, to warn of "letters it was getting from jitterbugs complaining about Shaw's display of sullenness" and adding that "while temperament was okay in its place, Shaw was not wise in letting these things happen."[34]

A Labor Day weekend misadventure in Buffalo showcased the tensions. The city's Crystal Beach Ballroom had booked Artie and his band, which included, the *Buffalo News* reported, "girl singer Helen Forrest." Ballroom manager Harold Austin promised there would be a "diversified offering of sizzling dance rhythm and romantic melodies," but on the night in question Artie tried everyone's patience as he showed up an hour and a half late. Some 2,500 restive fans grew increasingly agitated until the star finally showed and got the ball rolling. But after a short set of ninety minutes, Artie left the stage, done for the night. While a backstage dispute over the band's fee dragged on, angry fans who had paid one dollar for admission made such a racket that police were summoned to calm the waters. Artie split, leaving behind chaos in his wake. "At an early hour this morning they still were yelling, but with a lessened volume and with little hope of getting more than the hour and a half of dancing," the *Buffalo Courier Express* reported.[35]

Calling his own fans "morons" definitely went too far. Artie assured another reporter that the "moron" diagnosis only applied to 5 or 6 dancers out of a crowd of 2,000. That hardly calmed the waters. With a bit of cheek, at Artie's October 19, 1939, opening night at a New York City hotel, competing promoters distributed small cards declaring "We love jitterbugs." The cards were signed by Larry Clinton and the Roseland Ballroom, where Clinton was starting a two-week stand.[36]

The genie that had granted his Central Park wish for fame had, as always, imposed a hidden surcharge. Artie felt besieged by the crowds and boxed in by agents, lawyers, song pluggers, and flacks. Incidents piled up, one upon another. Artie was starting to unravel. In one mid-1939 recording session, he required an extraordinary seventeen takes instead of the usual one or two to wrap up "Comes Love."[37] Finally, on Tuesday night, November 14, 1939, during a performance at the Pennsylvania Hotel in New York City, a particularly irksome fan apparently pushed him over the edge. Artie abandoned the stage, went to his room, and called Andrew Weinberger. He told his attorney he was out, done with the whole damn business. Weinberger tried to reason with the fed-up bandleader. He had contractual obligations to meet, band members for whom he was responsible. He need only plug away another couple of years and then he'd have socked away a nest egg. While Artie had a reported $500,000 in the bank, he owed a bundle to the government. He had been, besides, a free spender on luxury items like the limousine that even his friends considered pretentious. He couldn't just walk away.

Sill, Artie would not be shaken. Increasingly desperate, Weinberger asked songwriter Sammy Cahn to come to the hotel room and talk some sense into the man.

"Artie, you know, it's not just quitting a band," Cahn recalled telling him. "It's quitting sixteen people and their wives, children, mothers, fathers, lovers, friends. You just can't do this. Artie Shaw is a million-dollar industry."

"I can do it."

"Please don't do this."

"I'm doing it."

"Don't you owe anything to these guys?"

"I owe them nothing," Artie said.[38]

Other bandleaders had abruptly bailed out before, as when a furious Tommy Dorsey abandoned his brother Jimmy on the stage of the Glen Island Casino in New Rochelle, New York, in May 1935, but Artie's walk-off struck a chord. It was, movie critic Benjamin R. Crisler said in the *New York Times*, an act of "Shakespearean sweep" and the "kind of spectacularly irreverent farewell to his work and his former associates that even the most timid soul must occasionally dream of, a beautifully incautious burning of all his bridges behind him."[39]

Artie ended up in Acapulco, still just a remote fishing village in Mexico. He finally returned to Los Angeles in mid-January 1940. There, he met, wooed, and wed teenage starlet Lana Turner in near-record time. Artie also returned to music, his eternal mistress. Still on the hook to RCA Victor for six more record sides, he pulled together a thirty-one-piece orchestra that included thirteen string players and recorded, most memorably, his take on a tune he'd picked up in Mexico called "Frenesi." It became another smash hit for the man who insisted he didn't want the crowd's acclaim.

In March 1941 Artie again broke up the orchestra he had been touring with for the past ten months. He holed up in his Central Park West apartment until tax hassles drove him to organize yet another band. A demanding schedule of one-night stands took them from the popular Sunset Ballroom in Carrolltown, Pennsylvania, on September 10 through some thirty shows to the Chicago Theater on October 31, followed by an additional run that landed them in Providence, Rhode Island, in December.

Then came Pearl Harbor.

# Chapter 4

# Battle of the Bands

Twenty-one bandsmen went down with the ship, the clarinet player among them.

Navy Musician Second Class Wendell Ray Hurley was a six-foot tall, 21-year-old Indiana native who had sung in his high school's glee club and followed his father into the carpentry trade until he enlisted in November 1940. He trained at the Naval School of Music in Washington, DC, with a band bound for the Pearl Harbor–based battleship USS *Arizona*. The outfit was designated Navy Band 22, reflecting its distinction as the twenty-second unit band to graduate from the military music school.[1]

The newly badged musicians joined the battleship's crew in June 1941. They were versatile, as every navy musician was required to know at least two instruments. They could play, as music historian Patrick Michael Jones put it, "ceremonial music in the morning, a concert in the afternoon and a dance in the evening, and in a variety of styles such as symphonic works, patriotic pieces, martial music, Americana and jazz."[2]

The young men of Navy Band 22 had a chance to show their stuff in an extended military "Battle of the Bands" that began in September of 1941. These contests, a popular custom in the civilian world as well, pit one band against another, with the winner selected by the length and intensity of the audience applause. The Pearl Harbor competition included bands from other warships and navy units, as well as the Marine Corps barracks, playing over the course of several months before crowds of up to five thousand at the navy's newly opened Bloch Arena.[3] The *Arizona*'s Band 22 had advanced in the initial two rounds of the contest, in which they outplayed the competition on a swing number, a ballad, and a jitterbug piece. On December 6, 1941, the *Honolulu Advertiser* warned audience members ahead of time that the arena crowds at that evening's competition would make "standing room scarcer than an unshined shoe at an admiral's inspection." *Arizona*'s men showed up to check out the teams from the battleships USS *Tennessee* and *Pennsylvania* as they went at it.[4]

The next morning, when the Japanese dive bombers roared overhead, the twenty-one musicians aboard the *Arizona* dropped their instruments and took up their auxiliary duties as ammunition bearers. All of them perished when the battleship sank, putting the entire roster of Navy Band 22 among the *Arizona*'s 1,777 dead that day. None of the bandsmen's remains were ever recovered.[5]

Musicians aboard Pearl Harbor's other ships fought as they were able. The bandmaster and several musicians aboard the battleship USS *Oklahoma* died in the surprise attack. The members of Band 17 aboard the battleship USS *West Virginia* were temporarily trapped below deck; one musician died. And on the battleship USS *Nevada*, duty-bound band members played on. "It never occurred to me that it was possible to stop playing 'The Star-Spangled Banner' once you had started, so we played to the bitter end, although the men in the band told me later we made an unrehearsed pause in the middle when another strafing plane came by," Musician First Class O. L. McMillan later recalled.[6]

The winners of the previous night's musical contest, Navy Band 8 aboard the USS *Pennsylvania*, were likewise in the midst of the daily 0800 "morning colors" flag-raising ceremony when the bombs fell. In the heat of the moment, the musicians made some remarkable choices. Clarinet player Eugene "Dutch" Albert, who had just celebrated his 26th birthday three days prior, diligently secured his $150 clarinet in its case before seeking cover.

"The first plane that comes in the channel is strafing," Albert recalled. "And here we're putting the instruments in the cases, and the paint is chipping off the turret above our heads!"[7]

The *Pennsylvania*'s musicians, once their instruments were stored and the initial strafing run was over, hustled to their battle stations. As the morning went on, the band members fought fires and hauled bodies. French horn player Frank Emond, a Rhode Island native who had enlisted in 1938, would recall decades later the overwhelming stench and how on some sailors' bodies, "the flesh was all burnt, so you couldn't pick them up by the flesh, you had to pick them up by the shoes."[8]

Though all of the *Pennsylvania*'s band members survived, the casualties aboard the *Arizona*, *Oklahoma*, and *West Virginia* made December 7 the worst-ever single-day loss of life for navy musicians. Bandsmen, though, would face danger throughout the duration of the war, exemplified by the harrowing experiences of saxophone player Horace "Saxie" Dowell.

Dowell, an amiable player known for his gags as well as his musicianship, had joined the navy in 1942. He was in his late 30s and enjoying a cozy stint with the highly regarded Great Lakes Naval Training Center Band in Illinois when the Great Lakes commander, Admiral Ralph Davison, was tapped in mid-1944 to lead a task force in the Pacific. Davison took Saxie Dowell's band with him aboard his aircraft carrier flagship, the USS *Franklin*.[9] On March 19, 1945, as the *Franklin* was supporting the Okinawa landings, a 550-pound Japanese bomb hit home, exploding below deck and igniting secondary explosions and fires that killed 724 men, including five of Dowell's fellow musicians, and wounding some 487 more.

Smoke filled the third deck, where Dowell had been stationed for general quarters in the machine shop. The men were cut off, trapped without communications or fresh air. They finally made their escape after several hours, and then went about fighting the fires and saving the ship. Finally, when the immediate risk settled down and the *Franklin* could start limping for the navy's big base at Ulithi, Dowell and his bandmates scrounged together some makeshift instruments and put on a show on the carrier's battered flight deck. "We tried to play everything the boys wanted," Dowell recalled. "Mostly, they wanted 'Don't Fence Me In.' When we got to the place where the lyrics said, 'Give me land, give me lots of land,' the whole ship's company joined in."[10]

By the end of World War II, the navy's music program included some seven thousand personnel and several hundred bands. Their legacy dated back to the early nineteenth century, when the earliest US Navy bands were dominated by talented foreigners who had the unfortunate habit of jumping ship at the first opportunity.[11] John Philip Sousa's leadership, starting in 1917, and the subsequent establishment of the Naval School of Music in Washington, DC, set the program on a steadier course. The school began graduating fully formed, twenty-member bands in 1936. The onset of conscription in 1940 and then the entry of the United States into the war in 1941 further deepened the potential talent pool, as draft-eligible musicians sought alternatives to the dreaded infantry.

Uniformed service was not for everyone. Some musicians, like bandleaders Woody Herman and Fletcher Henderson, publicly reasoned that they could contribute more to the war effort as a civilian than as a soldier. Others, like Benny Goodman with his bad back, were physically unsuited to military servitude. Even civilians, though, could contribute to the cause; the question was how.

Early in the war, Glenn Miller suggested recruiting musicians as air raid wardens. Denizens of the night, they could be equipped with whistles and flashlights and guide the populace to shelter when Nazi bombers appeared, say, in the evening sky over Manhattan. The notion, despite its comic potential, proved a clinker. In a more conventional vein, United Service Organization (USO) chair Walter Hoving announced plans a few weeks after Pearl Harbor to have 150 civilian bands perform free shows weekly at military bases throughout the country. Miller, Artie and Goodman were named as among the volunteering bandleaders. The idea never quite met its initial hype, though the individual bands did end up doing their part, one way or another.[12]

Composers, too, were mobilizing for total war.

"The nation is literally crying for a good, peppy marching song," Representative J. Parnell Thomas (R-NJ) declared in early 1942. "Something with plenty of pep, ginger, fire."[13]

The first musical offering was served up the night of December 7 at Ciro's nightclub in Hollywood, where Oscar-winning composers Ned Washington and Lew Pollack appropriated a napkin and scribbled out the lyrics to a patriotic ditty they entitled "We'll Knock the Japs Right into the Laps of the Nazis." Apparently with a straight face, singer Bert Wheeler belted out such lyrical lines as "when they hop on Honolulu, that's a thing we won't allow" and "I'd hate to be in Yokohama, when our bombers make a bow."[14] On Broadway Eddie Cantor inserted a number entitled "We Did It Before and We Can Do It Again" into the musical *Banjo Eyes*. The lyrics, promising to "take the Nip out of the Nipponese and chase 'em back to the cherry trees," foreshadowed the dreck that was to come. Songwriters subsequently cranked out the dead-on-arrival likes of "We're Going to Find a Fellow Who Is Yellow and Beat Him Red, White and Blue," "Let's Knock the 'Hit' out of Hitler" and "Yankee Doodle Ain't Doodlin' Now." The bloviating heartiness left troops unmoved.[15]

"Unfortunately for us, we had no songs to sing except those tuneless, pointless 'war songs' then arriving in a sticky flood," Marine Corps veteran Robert Leckie recounted. "Refrains like 'Just to show those Japs, the Yanks are no saps' . . . hardly fill a man with the urge to kill or conquer."[16]

Russian-born composer Andre Kostelanetz tried a more elevated approach by commissioning orchestral pieces honoring outstanding Americans. One contribution came from composer Jerome Kern, coauthor of the 1927 Broadway hit *Show Boat*. Kern had penned numerous songs that became part of the Great American Songbook, including "A Fine Romance," "I Can't Dance," and "I'm Old Fashioned." For the Kostelanetz project, Kern chose Mark Twain as his subject. The resulting fourteen-minute instrumental portrait got its radio broadcast premiere in June of 1942—about three months, as it happened, after Kern's daughter Elizabeth had married Artie in a civil ceremony. Critics considered the Mark Twain piece to be pleasant enough; it was easy to listen to.[17] It did not, however, rouse any fighting spirits to speak of. Soldiers and sailors wanted music that moved them. Army researchers in 1943 would survey 4,296 enlisted men about their musical preferences. Swing/jazz ranked number one, with classical coming in second place.[18] "Whether we like it or not, the fact remains that when it comes to entertainment, the men in our camps today prefer dance bands and popular music to any other sort," one official reported in March 1942.[19]

The military services met this demand with multiple outfits. The US Army, Navy, Marine Corps, and Coast Guard would all stand up their respective service bands; even the Merchant Marines would be musically represented. Some bands were attached to specific ships or units. Others represented installations. The army's Fort Dix band in New Jersey had a national reach, performing for radio broadcasts four times a week. The Great Lakes Naval Training Center in Illinois likewise boasted a stand-out group. In rural Vermont the 186th Field Artillery Band reached a statewide audience with weekly broadcasts on a Burlington radio station. Some of these military bands would spend the entire war without ever going in harm's way. Flush with newly conscripted musical talent in the months following Pearl Harbor, the navy organized the Navy Band Symphony Orchestra that would spend the war performing weekly on the home front in Washington, DC. Other outfits would serve on the front lines.

"We've been right up there where the only music was the whistling of the artillery and the singing of the shells," said Chief Warrant Officer Everett Rupert, director of the ninety-member 1st Infantry Division Band.[20]

# Chapter 5

# The Enlisted Man

Artie spun a streamlined version of his enlistment in the navy.

He "just went down and enlisted" following the Japanese attack on Pearl Harbor, Artie told filmmaker Brigitte Berman in the Oscar-winning 1985 documentary *Artie Shaw: Time Is All You've Got*. He told the House Un-American Activities Committee in 1953 much the same thing. Facing pointed questions about his participation in ideologically suspect organizations, Artie played the patriotism card with his description of his actions on December 7, 1941. "I turned to my band and said, 'you boys better start looking for jobs,'" Artie testified, "and by the first of the year I had canceled all of my engagements and went down and enlisted in the Navy."[1]

Not quite.

Even in the immediate aftermath of Pearl Harbor, Artie had obligations to meet. The very next day, December 8, he brought his band to Loew's State Theatre in New York City's Times Square. Artie then led his outfit on a run of one-night stands throughout the Midwest, capping it with a New Year's Eve show in Cleveland's Public Hall before some six thousand mostly young fans who "jumped and swirled and swayed" until three in the morning, one reporter recounted.[2] After a two-week vacation, Artie returned to the recording studio in late January. Finally, *Variety* reported on January 21, 1942, that Artie had folded his band; but it was not, according to the public reports, in order to enlist. Rather, the band's dissolution was attributed to doctor's orders. Artie had been in poor health for several weeks with a chronic cold and throat condition, the entertainment trade publication explained, and so he was going to cancel nearly a month's worth of scheduled shows and check into New York City's Roosevelt Hospital for several weeks. "He told the 29 men in his outfit to go ahead and get other jobs if they had the chance, but those that wanted to move back in with him when he reformed could do so," *Variety* recounted.[3] Similar newspaper accounts attributed the information to Artie's attorney, Andrew Weinberger, with the wire service version stating that "Shaw was taken suddenly ill and has been instructed by his doctors not to return to work for at least six to eight weeks."[4]

Artie had until then a 3-A draft deferment attributed to his being the sole financial support for his mother. Since his father had taken off, it had been Artie and his mother, Sarah, alone. While in New Haven, she took in sewing jobs to make ends meet. When Artie was living in Cleveland, earning $175 a week with the Austin Wylie Orchestra, his mother had insisted on coming out to live with him. Mother clung to son even as he moved onward and upward. "She was like a leech," Artie said. "She wouldn't let go."[5]

But despite Sarah's clutch, the draft board was starting to see Artie as ripe for the picking. *DownBeat* reported on February 1, 1942, without further explanation that Artie's draft status had changed to 1-A.[6] The periodical followed this up just two weeks later with a story filed from New York City asserting that the reports about a draft reclassification were incorrect. Artie, the magazine asserted, retained his 3-A status. This seeming reassurance that Artie would be staying a civilian coincided with news that the General Amusement Corporation had sold his contract to the William Morris Agency for the reported sum of $15,000.[7]

February and March of 1942 passed without Artie enlisting, even as other musicians were joining up. The young bandleader Dean Hudson reported to the Army Reserves in February. Paul Fredericks, a trumpet player in guitarist

Alvino Rey's orchestra, enlisted in the Army Signal Corps that same month. Tommy Dorsey's piano player Joe Bushkin and Jimmy Dorsey's piano player Joe Lippman both enlisted in the army. Trombone player and orchestra leader Jack Teagarden alone lost seventeen men to the army in just four months.[8] There were enough musicians entering the service that *DownBeat* attended their comings and goings in a column entitled "Ravings at Reveille," credited to "Sarj." "The Sarj is hearing nothing but rave reports about the Ft. Sheridan, Ill. Recruit Reception Band," one typical column item noted in the March 15, 1942, issue. The military maneuvers kept Sarj busy, as by one count thirty-nine civilian bandleaders would end up serving in the armed forces during World War II in addition to the myriad rank-and-file musicians who enlisted or were drafted.[9]

Artie, meanwhile, was keeping his powder dry. Any enlistment fancies that he might have entertained on the Providence stage seemed to have melted away. He subsequently let it be known in early May 1942 that he had a new idea. "I'm being fitted into a very careful plan by USO and Army-Navy Relief to give the services really decent recreation and entertainment," Artie declared.[10] He envisioned establishing full-blown recreation centers at assorted military bases, each with a band and the capacity for theater, dance, Hollywood star appearances—the works. Artie suggested dividing the country into different districts, with different bandleaders in charge of each district. He said he would spend two weeks or so in each camp, building up its band and library of arrangements. There was no end to the possibilities, and Artie seemed well-positioned to pursue them. A former William Morris Agency executive named Abe Lastfogel had taken charge of the USO's Camp Shows entertainment division and, conveniently, Artie himself had just joined the William Morris stable.

The Morris agency signed Artie to a two-year contract, effective March 6. The deal called on Artie to play only theatre runs and broadcast shows, no one-nighters. It was an endeavor that presumed continued civilian status, which was something Lastfogel might have been able to help with.[11] Dubbed "Affable Abe" by the nickname-slingers at *Time*, Lastfogel was a diminutive school dropout who had worked his way up from office boy to William Morris Agency honcho. He brought to the USO Camp Show work the same zeal that had made him so formidable in Hollywood and on Broadway. "He operated on the premise that entertainment for servicemen was not only desirable but essential," *Time* reported, adding that "by hook & crook he rounded up thousands of small-time entertainers" as well as big-time talent.[12]

The USO, originally called the United Service Organization for National Defense, had sprung from prewar conversations among leaders of the YMCA, Salvation Army, Jewish Welfare Board, and other groups intent on coordinating civilian efforts to boost military morale. A formal public-private partnership with the government was established, with the USO divided into several components. The most prominent was the Camp Shows operation, which would sponsor myriad performances that ranged from Al Jolson's solo gig all the way up to full-throttle orchestras.[13]

Artie's USO scheme entailed his remaining a civilian with a draft status of 2-A, akin to that of a defense industry worker. His personal status had already changed in another way, with his marriage to Elizabeth Kern, the daughter of composer Jerome Kern.

The parents of Artie's first wife, Jane Karns, had had the union annulled. His second wife, nurse Margaret Allen, secured a divorce in 1937. The union with his third wife, teenage starlet Lana Turner, didn't last.

Now came bride number four, the only child of Kern and his British-born wife, Eva. Elizabeth had been indulgently raised amid Broadway royalty. When songwriter Irving Berlin told her at the age of 4 that she was a very nice girl, she informed him that she knew it. A governess and private teachers serviced Elizabeth until she was sent off to private school in Bronxville, New York, at the age of 8, but she left school at 17 without graduating. She had her heart set on a career in the theater. Her father, though he treasured her, declared this was entirely beyond the reach of her limited talents. At 19 Elizabeth was married to her first husband. Not long after, she was divorced.

Despite the couple's eight-year age difference and Artie's womanizing reputation, her family blessed their union. Kern admired Artie's musicianship, and Artie in turn had faithfully covered some of his future father-in-law's tunes, such as "All the Things You Are." Accompanied by Eva Kern,

Elizabeth's mother, the couple drove from Los Angeles to Yuma, Arizona, where they avoided California's required three-day waiting period. Justice of the Peace R. H. Lutes, the operator of an ice cream business when he wasn't scooping out quickie wedding ceremonies, was on duty. He offered not romance but efficiency, sometimes servicing a dozen or more couples a day, and on March 3, 1942, he processed Artie and Elizabeth into a state of matrimony.[14]

Artie returned from the Arizona wedding with his future uncertain, though he was pressing ahead on his USO music proposal. He seemed to be making progress over the following month, as on April 8 *Variety* reported that he had gone to Washington, DC, five days earlier to "work out details with Major Howard Bronson, head of Army musical activity."[15]

Bronson was the man to see about wartime music. Like Artie, the major played the clarinet. Beyond that, they had little in common. Bronson had joined the South Dakota National Guard prior to World War I, becoming a member of the 4th Infantry Band. A big John Phillip Sousa fan, he played in or led a succession of military bands before being tapped in June 1941 to serve as the army's music advisor.[16] The one-time infantryman held firm views about proper wartime music. "We are emerging from a cycle of rather ineffectual and mushily sentimental popular music," Bronson told music educators in 1942, adding that "our songs and other forms of musical expression must express firmness, confidence and straight thinking."[17]

Bronson and members of an advisory panel called the Joint Army/Navy Subcommittee on Music were on the same page. The subcommittee members that year would report that "after careful discussion it was agreed that too many sentimental 'sob' songs should be avoided and that an effort should be made to select forward-moving, stimulating songs."[18]

Artie, meanwhile, had by April 10 reportedly filled out a twelve-page Justice Department questionnaire so that FBI special agents could begin a required background investigation for the anticipated USO job.[19] But only a few weeks after his USO civilian music role seemed within grasp, he made an abrupt U-turn. "The unpredictable Artie Shaw, with his inherent flair for making headlines, has done it again," the swing music fan periodical *Music and Rhythm* reported.[20]

Artie was not going the USO route after all. Instead, he was joining the United States Navy. His carefully constructed plans that would have allowed him to serve his country while staying a civilian had, it seemed, failed to satisfy the conscription machine. Artie had filled out his draft registration card on October 16, 1940, while he was in residence at San Francisco's Palace Hotel.[21] In the approximately year and a half since that San Francisco gig, draft boards had become stricter and exemptions harder to get. *DownBeat* in its May 15, 1942, issue reported that Artie had "cleared his USO camp job with everybody but his draft board." The magazine speculated that the draft board members, apparently feeling disrespected by the big-shot bandleader, "got huffy about the whole thing" and placed him atop the to-be-inducted list.[22]

This account, though unattributed, made some sense. Military and Selective Service System leaders were increasingly sensitive about reports of privileged entertainers enjoying special treatment. In the months before Pearl Harbor, singer Tony Martin had sought a navy sinecure, allegedly with the help of a procurement officer, Lieutenant Commander Maurice Nathaniel Aroff. The navy suspected Aroff of taking bribes, and in July 1942 he was tried in a nationally publicized court-martial, with one of the charges being that he had accepted a $950 Studebaker President sedan from Martin in exchange for assistance. Aroff was also charged with obtaining fancy cufflinks from several Stanford men looking to become quickly anointed navy ensigns.[23]

The navy ended up dismissing Aroff and pushed out Martin as well, though he later joined the Army Air Forces. The notoriety of his case and others like it complicated things for entertainers who might be seeking their own accommodations. Members of Congress denounced the privileges being accorded to those who, as one riled-up House member put it on February 9, produced nothing more than "salacious bedroom drama, low comedy and propaganda."[24] Hanging tough with Artie Shaw, if that's, in fact, what was happening with the draft board, could have been intended as a salutary signal that all was on the up-and-up.

As Artie made public his navy plans, his attorney, Andrew Weinberger, insisted that the service had not given any indication of what the bandleader might do, while adding that his talents were wasted on anything but playing music. Weinberger was well-practiced at protecting Artie's interests. It was Weinberger, Broadway columnist Louis Sobel wrote, who managed to free the bandleader from an onerous contractual obligation that had divided him "into more parts than Gaul."[25]

About eight years older than Artie, Weinberger had come to the United States as a young child from his native Hungary. He had graduated from New York Law School, attending at night along with other upwardly striving immigrants. An attorney with a pronounced liberal bent, in time a vocal supporter of the NAACP, Weinberger got his start in show biz by representing crooner Rudy Vallee. The work eventually connected him with Artie and other musicians, including singer Rosemary Clooney, trombone ace Jack Teagarden, and saxophonist George Auld.[26]

Weinberger deftly finagled Artie's contractual conflicts and Teagarden's 1940 bankruptcy petition, but against the Selective Service, he could only do so much. The draft board would not be denied its claim. Max Kaminsky, in a fanciful-sounding account, claimed that Artie was with his band in a recording studio when he was handed his draft notice by his manager. Artie, Kaminsky asserted, thereupon dismissed the band immediately. "Well," Kaminsky recounted telling drummer Dave Tough as they packed up their instruments in the studio, "that's the way it goes. The minute we get a chance to make a little money, they have to go and have a war."[27] Like any number of Kaminsky's other anecdotes, this accounting made for a good story but seems questionable. Kaminsky's last recording session with Artie was in January 1942.

At any rate, the conversations with Major Bronson and USO officials having apparently borne no fruit, Artie stepped up. On Monday, April 27, nearly five months after Pearl Harbor, the bandleader and his wife Elizabeth traveled from their New York City apartment at 67 W. 44th Street to the Navy Recruiting Station at 90 Church Street.

The 90 Church Street station had been going great guns since Pearl Harbor. In just the first week after the Japanese attack, 1,723 new navy recruits passed through its doors. The rush was such that the navy had to borrow bed space in the Brace Memorial Newsboys' Home and the Brooklyn Supply Armory to stash its men overnight.[28] The Marine Corps Recruiting Station at 90 Church Street received more than 2,300 enlistment applications during the same period.

Artie dressed up for the occasion, complete with a perfectly knotted tie and a handkerchief peeking out of a pocket on his double-breasted jacket. With a newspaper photographer capturing the moment, Artie raised his right hand, fingers casually splayed, and was sworn in as a seaman first class in the US Naval Reserve by Lieutenant Commander Leon J. Carro, a lawyer and World War I veteran who was in charge of naval recruiting in New York, Connecticut, and parts of New Jersey.

In the weeks prior to Artie's arrival, Carro had been seeking fishermen, yachtsmen, and others with small boat experience for service aboard what he told one reporter would be "local defense vessels" patrolling the "home waters" in the vicinity of Long Island Sound.[29] Carro said that men could choose among fifty-three enlisted rates in the Naval Reserve, from quartermaster and coxswain to ship's cook. Artie told reporters he was ready to serve wherever the navy wanted him, explaining that he chose the sea service because he had considerable experience with small boats. Asked why he didn't apply for a commission, Artie said he didn't think he was entitled to it. He sounded very much like he was surrendering his celebrity stripes for the good of the service.

The night of his enlistment, Artie was, for a change, in the audience instead of on stage for a program at the New York City's Metropolitan Opera House billed as "Entertaining the Entertainers." Navy Seaman Second Class Hiram Sherman, a chubby 34-year-old comedian and one-time playwright formerly with Orson Welles's famed Mercury Theater, served as a master of ceremonies. Sherman joked that he was well suited to the task, as his navy career had thus far consisted of picking up garbage. Members of the audience ate up the cornpone like it was their patriotic duty. Joining Artie in the audience were military leaders, entertainers, and socially connected representatives from the New York City Defense Recreation Committee. The army portion included a slapstick skit featuring characters identified as Fritz, Spaghetti, and Jap.[30]

New York City Mayor Fiorello La Guardia played his own distinctive part. "The mayor stationed himself in the orchestra pit with a baton and worked himself into a lather directing at one and the same time the bands of the Police, Fire and Sanitation Departments and the Police and Fire Department Glee Clubs," the *New York Herald Tribune* reported.[31]

Artie slept in his own bed that night; no barracks, yet, for him. Instead, the bandleader continued on a sayonara tour that music industry cynics sniped was little more than a last-minute squeeze for the William Morris Agency. On May 26 the *Washington Star* announced Artie and his orchestra would be appearing at Loew's Capitol Theatre in DC in his last appearance for the "duration." If there was any ambiguity as to what duration was meant, the same page featured a gun-toting Gary Cooper in an ad for a war flick called "The Real Glory," described as "the thrilling story of the heroic Americans" who battled the Japanese in the Philippines.

Artie's final tour would take the band to Pittsburgh, Akron, Youngstown, and finally Detroit, where on Friday, June 12, the band settled into the opulent, 4,023-seat Michigan Theatre for its final weeklong run of performances. Normally the most unsentimental of men, Artie was temporarily roused to something unexpected in his eve-of-battle Detroit show. For just a moment, he waxed elegiac on patriotic themes. The audience rewarded him with a standing ovation, though for Artie the moment, shorn of all cynicism, didn't last. "I imagine it touched everybody about a millimeter deep," Artie said.[32]

With the Detroit show, Artie had cleared the deck of his civilian obligations, and he told a radio audience listening to the CBS "Hobby Lobby" show what came next. "I said goodbye to my gang, and Friday morning I was in dungarees aboard a Navy ship," Artie said. "From that time, music became my hobby. My profession is to become one of Uncle Sam's good sailors."[33]

# Chapter 6

# From Minesweeper to Bandstand

Artie reported for active navy duty on June 19, 1942, seven months after Pearl Harbor. In the meantime, the war had been getting along without him.

British soldiers in North Africa that month were defending the besieged Libyan city of Tobruk. In the Pacific, US naval strategists were plotting their course following the previous month's Battle of the Coral Sea, in which US and Japanese aircraft carriers had flung warplanes at each other from over the horizon. President Roosevelt and British Prime Minister Winston Churchill were meeting in Hyde Park and Washington, DC, to settle on the selection of then Major General Dwight Eisenhower as commander in chief of the US forces in the European theater.

Artie's service started off with the basics. Military doctors measured him, noting that he stood a little more than five feet and nine inches tall and had a thirty-three-inch waist. He had twenty-twenty vision and a resting pulse of seventy-six beats per minute. Under the category for "abnormal psyche" that included the specifications of "depression, instability [or] worries," the examiners reported "none."[1]

Once he was assessed, Artie was immediately granted a nine-day furlough. He and Elizabeth spent it in part at the well-appointed Sekon Lodge at Upper Saranac Lake in upstate New York. Finally, on June 28, Artie was back with the navy for keeps. Unlike some of the musicians who would eventually join his military band, Artie undertook rudimentary navy training; according to a brief August 19 item in *Variety*, this boot camp was at Newport News, Virginia. Comedian Lenny Bruce, in his quasi-autobiography *How to Talk Dirty and Influence People*, recounted that he attended the navy's three-week boot camp at about the same time as Artie. "During that 21-day incubation period, the excitement of war was dwarfed by 'Artie Shaw is here!'" Bruce wrote, noting the contradictory mix of solicitousness and resentment that the celebrity recruit attracted. Artie, Bruce discerned, "would have been as glad to have been as I was then, an ordinary seaman with a serial number, willing to fight for his country."[2]

After boot camp Artie was assigned to a minesweeper at the Naval Frontier Base at Tompkinsville, Staten Island. Located about ten miles from Manhattan, the drab installation was home to an antisubmarine warfare training center, a boat repair unit, and some unglamorous coastal mine-sweepers. Artie's minesweeper service would not last long, but the experience would stay with him. He would later recall that the ship's galley served decent grub, and his fellow enlisted men were friendly. It was honest sailor's work; though he retained some of his celebrity swagger, he was not above some of the military's petty humiliations. He would eventually have his navy uniform custom-made and tailored by the top-end crew at New York City's Rogers Peet and Company, a shop that had served high society since the nineteenth century. But before he managed that, he would on occasion be summoned into line. "A sailor was wandering down Broadway with his cap turned over his eye when he met the Shore Patrol and was advised sharply to straighten his headgear," *Stars and Stripes* reported in late July 1942. "Meekly, Artie Shaw, former band leader, complied."[3]

The novelty soon wore off, and Artie's chronic appetite for something different returned. He recounted that "after about six or eight weeks of mine-sweeper duty off Staten Island, this, that and the other," he got fed up with the duties of an apprentice seaman. "I thought the Navy would have enough rationality to put me into the job I could do best for them and then give me whatever rate or rank I needed for that," Artie recalled. "I was very naive, you know. I didn't realize that the military service doesn't operate rationally. They looked at one stripe or no stripe, and they gave me a swab, 'swab the deck, sailor.' Well, that's kind of stupid."[4]

He had spent years perfecting his craft. His obvious role was as a musician, and he knew it, despite whatever fancies he might have once entertained about manning a warship. The navy finally reached the same conclusion. By midsummer Artie had been reassigned from the Staten Island minesweeper base to lead a fourteen-member navy band in Newport, Rhode Island. A *Metronome* magazine reporter, in a piece that sounded like it was Artie speaking, wrote that "he did not request the transfer." The reporter added that "Navy officials made the change (and jumped him from a seaman to a Chief Petty Officer) of their own accord, without Artie making application or any kind of request whatsoever."[5]

Newport made more sense as a base for the bandleader, but the available musical talent could not meet his standards. Artie was accustomed to playing with the best. At Newport he was put in charge of well-meaning amateurs and hobbyists for whom the band might be an alternative to assignment as a boatswain's mate or an aviation machinist.[6] "I had two men who could blow good," Artie recalled. "The rest were terrible. I was back where I started as a kid, with the Peter Pan Novelty Orchestra."[7]

Other professional musicians shared Artie's harsh assessment of the military talent pool. Army and navy field bands struggled to make the grade, their recruitment efforts hindered by their reputation for mediocrity. "Many men entering the Army preferred not to mention their musical ability because of the poor quality of the bands and the fact that bandsmen have to do so many menial jobs and had no time to practice," members of the Joint Army/Navy Subcommittee noted in February 1942.[8]

In the absence of complete personnel records, ambiguity clouds the chronology of Artie's time at Newport, including the formative moments and various comings and goings of what would become his navy band. But on Friday, October 2, his exact whereabouts were recorded in his medical file as Artie checked himself in at sick call with complaints of gastrointestinal distress. Doctors examined him and were alarmed enough at what they found to admit him to the Newport US Naval Hospital.[9] Although Artie had previously reported to sick call with similar complaints of abdominal cramping, his GI tract seemed to be the least of his problems. One doctor identified Artie as an "emotionally unstable individual with anxiety and depressive trends," and a navy lieutenant wrote bluntly that Artie should be studied closely to determine "the exact physical and neuropsychiatric situation and fitness for the Service."[10] "At times, he has appeared to be nervously tense and dissatisfied with his position in the Navy," Lieutenant Commander R. S. Bray wrote, adding that Artie's abdominal distress appeared to be related to "an underlying emotional over-activity."[11]

The doctors monitored Artie in the Newport Naval Hospital for some time, with his medical file recording that he was not discharged until October 24. During his extended hospital stay, the band members he sought were left dangling. Two men who would later join his navy band, guitarist Al Horesh and saxophone player Dick LaPolla, both later recounted how they arrived at the Newport Navy base in October and heard that Artie was hospitalized with migraine headaches that could be serious enough to force his medical discharge.[12]

As an accommodation, Artie at some point during his time in Newport was also given the opportunity to live off base with his bride Elizabeth. Some gossip columns had briefly spread a rumor that the couple had separated. With the subsequent reassuring report that Elizabeth had rented a "little white cottage with picket fence and roses and everything just to be near," it was speculated, sassily, that Artie was no doubt "blowing sweeter notes on his flute."[13] The cottage timing is unclear, but it may indeed have worked its magic. By late November gossip columnist Louella Parsons would pass along the scuttlebutt that "Artie Shaw and Betty Kern are expecting the long-legged bird."[14] Eight months after that report, Elizabeth would give birth.

Artie's own release from the Newport Naval Hospital enabled him to resume a recruiting effort he had begun, he later recounted, under an arrangement with the Navy Undersecretary James Forrestal. This arrangement—seemingly undocumented, so far as a search of archival records could determine—appeared to be a remarkable power play by a lowly enlisted man.

But then, neither Artie nor Forrestal were averse to taking power and using it to their advantage.

James Forrestal was the first person to hold the newly created position of undersecretary of the navy. He had the combination of military, management, and political experience that made him a natural for the position. Following stateside service as a navy aviator in World War I, Forrestal had rejoined the investment firm Dillon, Read and Company as a bond salesman, rising to vice president in 1926 and president in 1938. Boosted by Roosevelt administration insiders, including adviser Tommy Corcoran and Supreme Court Justice William O. Douglas, Forrestal had joined the White House as a $10,000-a-year special assistant in 1940. Shortly thereafter, he was named undersecretary of the navy that August.[15]

It's not clear how Forrestal and Artie knew each other. The Wall Street financier and the celebrity bandleader might have had several occasions to cross paths. However it was that Artie and Forrestal first met, they evidently connected. As Artie subsequently recounted to interviewer Terry Gross, Forrestal "had said to me, when I joined the Navy, 'You're going to be in some trouble. When you get in real trouble, come see me.'" Artie cast it somewhat differently in 1953 when he told the House Un-American Activities Committee that "before I had joined the Navy at all, I had asked [Forrestal] if there was room for anyone like me in the Navy."[16]

The two versions have in common the recollection that Artie had effectively secured an open-ended invitation from the undersecretary. One potential hint of a prior conversation may be found on Forrestal's telephone log for January 20, 1942. The log records that at 1:54 p.m. that day, amid a flurry of calls with Navy Secretary Frank Knox and assorted admirals and congressional offices, Forrestal or someone from his office left a message for a "Mr. Shaw." A second message for "Mr. Shaw" was recorded as having been left about three hours later.[17] Perhaps this was a reference to Artie, although the timing so early in 1942 is curious; in any event, there do not appear to be other documented references to Artie in Forrestal's papers held at Princeton University. Artie's own accounts of his dealings with Forrestal fluctuated over the years, though the gist was conveyed in a

1992 Smithsonian Jazz Masters interview conducted by Bruce Talbot. Artie described how he got fed up with his inadequate Newport band and determined to do something about it. First, Artie said, he sought permission to leave the Newport base from a superior whom he called "Red Mike." This was a senior enlisted man, Artie explained, "whose face gets red when he says [things like] 'stand up and salute, sailor.'"

"I just asked if I could see the captain, the head of the base," Artie recalled.

Red Mike thought poorly of the idea. Artie then recalled that he "went AWOL" after a fashion, donning civilian clothes and making his way to Washington, DC. In his various public retellings of the story, Artie never mentioned a date for this trip. His destination, Forrestal's office, was on the second deck of the Main Navy Building, erected as one of several supposedly "temporary" structures along the National Mall near the Lincoln Memorial. One of Forrestal's outer offices was manned by Captain John Gingrich, a 1919 Naval Academy graduate who had served aboard several warships before becoming, in August 1940, aide to the undersecretary. Gingrich was a highly capable man, trusted by Forrestal on military matters—so much so that the hot-tempered chief of naval operations, Admiral Ernest King, came to suspect Gingrich was the string-puller in the undersecretary's office.[18]

Among his other tasks, Captain Gingrich was a gatekeeper to Forrestal's inner sanctum, and Artie remembered his name years later.

"I said, 'I'd like to see Mr. Forrestal,'" Shaw recounted. "[Gingrich] said, 'What do you want to see him about?' I said, 'Well, sir, it's a long story.'"

"Yeah, everybody wants to come in and see him and get favors," Gingrich said.

"I don't want any favors. I'm already in the Navy," Artie said.

"What are you?"

"A seaman," Artie said.[19]

Captain Gingrich shook his head at the impertinence, Artie recalled, but he dutifully went in to check with the boss. In a minute the aide came out. Yes, the undersecretary of the navy would see enlisted man Shaw.

Forrestal was a brusque hard-charger and a fierce bureaucratic battler. He maintained a tickler file with the birthdays of useful people, and he never missed a chance to congratulate the freshly ascended. He would have seen the value in helping a celebrity like Artie Shaw even as he brushed off other pleas for help with obtaining a safe navy commission. Artie might be impertinent, but he was also a special case.

"Jesus. I knew you would be in trouble. You're AWOL. You know what that means?" Forrestal said, in Artie's subsequent retelling.

"Sure, but you're the boss man here," Artie said.

"What do you want?" Forrestal asked.

"I want to get a good band together," Artie said. "Give me the right to get some men together."[20]

Forrestal was accustomed to special pleading. Only one month after he had joined the Navy Department in the summer of 1940, the Selective Service Act was signed by President Roosevelt. This prompted draft-vulnerable men to seek some safe haven, and Forrestal received so many pleas he had to find new ways of saying no. He learned to couch rejection as praise, diplomatically advising one petitioner in March of 1941 that "it is difficult to find places which will fully utilize men of your intelligence and experience where you would feel that you were really doing constructive work in the national defense."[21]

For Artie, though, the undersecretary apparently said yes. Whether swayed by celebrity, finagled by friendship, or sold on the merits, Forrestal, by Artie's recounting, called on the enlisted personnel chief at the Bureau of Navy Personnel, Captain Albert H. Bledsoe. A 1918 Naval Academy graduate, the Texas native knew how to salute his superiors.

"Old Forrestal had said, 'Pay attention,' so he paid attention to me," Artie recalled.

Artie said he subsequently told Bledsoe he wanted to go where the action was. Informed that that was the Pacific, Artie said, good, then he wanted to go to the Pacific.

"Mr. Forrestal says I should get a big band together. Can you give me some kind of orders that allow me to do that?" Artie asked.

"How long do you need?" Bledsoe asked.

"Two or three months," Artie recalled saying. "I'm going to get a bunch of 1-A-classified guys who were not in the service yet, and I'll talk them into joining my band."[22]

However, precisely, it happened, Artie got his marching orders, and he returned to Newport to recruit the men he wanted. He could dangle several inducements. Though Artie had a reputation as a demanding and sometimes mercurial boss, he was also known for his musical excellence. To play with him would be to play with the best. Not least, Arie could offer musicians the chance to avoid the alternative.

"They'll get you in this war anyway, and they'll put you to work doing something else," Artie would tell the prospects, "and when you get out, you won't be able to play. Your lip will be gone."[23]

Word soon reached the street about Artie's new recruiting drive. "Now that Artie Shaw has won his commission the hard way, he's been given the green light by the government to build the finest band from our forces than has yet been gathered together," gossip columnist Hedda Hopper reported in early November, adding enigmatically that "if he's not careful, he's going to become the John Phillip Sousa of this war."[24]

# Chapter 7

# "A Pretty Good Group"

**D**ave Tough was one of a kind.

The 35-year-old drummer weighed a scant 112 pounds when he registered for the draft in October 1940. He stood five feet and five inches tall, or thereabouts. He had, *New Yorker* jazz critic Whitney Balliett observed, "a long, wandering, bony face, a high domed forehead and black hair with a widow's peak; it was a face, perched on his tiny shoulders, of a bigger man."[1] His blue eyes gleamed with curiosity, intelligence, and mischief. Often shy, he spoke precisely, attended readings by the likes of Langston Hughes, and admired the Cezanne exhibits at the Art Institute of Chicago. While living in Europe, he reportedly swapped limericks with author F. Scott Fitzgerald.[2] The poet and intellectual omnivore Kenneth Rexroth, in his *An Autobiographical Novel*, cast Dave as a character named Dick Rough. The Rough/Tough cat, Rexroth wrote, was a "skinny little boy" who also happened to be "the first and greatest of the hipsters."[3]

Musically, he was in the top ranks, with *Variety* recognizing Tough in 1936 as an "ace swing man with the sticks."[4] He drove bands led by Tommy Dorsey, Bunny Berrigan, Red Norvo, and Benny Goodman, sitting trim and erect behind his kit while he worked what biographer Harold Kaye described as his "piston-like wrists."[5] Tough placed third among drummers in *DownBeat*'s unscientific but closely watched readers' poll in 1938, and he moved up to second place in 1942.

"An extraordinary pulse resided within him," jazz critic Burt Korall observed. "When he played, Tough energized and elevated music in an almost unbelievable manner."[6]

He was also a serious lush. Dave had reportedly discovered booze at the age of 14, and as an adult he was not infrequently falling-down drunk, though he stayed sober enough over the years to satisfy some of the most demanding bandleaders of the Swing Era.[7] When he was in the throes of his dissolution, trumpet player Max Kaminsky recalled, Tough looked like an "emaciated imp," and his usually sublime playing could fall to pieces.[8] Some thought he was epileptic. In search of a high, he knew all the street-wise tricks. For a pick-me-up, he might remove the Benzedrine strips from asthma inhalers, drop them into a Coca-Cola, and blast off. When really desperate, he might resort to buying canned heat and siphoning off the alcohol to drink. Leonard Feather, an influential critic and prolific *DownBeat* contributor, recalled a time when Dave showed up at Feather's New York City apartment gaunt and vacant-eyed. "I haven't eaten in three days," the desperate drummer told Feather. "I don't know where I'm staying. I forgot what happened. Just let me lie down and rest."[9]

Artie knew all about Davey's dissipations as well as his potential. They had played together for part of 1941 in one of Artie's large orchestral configurations, and Artie had seen what Tough could bring to the table when he was sober. He was, Artie determined, the best drummer possible for this new navy band. Enlisting him, though, was no easy matter.

Artie first had to convince the percussionist that he should leave his gig with the Charlie Spivak orchestra. Spivak was displeased that his talented drummer was being lured away by a competitor, but he couldn't have been too surprised. Poaching was common practice among the competitive big bands. Artie assured Tough that this new navy band was the place to be. The drummer fell for the pitch, but then he had to pass the navy's physical in October. According to Max Kaminsky's recounting, Dave stuffed himself with pasta for several weeks to pack on some pounds and meet the military's minimum weight requirement of roughly 110 pounds. Several versions of Tough's subsequent navy physical examination differ in detail but generally recount that Artie somehow managed to attend the proceeding. According to Kaminsky's version, when Dave stripped for his physical, the medical officer took one unbelieving look and shook his head.

"Do you really need this man in your band?" the doctor asked, in this account.

"This is the world's greatest drummer," Artie snapped.

"Then get him the hell out of here before somebody sees him," the doctor ordered.[10]

However it happened, the Oak View, Illinois native was admitted into the service. It was but the latest turn in an unlikely life.

Dave Tough was born in 1907 to Scottish parents. After his mother died in 1916, his bank-teller father married the late mother's sister, young Dave's aunt. Dave, who had first been introduced to the piano and then took up drums, dropped out of high school and was playing professionally by 1925. He knocked around before Tommy Dorsey hired him in 1936 and kept him gainfully employed for about two years. Decades later, Whitney Balliett praised Tough's work as "lifting [the] soloists and giving what was basically a big Dixieland band a fresh and buoyant feeling."[11] For a time *Metronome* magazine retained Tough for a column in which he might enumerate jazz drummers' favorite chewing gum brands, elucidate stick techniques, or, as he did on one occasion, adroitly parody Ernest Hemingway: "But I can say this, sir, that Chick Webb is much better than whom and who and he's good and he's very, very good and he does everything there is to be done to a drum and he does it beautifully," Tough wrote.[12]

Though a bit of a recluse who would characteristically avoid playing solos, Tough shared with Artie a love of both reading and hot jazz. In the 1930s they would venture up to Harlem together to catch the latest jams. He knew Artie's library. During a September 6, 1941, broadcast appearance at Atlantic City's Steel Pier, Dave was part of the aggregation that ran through a set that started with Artie's "Nightmare" theme, followed by "Frenesi," "Dancing in the Dark," "Time Was," "There'll be Some Changes Made," "Blues in the Night" and "Little Gate's Special."[13] Artie knew that with this background, Dave Tough could be the foundation of the new navy band.

Artie wrangled some other former bandmates as well. His old friend from Cleveland days, pianist and arranger Claude Thornhill, was now a bandleader in his own right. Artie called him "not only a damn good musician, but far and away one of the best piano players I had ever heard."[14] The Indiana native could seem a softy, with one music magazine referring to him as "the chubby one," and Artie unkindly described him as "a funny looking gent, with that potato nose and round Germanic face." Still, for all of the soft impressions he conveyed, Thornhill could also be willful. "It wasn't easy for him to express himself," Artie said. "He hid inside himself. But he was more guileful than he appeared, because he generally got what he wanted."[15]

Claude's piano touch was light, sometimes barely a whisper. Whitney Balliett said his arrangements, featuring distinctive voices such as French horns and tubas, "were more like tone poems than dance-band arrangements [that] spoke of deep velvet, of Matisse reds, of melancholy without tears."[16]

After rooming with Artie in Cleveland, Claude through the 1930s had served a varied apprenticeship. He accompanied the trumpet-wielding showman Louis Prima in 1934 and the next year he joined Ray Noble after the highly popular British pianist and bandleader came to the United States and was compelled by union rules to hire American musicians. Noble turned to Glenn Miller for help in organizing the new band, and Miller brought in Claude, among a number of other talented players.[17]

Thornhill composed his own best-known song, "Snowfall," while he was with Noble. He later made his mark as an arranger in 1937 with a reworking of the Scottish folk song "Loch Lomond." Singer Maxine Sullivan turned it into a hit even after, as historian David W. Stowe recounted, her song was "cut off in mid-broadcast by a Detroit station manager who had supplied a list of songs not to be jazzed." The station manager's order, Stowe added, "was quickly rescinded."[18] It would not be the last time Thornhill's musical conceptions ran afoul of conventional opinion.

Claude made his public debut as a bandleader in April 1940 with an outfit that launched from Hartford, Connecticut, and belly-flopped that September at the Mark Hopkins Hotel in San Francisco.[19] Chastened by the indifferent reactions, Thornhill returned to the stage with an orchestra that *Metronome* magazine described somewhat patronizingly as a "good hotel prospect [that] never plays so loud that you can't talk above it," while Thornhill himself was portrayed as "a cultured chap [who] can talk intelligently with all customers."[20]

When war came, he was willing to do his part. In a March 1942 morale-building concert at the Hollywood Palladium, Thornhill led his band through another composer's new flag-waving ditty entitled "Carry on for General McArthur."[21] As the post–Pearl Harbor months passed, the draft had directly or indirectly peeled away members of Thornhill's orchestra. Musicians were either having their number called or joining up in order to snag a military band slot they hoped would be a sinecure.[22] Claude could see his own number coming up, and he told a reporter conducting a survey of musicians' military service plans that he would choose the navy over the army. It was, he said, just his nature that he'd prefer someplace "on the water."[23] He enlisted in the Naval Reserve as an apprentice seaman on Monday, October 5, and was immediately placed on inactive duty. *DownBeat* reported the following week that "in enlisting, Claude insisted that he wants active duty . . . that he wants no music."[24] In fact, his placement in a navy band slot may have already been secured several weeks before. "I heard Artie Shaw was recruiting a band, so I phoned him in Newark, New Jersey from where I was playing in Nebraska," Claude explained to a reporter later. "We struck up a deal."[25]

Claude had been in Nebraska in mid-September for some shows including a September 12 "Salute to our Heroes" war bond rally in Omaha. His recollection of the timing suggests that he knew exactly in September what type of action he was heading for when he enlisted in October. Claude broke up his civilian band on October 24 and went on active duty on October 26, assigned to Artie's growing outfit. His timing was, so far as his own career went, somewhat poignant. John Skelton would note in *Metronome* that Claude was "within almost measurable inches of hitting, of becoming not only one of the great bandleaders of popular music from a musical point of view but from the commercial, too."[26]

Dave Tough and Claude Thornhill were standout draft picks for the new band. The roster expanded with the addition of 34-year-old trumpeter

Max Kaminsky. His friends knew him as Maxie, a diminutive and colorful jazz man. The youngest of seven children, Max was born in Brockton, Massachusetts, on Labor Day 1908. His father, who emigrated from Russia in the 1880s, ran a grocery store. Max and his twin sister both contracted pneumonia when they were about 1 year old. Max fell into a coma but survived. His twin sister did not. Physically, Max remained a runt. During his teenage years, he recalled feeling such "agony" over his small stature that he wouldn't leave his house. Desperate, he bought a pair of shoes with awkward four-inch lifts.[27]

"Maxie is a very small, good-looking little guy with an accent that still bore traces of his Boston origin," critic Leonard Feather observed in 1944, adding that "he happens to be one of the best-natured musicians you'll ever meet and he hates to say a word against anybody for fear of hurting feelings."[28]

Like others in Artie's circle, Max picked up his first instrument, a cornet, when he was young. He and his early bandmates dressed in sailor suits, played on their backs, and called themselves the Six Novelty Syncopators.[29] Max matured musically when he was about 17 and saw Bix Beiderbecke in a Boston battle of the bands; like others before him, Max had his ears opened by hearing the great jazz cornetist. Max and Artie had first met in New York City sometime around 1930, when Artie was in town with Irving Aaronson's Commanders. At a party Artie and Max got to talking about jazz and drinking bootleg corn whisky—the kind, Max wrote, that "started off as the worst taste you ever tasted but after three or four tastes it tasted fine."[30]

The two young jazz-obsessed musicians would venture to Harlem to hear the real deal whenever they were in town together. Max played with Tommy Dorsey's band in 1936 and then bounced around before joining Artie in January of 1938, an initial pairing that lasted until that June. He could testify to Artie's recruiting skills. "Artie turned on the old charm, with his marvelous laugh and his wonderful way of making you feel he was a real friend," Max wrote.[31]

In truth, their relationship was a complicated one, as was the case with almost everyone who drew close to Artie. What Artie turned on, he could most emphatically turn off. At times Max and Artie more or less stopped talking. Come wartime, though, circumstances changed. Kaminsky heard while playing a gig with clarinetist Joe Marsala's outfit at a roadhouse in Armonk, New York, that his old bandmate was pulling together a new outfit for the navy. Max called to check out the story.

"'Maxie!'" Artie said. "How would you look in the Navy?"[32]

In his not-always reliable autobiography, Max recalled that "although Artie and I had plenty of battles ourselves, going into his Navy band seemed a better idea than going into the Army."[33] Kaminsky said he was in. But it wasn't that simple.

Several weeks after accepting Artie's recruitment pitch, Kaminsky received his Navy Department order to report to New York City's 90 Church Street recruiting station. There, a medical officer informed the trumpeter that he was too short. The navy's minimum standard was five feet, although the standard could be elastic. Sent home, Kaminsky several weeks later received another letter from the navy. He returned to the 90 Church Street station, where the fix might have been in, as he was quickly processed and was sent to the Pier 92 receiving station, where 54th Street met the Hudson River. There, Max joined hundreds of other men in a three-story former passenger terminal previously leased by the Italian Line. The navy had commandeered it in August 1941 to temporarily stash sailors and recruits on their way to somewhere else. It had the smell of navy beans and worse.

"When I finally found an unoccupied cot way up on the fifth tier of bunks, [a] chilling thought occurred to me, 'Buddy, you're in the Navy now.'" Max recalled.[34]

Artie kept recruiting.

Saxophonist Sam Donahue was a movie-star handsome Michigan native who had turned 24 in August of 1942 and who had proven leadership potential. His mother had played piano and sang, and she got him started on the clarinet when he was young. He dropped that for the saxophone, which he played in the Redford High School band in his native Detroit and at beer garden gigs near his home. Donahue had done time with drummer Gene Krupa starting in June of 1938, later joining Harry James in his way up through the ranks. His 1940 draft registration card recorded his then-employer's name and address: Mr. Ben Goodman, 3 East 69th Street New York, New York.

By early 1941 Sam was running his own show. Bandleader Stan Kenton described his musicianship approvingly, as "manly," adding that "it wasn't only the way he handled his horn, it was the positive way he blew."[35] Donahue also looked like a leader. A one-time auto factory worker while he was still in school, he was six feet and one inch tall and weighed a solid 160 pounds. *DownBeat* added that he "sings amiably . . . dresses sharply and is a terrific bandstand attraction himself."[36] He was a road warrior, through and through. After the war he would marry a one-time singer named Patricia; when they separated in 1954, Patricia would tell a judge that her husband had spent only six days at their Southern California home over the past year. "He said he preferred living this way," Patricia Donahue testified, "and if he had to choose between being on the road and living at home, I was at liberty to divorce him."[37]

Donahue's band in early 1942 was a promising young outfit, but by May there were reports that his Detroit-area draft board was scrutinizing his 3-A draft status, the same one Artie once held. A number of musicians and composers were similarly low priority for the draft because they were deemed to be their family's sole economic provider. Like Artie, though, Donahue could apparently anticipate the impending loss of this protected status. It seemed, a *DownBeat* critic lamented in October, "a shame that Sam is having to bust up his band just as he was really getting somewhere with it."[38] Several of his civilian bandmates, including trombone players Earle "Dick" LeFave and Tak Takvorian would join him in Artie's navy band. Donahue would end up chafing under Artie's management, but then would arguably surpass him as a leader of the outfit.

Trumpeter John Best Jr., a 29-year-old North Carolina native, was another former bandmate of Artie's. Best had studied at Davidson College before being initiated into the professional band business with an outfit called Elga and Her Melody Men, an eight-piece dance orchestra founded around 1930. Elga was described in newspaper accounts as the South's only girl orchestra leader; Best recalled she was "thin as a slat and played a saxophone that sounded like a kazoo," while her husband "was a tough guy who carried a gun." Best moved on to other bands, each instructive in their own way.[39] "We never made any money," Best recalled. "If we did make it, the leader would go off with it in those days. I remember we did a whole bunch of college stuff in North Carolina and Virginia, and this guy took all the money. The next time we saw him, he's smoking an expensive cigar and has a beautiful new suit."[40]

Best knocked around a bit before landing in New York City in 1936. Newcomers had to maintain their New York City residency continuously for six months before they secured their card with the American Federation of Musicians Local 802, but soon after Best arrived, Artie offered him $75 a week to join his new traveling band. Best told Artie he didn't want to leave the city if it meant losing credit with the local union for the three months of residency he had already put in. Artie reassured him it would be taken care of. So Best joined Artie's band, traveled with it to out-of-town gigs, and then learned that Artie had dropped the ball. Best said he learned his lesson: Don't trust Artie Shaw.[41]

Best quit that band, but then about eight months later was recruited again by Artie. In 1939 Best quit Artie a second time to join Glenn Miller's outfit, apparently after a nonmusical dispute. The talented trumpet player, a brown-haired, brown-eyed man who stood a bit above five feet and ten inches tall, would only say later that this conflict with Artie involved an individual of "another sex."[42]

While with the Miller organization, Best recorded a solo on the hit "Stardust" that remained one of his personal favorites for years. He was later for a short while with Bob Crosby, the younger brother of Bing, the crooner. Then, as he later recounted to writer Warren Vache, Best happened to be backstage after a show when the phone rang. Best answered it. Artie Shaw was on the other end, and he got right down to business. "I have permission to recruit a band of professional musicians for the Navy," Artie told Best. "I have a place in it for you if you want it."[43]

Best's prior experience with Artie had soured hm, but Artie wanted to look at the future and not the past. He told Best who else had signed on: Claude Thornhill, Davey Tough, and Max Kaminsky and the others. "It sounded like a pretty good group," Best said. "And it was."[44]

Player by player, Artie's navy band was becoming a hot shop, and talented youngsters like trumpet player Conrad Gozzo wanted in. In time

Gozzo's peers would recognize him as, in Best's words, "the Enrico Caruso, Jack Dempsey and Babe Ruth of the trumpet."[45] But when Artie got hold of him, Gozzo was a 20-year-old kid with loads of potential and plenty of rough edges. He was something of a fireplug at five feet and six inches tall and 180 pounds. His father, an Italian immigrant, had been a professional trumpet player and a demanding music teacher who started his son on the instrument by the age of 5. Goz did poorly in high school, but he practiced incessantly, driven by his father's slaps and shouts. As an adult Gozzo hunched when he played, his head tucked as if protectively into his shoulders.[46] "Goz used to recall his dad's first words when he got home from work," a friend recounted years later. " 'Conrad, how much did you practice today?' If he didn't get the right answer, Conrad would get the belt."[47]

Like Artie, Goz abandoned high school for the band circuit. By the time he was 19, he was having, he told a *Hartford Courant* reporter in early 1942, the time of his life and "couldn't be happier."[48] Affecting, for a while, a mustache that couldn't disguise his youth, he played with Red Norvo and other leaders, including Claude Thornhill. The bandleaders saw in the young man tremendous energy and potential, though it required special handling. Goz blew his trumpet so hard that in the recording studio he would have to be placed several feet behind the other musicians. He played with Thornhill's outfit until its final performance on October 24, 1942, at the popular Elms Ballroom in Youngstown, Ohio. Days later Thornhill went on active duty with Artie's navy band, and after a brief stint with Benny Goodman, Goz joined up as well on November 11.

Goz's recruitment came after Artie's outfit had transferred from the Newport, Rhode Island, navy base to New York City. *Variety* reported on November 4 that Artie had convinced the navy command that it was too difficult to secure musician recruits in remote Rhode Island and that in New York City the band could fill its open chairs and rehearse. *Variety* and *DownBeat* tracked every development, including various tips that trumpet player Lee Castle or Canadian tenor sax player Georgie Auld were slated to join Artie's navy band. Castle and Auld both ended up elsewhere, but Artie, with the move to the big city, was able to complete his roster.

# Chapter 8

# Meet the Band

Introducing the remaining members of Artie Shaw's Navy Band.[1]

Joining Sam Donahue on saxophone:

Joe Aglora was a trim, five-foot and seven-inch tall, 24-year-old New York native who, like Artie, had sanded the ethnic edges off his birth name—in Joe's case, Aglialoro. He had a recording history dating back to 1939 and had been with an orchestra led by Eddie DeLange, the lyricist of hits including "Darn That Dream" and "String of Pearls." Aglora was a capable supporting player on alto sax and a bit of a neatnik. Once the navy band hit the road, he would earn some additional money on the side by meticulously laundering the other musicians' widely loathed white sailor uniforms.[2]

Baritone sax man Charlie Wade was a Fall River, Massachusetts, native who turned 38 in in November 1942. He was one of the oldest members of the band and, standing all of five feet and three inches, one of the shortest. Wade was born into a musical family that he said used to sing together because they were too poor to buy instruments. Though he reportedly earned a scholarship to the New England Conservatory of Music, the lure of playing professionally proved too great to resist. He was a bit of a journeyman; as a member of the NBC Orchestra in 1938, he had backed up Kate Smith's indelible rendering of "God Bless America." "I chose to become a musician because I'm lazy," Wade declared. "I knew I had to do something that came easy to me and music fit that category."[3]

Mack Pierce Pitt was a slender six-foot tall musician in his early 20s. A name changer like Shaw and Aglora, he was born Mack Leb Pitkowitz in Detroit and had been introduced to the mandolin and the fiddle at a young age. By the time he was 8, he was performing with the Workmen's Circle Mandolin Orchestra in Newark, New Jersey. He later picked up the vibraphone and, finally, the saxophone. After dropping out of high school, he initially landed a gig with the pit orchestra at Radio City Music Hall before starting with traveling bands. His last name was sometimes rendered as Pitt and sometimes as Pierce.[4]

Ralph LaPolla was a Rhode Island native who turned 21 in September 1942. His sax-playing career was boosted by his father and his own adaptability. Ralph had studied clarinet under a member of the Boston Symphony Orchestra, worked for the Providence radio stations WEAN and WJAR, and played jazz at night to pay for the lessons. He'd arrived in New York City at 18 and played with Vaughn Monroe's outfit.[5] After reading about Artie's navy band in *DownBeat*, Ralph's father reportedly arranged for his son to have an audition. But on the day in question, when his accompanist began playing, LaPolla realized the piano was flat. Without missing a beat, he deftly adjusted his alto sax mouthpiece, transposing the tune into the proper key.

"That's quick thinking, lad," Artie told him.[6] And with that, the quick thinker was in.

On trumpet:

Frank Beach competed the powerhouse lineup of Max Kaminsky, John Best, and Conrad Gozzo. Beach was a 21-year-old native of Winnipeg, Canada, who had been with Stan Kenton's orchestra when he was still a teenager. Artie's navy band was only the second outfit he'd played with.

On trombone:

Wilson "Gene" Leetch was a soft-spoken native of Kankakee, Illinois, in his mid-20s who had studied at Illinois Wesleyan University before enlisting in the navy in 1941 prior to the Pearl Harbor attack. He was stationed for a time at the Great Lakes Naval Training Station, a facility that hosted one of the best service bands. Along with Artie, he would be one of the navy band's married members. Unlike Artie's, Leetch's 1942 marriage would go the distance.[7]

Earle "Dick" LeFave was a Boston-area native born in 1914. He'd been playing professionally since he was 18 and had spent time working the society circuit. A former member of both the Benny Goodman and San Donahue prewar bands, LeFave could cut up on stage, with one jazz reviewer recounting his "burlesque trombone solos that would leave not only his audience but his fellow bandsmen in a state of helpless laughter."[8] LeFave was also a licensed barber, which a reporter pointed out was "a break for the Donahue bandsmen, none of whom has had to visit a barbershop since Dick joined the outfit."[9]

Vahey "Tak" Takvorian turned 20 in August 1942. The Somerville, Massachusetts, native was one of the heftier recruits, weighing in at 195 pounds and standing five feet and ten inches tall. His athleticism and physicality would come in handy down the road, when the notion of a battle of the bands took on new meaning. Tak had started on cello before picking up the trombone, and by the time he was in high school, he was gigging with a band four nights a week. He went on to play with the Sam Donahue outfit, along with LeFave.[10] Tak's twin brother, Vasken, played bass, and the two enlisted in the navy on October 15, 1942, on the advice of their father, a World War I veteran who urged them, above all else, to avoid the army. Donahue suggested Tak's name to Artie as a good candidate for Navy Band 501, and so the navy summoned V. Takvorian to New York City.

But they got the other Takvorian brother, Vasken instead of Vahey.

"He got there and he told Shaw, 'I think you've got the wrong Takvorian,'" Tak later recounted. "And Shaw said, 'How many musicians named V. Takvorian can there be?'"

Two, it seemed.

The navy straightened out the brothers and brought Tak to join Artie's group. Vasken was retrieved by the personnel bureau and eventually joined an aircraft carrier band.[11]

Some musician's names initially got attached to the band, but then they fell off the roster. Guitarist Turk Van Lake, another veteran of Sam Donahue's civilian band, was reported in the December 1, 1942, issue of *DownBeat* to have been recruited, but that putative assignment didn't last. Ray Heath, a trombone player from Vaughn Monroe's outfit, joined Artie's navy band in late September. Shortly before Navy Band 501 departed the East Coast, though, Heath was, in the somewhat enigmatic phrasing of *Variety*, "caught sleepwalking." "Since the Navy prefers musicians who don't sleepwalk, Shaw was obliged to replace him," the entertainment newspaper reported.[12]

Heath's abrupt departure left Artie scrambling for a last-minute replacement. Claude Thornhill suggested another member of Vaughn Monroe's outfit, a 23-year-old Pittsburgh native named Tasso Harris. Harris had previously played with Thornhill as well as vibist and bandleader Red Norvo. He was well regarded by his peers as a musician who could play, as one admiring critic put it, "wonderfully phrased solos with a queer, pulsing vibrato that is all his own."[13]

Over dinner at New York City's Villa Nova restaurant, Artie made his pitch and Harris bought it. The next day, November 30, the young trombone player went to the 90 Church Street recruiting station and signed up. He was immediately issued his uniform and that was it: Tasso Harris was now Seaman Harris. At least, that's what his piece of paper said. Like many of the other hastily recruited members of Navy Band 501, he apparently skipped anything resembling boot camp. This streamlined the band's formation but would later complicate relations with the traditional navy.

On the upright bass, Bernhard "Barney" Spieler provided the band a solid footing. Born in Newark, New Jersey, in 1922 to Yiddish-speaking Russian immigrant parents, Barney had spent his formative years in Brooklyn, in what his bandmates would later come to understand had been an unhappy family. By the time he was fully grown, he could manhandle his instrument. Spieler stood nearly six feet and four inches tall and weighed 230 pounds at the time of his Selective Service physical. He was, one civilian violinist recalled, a "Falstaffian figure," with a scar beneath his chin behind which there was no doubt a story.[14]

Artie had one piano player already in Claude Thornhill, but he added another with the recruiting of Rocco Collucio, inevitably known as Rocky. Collucio was a personable native of Rome, New York, who had just turned 22 in August of 1942. He struck some of his bandmates as a bit of a glad-hander, everyone's friend. In later years he would be a natural on Las Vegas stages.

In a farsighted move, Artie recruited Harold Wax, a 20-year-old accordion ace. Harold had begun playing the instrument in public when he was 13, first at his father's tavern in Newark, New Jersey, and later in performances broadcast over Newark's WAAT radio. That, apparently, is how Artie first heard him. The bandleader called the studio and asked for Harvey. After convincing the skeptical youngster of his bona fides, Artie invited him the next day to his place at The Whitby in Manhattan's Theater District. Wax later said that Artie told him the navy band's plan was to go to Hawaii and then return stateside to perform for bond rallies. There was, apparently, no talk of venturing into war zones. The accordion was an unconventional addition to a jazz band, but Artie was thinking ahead to circumstances where the portable keyboard might be just the ticket.[15] Harold, in any event, thought the deal sounded good, and he signed up on November 2.

Al Horesh was not Artie's first choice for guitar, but the bandleader was impressed when he heard the 22-year-old Cleveland native play at the Hotel Pennsylvania while scouting another musician in the Bob Allen orchestra. A big, lanky guy, pleasant to all, Horesh would go off and practice by himself when the other band members were horsing around.[16]

Arranger Richard "Dick" Jones was, at 36, another one of the older recruits snagged by Artie. The two men had known each other for about six years, having met at the storied 1936 concert when Jones was with the Tommy Dorsey Orchestra and Artie had unveiled his "Interlude in B-flat." After leaving the Dorsey organization, Jones had turned to full-time arranging with Glen Gray and the Casa Loma Orchestra, and it was for his arranging that Artie picked him up.[17]

Artie added New York–based arranger David Rose, who shared a name with composer David Rose. Artie's recruit had previously worked with Vaughn Monroe and several other groups, but Rose was also young, and street-seasoned characters like Davey Tough considered him a bit of a square.[18]

When he was done recruiting, Artie had himself quite a band. Many already knew each other. Artie had played with Best, Kaminsky, Tough, and Thornhill. Thornhill had played with Harris. Donahue had played with Takvorian and LeFave. Taken together, Artie's new outfit had several stand-out soloists backed up by rock-solid support players and two adroit arrangers. In Thornhill and Tough, the band had name players who amplified the orchestra's celebrity appeal. Live wires like Kaminsky could inject some New Orleans zest into performances, while Donahue was a leader in his own right, a man upon whom others might rely. It was a happening outfit.

"Artie Shaw has developed an unusual band for the Navy," jokester Milton Berle wisecracked in his November 11, 1942, *Variety* column. "It's composed of 67 bosn'n mate's whistles and a foghorn."

The men wore uniforms. They saluted their superiors, after a fashion. They would have a unit designation, Navy Band 501. The lash of military discipline could reach them. They were a navy band, no doubt. At the same time, the band stood apart. The men had not been forged by a common basic training. Some had just been thrown a duffle bag and ordered aboard. Some had no business being in the military at all. The rank of chief petty officer, which customarily reflected years of sea service, was simply bestowed upon Artie. In public Artie took pride in the enlisted man's rank. There was nothing ostentatious about it. As he learned more about military protocol, though, Artie would eventually kvetch about how he lacked sufficient rank to work his will or avoid harassment from the brass.

The Navy Band 501 musicians were young. Most were under 24, and several were barely out of their teens. In this they more or less matched the overall World War II US Navy, in which more than 60 percent of enlisted men were aged 24 or younger. Age did not necessarily comport with leadership or even maturity. At 35 Dave Tough was among the more senior band members and, musically, one of the most well respected. For all his road wiles, though, he was not well suited to take charge of anything but the beat. Offstage he'd lose himself in books or in the bottle, or in both. Sometimes he would disappear altogether, only to be found curled up with a bottle and some blankets in a little nest beneath the bandstand.[19]

The bandmembers were not well educated. Many had dropped out of high school to play music professionally, including Artie, Max Kaminsky, Conrad Gozzo, Mack Pierce Pitt, and Charlie Wade. This was not unusual at the time. In 1940 some 64 percent of US adults aged 25–34 had not graduated from high school. The musicians were all white. The US military would remain segregated throughout the war, and one navy band was not about to challenge that. But in other ways, Artie's outfit reflected America's diversity. Artie's father was born in the Ukrainian city of Odessa. Max Kaminsky's and Barney Spieler's fathers were born in Russia. Rocky Collucio's and Conrad Gozzo's fathers were born in Italy. Tak Takvorian's father was born in Armenia, Davey Tough's in Scotland, Frank Beach's in Canada, and Harold Wax's in Poland. Both of Tasso Harris's parents were Greek immigrants. Six of the band members were Jewish. Navy Band 501 was in many ways a proverbial melting pot.

The formation of Artie's band throughout the fall of 1942 and its ultimate destination captivated the music world. On November 15, 1942, *DownBeat* floated the rumor that "the boys will move out to the West Coast as soon as they are thoroughly organized [and] make a movie to match the Army's 'This is the Army' picture." In time, this idea of a navy flick sank without a trace.

Meanwhile, other bandleaders had been making moves of their own. In mid-September 1942, Glenn Miller seized the spotlight when he enlisted in the Army Air Forces at the immediately bestowed rank of captain. "I feel I wasn't doing enough, and I wanted to do more," Miller explained, adding that "I'm in for the duration."[20]

Glenn Miller was stubborn that way.

An Iowa native, Miller had gotten his performing start as a 13-year-old, playing trombone in a Sunday School band. He did a brief stint at the University of Colorado and continued moving up the musical ladder. Through the Great Depression, Miller played with a succession of bands that included those led by the Dorsey brothers, Tommy and Jimmy, and alongside Claude Thornhill. In 1937 Miller organized his first band as a leader. He kept plugging away until he broke through with a combination of radio broadcasts and recorded hits including "Moonlight Serenade" and "Little Brown Jug," both released in 1939. His live performances during an extended engagement starting in May of the same year at the Glen Island Casino located in New York's Long Island Sound drew record-setting crowds and propelled him along the celebrity path.[21]

At 38 Miller was getting long in the tooth for military service, but he wanted to serve. He first applied for a commission in the Naval Reserve, offering letters of recommendation from the likes of crooner Bing Crosby. The navy, though, was facing scrutiny over alleged bribes being paid by entertainers seeking sinecures, and his application was rejected.[22] The willful bandleader pivoted, and on September 8, 1942, the War Department announced Miller's commission as an Army Air Forces captain. He retained his own dedicated public relations man, George Evans, who would, *DownBeat* explained, "attempt to keep Glenn's name before his millions of fans by press stories of GM's activities" and by getting his records played over the radio.[23]

Miller and Artie were the best known of the prewar bandleaders to enlist, but the services kept claiming others as well. Bobby Byrne, a talented trombonist and notoriously demanding leader, joined the Army Air Forces along with four of his men in November 1942. The next month, violinist and trombonist Ted Weems and his entire fourteen-member orchestra joined the merchant marine force for duty in the San Francisco Bay Area. Phil Harris, who led the musicians on Jack Benny's radio show, also joined the merchant marine about the same time for duty on sunny Catalina Island in Southern California. There were also many who did not serve. Benny Goodman, who turned 33 in May of 1942, was classified as 4-F because of a bad back, and there was a parade of other performers deemed physically unfit for service from crooner Frank Sinatra to trumpet ace Harry James. "One of the reasons often given for the high rate of rejectees among music men is the fact that bandleaders, side-men and singers live a fast, tense life which tends to throw their nervous systems out of gear, thus making it impossible for them to adapt themselves without mental breakdowns to the rigor and disciplined of a serviceman's life," *DownBeat* reasoned.[24]

Those musicians who made the grade were in for a shock. As civilian band members, they lived by night, intoxicated themselves freely, and escaped from domestic responsibilities. Although notoriously demanding leaders like Benny Goodman and Tommy Dorsey kept their men in line, military discipline was a slap in the face. The navy's new recruits were rising with the sun, deciphering alien orders, and marching, more or less, in line.

Sometimes they made a hash of it, shuffling out of step or veering off in the wrong direction altogether. At one point early in the formation of Artie's navy band, Claude Thornhill fielded, absurdly, a set of cymbals while he stumbled along on his two left feet. "For men with a professional sense of rhythm, my band marked up records for poor marching," Artie said. "I think a troupe of baboons could have been trained to do it better."[25]

Trumpet player John Best ruefully acknowledged the mess they made of the most basic of military drills, recalling that "if anybody could have seen us, they might have taken us for a comic routine in the movies." The bandsmen even flip-flopped their way through the occasional morning calisthenics, that military staple also known as PT. Best described it as the "Gene Tunney routine, where you jump up and down waving your arms." The musicians were a sight to see at sunrise. Drummer Dave Tough's skinny legs, Best said, "never left the ground, but his arms kept moving."[26]

A few other military obligations came with the territory. Best recalled that one cold night when the crew was at New York City's Pier 92, he saw Artie dutifully standing guard over the wreck of the USS *Lafayette* at nearby Pier 88. The ship, formerly a French passenger liner called the *Normandie*, had been seized by US authorities in 1940 and renamed. It was in the process of being converted to a troopship when it caught fire in February of 1942. The wreck needed little protecting, other than against curious passersby, but the assignment gave Artie a taste of conventional navy duty.

A little of this went a long way, and the men couldn't get out of Pier 92 fast enough, though where they were bound for was still uncertain. Citing "Navy officials familiar with the situation," *Variety* reported on November 11, 1942, that Artie and his band had "definitive orders to move out of New York early in December and head for the Pacific area." On November 30, the band members boarded trucks for the trip from Pier 92 through the blacked-out city to Pennsylvania Station.

"Take a good, long look," Dave Tough said softly when the truck carrying the men turned down Broadway.

"I feel like I've been shanghaied," Max Kaminsky told his bandmates.[27]

At the train station, family members, associates, and assorted others gathered to see the navy band off. The energetic bookers Joe and Si Shribman, who were watching some of their biggest earners slip away, were said by one sardonic reporter to "be seen weeping quietly into their billfolds."[28] Si Shribman mordantly urged one musician to return with all of his arms and legs intact, while Hermine Wax, the distraught Austrian-born mother of young accordion player Harold Wax, made her own tearful plea.

"Please take care of my little boy," Hermine asked Chief Petty Officer Shaw.[29]

# Chapter 9

# Shipping Out

And so Shaw's Rangers trained for they knew not what.

No one seemed to know their destination for sure. One reporter suggested that "Artie Shaw's Navy orchestra may tour the country or promote War Bond drives."[1] Others still entertained the notion of a Hollywood movie gig similar to the once-touted *This Is the Navy*. Even those who placed their bets on Pearl Harbor lacked details about what, exactly, that entailed.

At Penn Station on the night of November 30, the musicians boarded their own train car. There, for the next few days, they could shoot craps, play cards, swap yarns, and, when all other distractions failed, simply stare out the windows at America passing by. Some might have wondered what it was, exactly, that they had gotten themselves into. The newspapers could have clued them in. On the third day of the band's cross-country trip, a widely distributed Associated Press account reported that on the island of Guadalcanal, one Marine Corps patrol "had the best bag" by killing twenty-five Japanese soldiers along the Lunga River. The Lunga was an alien name that the band members would come to know.[2] The December 1 copy of *DownBeat*, if they managed to get one aboard the train, would have informed the band members that Coca-Cola was planning to sponsor two bands on tours of overseas US military bases. Bandleader Kay Kyser was planning his own morale-building tour, and the irrepressible Cab Calloway was thrilled to learn that a B-25 bomber in North Africa was nicknamed "Minnie the Moocher."[3]

Traveling took a toll, but the bandsmen could be grateful they weren't being bounced around on their customary bus with hard seats, worn springs, and no room to move. On the train they could stretch out, stand up, and walk around. They could feel the charge from the start of a new road adventure. Artie himself was still getting to know his men. He could be quite winning at the start of new relationships. An alto sax man from one of his prewar bands, Charles DiMaggio, noted that Artie "was not aloof as many people think. He joined in the dice and card games" with which musicians passed the time while on the road.[4]

After some delays the train pulled into San Francisco on Sunday morning, December 6, just as the city was preparing to mark the one-year anniversary of the Japanese attack on Pearl Harbor. Weary from the cross-country trip, Artie's men were transported to their new temporary quarters at the navy station on Treasure Island. A four-hundred-acre artificial outcrop in San Francisco Bay, Treasure Island had been constructed by the Army Corps of Engineers for the 1939–40 Golden Gate International Exposition. The navy had subsequently moved in, turning the island into a major communications and personnel processing center. The band members were assigned to barracks on the island, but Artie appropriated for himself a room at the Mark Hopkins Hotel in the heart of San Francisco. Artie's pregnant wife Elizabeth and his father-in-law Jerome Kern joined him at the hotel, a popular venue for top bands

Artie took the luxury as his due. He said that he had learned as a civilian bandleader to separate himself from the rank and file, reasoning that this would avoid embarrassing musicians who might be accused of apple polishing if they were to be seen dining with the boss.[5] It was a flimsy cover story that could not prevent Artie from getting a reputation as a man who took care of himself. Still, he joined the band members on Treasure Island as they practiced and pulled together toward a common goal. "Any band," Artie noted, "takes time to work itself into a good ensemble. A certain period is necessary before the men get the feel of each other and learn the music well enough to play freely and uninhibitedly."[6]

During such orchestral formative periods, Artie could be an exemplary leader. He might tinker obsessively, so intently focused that he would forget about calling bathroom breaks, but he communicated clearly what he wanted. His quest for perfection would infect other musicians. In the end, said Neely Plumb, a saxophone player in one of his prewar bands, Artie "almost always got exactly what he was looking for."[7] Shaw's Rangers, as they would be known, squeezed in about a week's worth of practice sessions before they made their West Coast debut. "This aggregation of 20 men is now hard at work on Treasure Island whipping into shape for the biggest engagement of their lives," the military's *Our Navy* magazine reported.[8]

The band played a gig on Treasure Island that *Our Navy* rhapsodically described as a "jive session [for] an impromptu audience of fellow blue-jackets [who] were so impressed that they stepped up and bought more than $7,000 worth of bonds."[9] A more public performance happened the night of December 15, when the band played at San Francisco's Veterans Auditorium on a program honoring the WAVES, the Women Appointed for Volunteer Emergency Service. The head of the new navy auxiliary branch, Lieutenant Commander Mildred McAfee, was in attendance, on leave from her position as president of Wellesley College. McAfee did not let her relatively low rank confine her ambitions. She saw her WAVES as an integral part of the navy even as many insisted on keeping the ladies in their traditional place. At the December 15 concert, some of her enlisted WAVEs were serving as "usher-ettes," as the *San Francisco Chronicle* put it with a patronizing pat on their heads. By war's end McAfee would secure the rank of captain and command some eighty-two thousand women.[10]

Trumpet player John Best excelled at the San Francisco concert with his solo on Jerome Kern's and Johnny Mercer's "Dearly Beloved," a winning song penned for the 1942 Fred Astaire and Rita Hayworth musical comedy *You Were Never Lovelier*. Best's stand-out performance earned him an invitation to a party with Kern, who was in the audience for his son-in-law's show.[11]

The Treasure Island sojourn ended on December 20, when the band boarded the *Lurline,* a converted luxury liner. Some five thousand men were crowded intro all of the ship's nooks and crannies, but the navy musicians enjoyed relatively comfortable cabin arrangements. The ship itself had quite a legacy, having spent years ferrying to Hawaii the well-to-do as well as, in April 1935, the six Black members of a Honolulu-bound dance hall band that would initially be billed as Bernard Banks and his Five Clouds of Rhythm. The outfit would evolve with time into the much-hipper sounding Brown Cats of Rhythm.[12]

On their first day out at sea, Max Kaminsky was in the chow line when a surprised ship's purser called out his name. The purser was a jazz fan and recognized the distinctively small-statured trumpet player. The purser introduced Max to the ship's chef, another former New Yorker, who served up a piece of fresh lemon meringue pie. The chef and the purser thereafter treated the musicians with daily offerings of fresh fruit and full-on meals. Thus fortified, the men settled into the cruise. The ship arrived at Hawaii on Christmas Eve, spent the night outside the submarine net–protected harbor, and then entered the harbor on Christmas Day. A commanding headline in the *Honolulu Advertiser* on the day of their arrival confirmed their entry into the anteroom of war: "Allies Must Kill Japs to Win, Halsey Says."[13]

The blunt pronouncement by Admiral William "Bull" Halsey Jr. showcased the aggressiveness that in October had won him the job of South Pacific area commander, replacing the hesitant Admiral Robert Ghormley. It was also a wake-up call for the men of Navy Band 501, alerting them to the approaching war that had seemed so distant back on the mainland. There were other clues, as well. Oil from warships sunk a year before on December 7, 1941, still oozed into Pearl Harbor. The lei sellers who once greeted new arrivals to the Hawaiian islands in peacetime were now gone, off making camouflage. The island bristled with gun placements, air raid shelters, warehouses, and ammo dumps.[14] "The Territory of Hawaii is no longer a tourist's playground, a Pacific paradise," the *Pearl Harbor Bulletin* advised newcomers in 1943. "It is a great fortress, a Pacific outpost."[15]

Still, six months after the US Navy victory in the Battle of Midway, Hawaii was no longer considered at imminent risk of invasion. Authorities had lifted Honolulu's evening curfew from 8:00 p.m. to 10:00 p.m. in October of 1942. Two months later the restriction on nighttime driving was likewise lifted by two hours, to 10:00 p.m.[16]

Shaw's Rangers claimed their barracks at the US Naval Receiving Station in Aiea, a modest outpost just outside of Honolulu that had been transformed into a 130-acre base eventually containing 117 single-story barracks, four mess halls, two recreation halls, and one administrative building. Artie secured for himself a room at the congenial Halekulani Hotel on Waikiki Beach, eleven miles from the drab Aiea barracks. For Chief Petty Officer Shaw, celebrity status brought other privileges as well, including some bestowed by Vice Admiral William Lowndes Calhoun. A 1906 Naval Academy graduate and former submariner, Calhoun was commander of the supporting service force of the US Pacific Fleet. This made him the man to see about fuel, housing, and any of the myriad other items required to sustain the war effort. He quickly understood Artie's requirements and moved the necessary levers. "I had a station wagon that Admiral Calhoun gave me, that I could drive around the island and see the different bases and see where we should play," Artie recalled.[17]

While Artie was securing his reconnaissance car and his beachside lodging, his men in the Aiea barracks were braced by elementary navy tasks like guard duty, KP, and cleaning details. So it was, not long after the band's arrival in Hawaii, that trumpet players Frank Beach and Conrad Gozzo and piano player Rocky Collucio were shuffling along outside while they halfheartedly stabbed at paper trash. Trombone player Tak Takvorian and piano player and arranger Claude Thornhill were sweeping the tennis courts. Recorded music played over the loudspeakers.

"Suddenly, the loudspeakers went quiet," historian Harold S. Kaye recounted. "A voice came through: 'Now hear this. Now hear this. We are bringing you the music of the amazing Claude Thornhill and his orchestra.'"[18]

The men of Navy Band 501 stopped what they were doing and listened. Sure enough, the 1941 Columbia Records recording of Thornhill's impressionistic civilian theme song "Snowfall" was shimmering over the loudspeakers. Leisurely paced and sweetened with strings, "Snowfall" was about as unmartial as a song could be. The musicians cracked up at the incongruities until the music faded and they had to return to their base-tending duties. The duties, though, also diverted the musicians from preparing for their intended purpose. Apparently with Artie's intervention, they later were said to have gained exemptions from routine details so they might practice.[19]

Such exemptions, or the rumors about them, rankled other enlisted men and prompted speculation about what else Shaw's Rangers might be enjoying. There were always stories circulating around Artie's navy band, along with entertaining vignettes about swabbies crossing paths with the musicians. A tidbit in the January 12, 1943, edition of the *Honolulu Star-Bulletin* recounted the time that "a 'hep' sailor, standing outside a Navy barracks from which hot, sweet music was sweeping, yelled excitedly to a pal. 'Hey, Mac,'" the sailor shouted. "'There's a bunch of boots in there, and a guy playing a clarinet, and, boy, can they whittle!'"[20]

In their Aiea rehearsal hall, the band members picked up where they had left off on Treasure Island. Dave Rose set to work preparing arrangements for tunes from Artie's library, including "Dancing in the Dark," and "The Man I Love." Rose recounted that Artie praised the work he did on arranging the Cole Porter classic "Night and Day." It was, Rose said, "the only compliment I ever heard him give anybody."[21]

The band's job was to play the hits, the familiar songs from peacetime, and play them over and over again. This was, for Artie, the definition of musical hell. He required room to improvise and grow. Still, given a job to do, Artie drove his band hard to perfect even the same old, same old. He described himself as "absolutely meticulous" about rehearsing. Some of his younger navy men would use more pungent words to describe him, but they respected his craftmanship and scrupulous attention to detail. Blessed with what he described as "an almost eidetic memory," Artie had his men run through a number while he would mentally note what went wrong, jot down a word or two as a reminder, and then start over. "Sometimes we'd fall into a bad habit or a trumpet player would do something. Sometimes good," Artie recalled. "Then I'd say, 'let's everybody do that.' Or sometimes bad, and I'd say, 'look, you're falling into this and I don't want it. I want this. Cut that note short. Don't hold it longer.'"[22]

The Hawaii practice sessions were just getting underway when *Down Beat* magazine came out with its latest annual poll of some fifteen thousand readers. The fans named Artie Shaw's as the best military service orchestra. The first-place finish was presumptive, a reflection of civilian reputations, but the time was finally arriving when Artie's men would be put to the test. After not quite two weeks of practice, Navy Band 501 kicked off its Hawaii run on Sunday, January 10, with an afternoon appearance at a new enlisted man's club. It was called The Breakers.

# Chapter 10

# The Breakers

Navy Commander Stockard R. Hickey wanted fighting men to have some fun.

The Seventh Fleet's recreation and morale officer, Hickey held a job that the *Honolulu Star-Bulletin* reported in a December 6, 1941, article meant "plenty of sweat, worry and work, cheerfully given." After all, as the feature article blithely pointed out, "All work and no play makes Jack a dull boy [and] the U.S. Navy has no use for dull boys."[1] A native of the Deep South, Hickey was a World War I veteran who had been assigned the recreation and morale job in May 1941. He took it seriously. "We cannot overestimate the value of recreation," Hickey declared several weeks after the Pearl Harbor attack, adding that "Americans need relaxation. They work hard, and the combination is what makes for spirit, efficiency and happiness." Indeed, the navy commander opined that the recreation program "paid heavy dividends" on December 7, when, he declared, "our men of the fleet showed definitively they were no softies."[2]

Hickey's turf included softball fields, boxing rings, bowling alleys, an archery range, swimming pools, handball courts. and church services. The jewel in the crown was The Breakers, a one-story enlisted men's club located alongside the southern edge of Waikiki Beach. Outside, the club offered volleyball, handball, and badminton courts. There were horseshoe pits and facilities for those using the beach. Inside, the handsome club building included two long bar counters, a library room, a twenty-thousand-square-foot teak dance floor, and a four-hundred-square-foot stage. A preopening *Honolulu Star-Advertiser* ad depicted its future clientele as a grinning swabbie, as innocent as an Iowa cornfield. "Yes, sailor," the ad stated, "the Navy has spared no expense to make your new club 'The Breakers' up to the minute in every respect, and naturally good, rich Dairymen's Ice Cream will be there on the bill of fare!"[3]

The Breakers had formally opened on December 2, 1942, in a ceremony attended by a capacity crowd of some three thousand people led by Honolulu's civic and military luminaries. Admiral D. W. Bagley, commandant of the 14th Naval District, enthusiastically described the club as a place where "men of the armed forces could find amusement and relaxation that will sustain the spirit that makes victory possible." A navy band played "Anchors Aweigh," and Admiral Nimitz dutifully waltzed with a USO showgirl.

A month later, *DownBeat* kicked off the new year with a January 1, 1943, edition that featured a front-page picture of Army Air Forces Captain Glenn Miller, along with tiny digs directed at both Miller and Artie. The photograph, according to the periodical, showed a proud-looking Miller "in full regalia, striding off in the general direction of Montgomery Field in Alabama." It noted, as well, that the cigarette-holding bandleader, in apparent homage to his former commercial sponsor, was still "Chesterfield conscious." A smaller front-page item, inserted in a column by Rod Reed, offered an insider's gag that "Artie Shaw's band is well known for a secret mission. Jam men in the band have often proved their ability to make a secret of whatever they were playing."

Artie's band made its Hawaiian public debut at The Breakers on the afternoon of January 10, 1943. After the unsettled months of recruitment, rail, and ship travel, the band was finally being invited into a groove, with its new schedule that called for shows at The Breakers on Sundays and Thursdays from 1:00 p.m. to 4:00 p.m. Wearing a tie and a khaki uniform, Artie was on his best behavior at the kickoff show. Notorious for turning his back on the audience in his civilian days, he dutifully signed autographs for young female fans. He similarly charmed *Honolulu Star-Bulletin* reporter Betty MacDonald, who described Artie's clarinet as a "magic wand" that drew thousands of people to the club. "He says he'd rather be doing band work than fighting in the Pacific because 'music is something I know a lot about. I'd only be in the way on a warship,'" MacDonald reported.[4]

MacDonald would write more stories about Artie's navy band and its individual members over the next few months, until she joined the Office of Strategic Services for an adventure of her own in India and China.[5] Before she shipped out, she turned her attention to Sam Donahue, praising him as "one of the best tenor sax players in the swing business." She quoted Donahue as saying that he intended either to blow his horn "right in der fuehrer's face" or lead a victory march through the streets of Tokyo.[6] Lesser-known members of the band got some attention as well, including Mack Pierce Pitt. The 22-year-old saxophone player earnestly praised Artie as having "done more for swing than any other bandleader," and he enthused over the supposed benefits of military service. "Navy life is a great chance," Pierce assured a *Honolulu Star-Bulletin* reporter. "I've learned to do without luxuries and to appreciate many of the things I took for granted before."[7]

Artie, too, puffed up and blew for the benefit of Hawaii's reporters. He told one scribe that once the band members "played together a little longer," they were going to be one of the best bands anywhere, and he proffered mighty ambitions for himself, as well. "When my grandchildren climb on top of my knee and say, 'Granddaddy, what did you do during the war?' I'm going to tell them that I led the march into Tokyo and played at the victory ball at Hirohito's palace," Artie declared.[8] Of course, Artie could tell any old war story he wanted, regardless of the facts. The same was true for members of his navy band. Their war stories would always remain subject to whim and improvisation.

The band followed up the inaugural show at The Breakers later in January with an appearance in the unusual factory setting of Shipfitters Shop 11, part of the sprawling Navy Yard on the island of Oahu. Since being established as a repair station in 1908, the Navy Yard had grown into a bustling industrial city with administrative buildings, barracks, warehouses, a power plant, and one of the world's largest dry docks. The place hummed around the clock.

"Men worked long, hard hours, with little sleep and little recreation," a Navy Yard history recounted, adding that "repair records were broken as the work of keeping the Fleet 'fit to fight' went into high gear."[9]

Managers tended the workers' morale with tours, lectures, games, and shows. The Navy Yard's Welfare Department loaned instruments to the rotating members of a civilian band. The mid-January appearance of Artie Shaw and his navy band, though, was a cut above the Yard's usual morale-building efforts. The musicians were still fresh and the workers were thrilled that, as a Navy Yard newsletter put it with some asperity, they were "at long last" being remembered by the entertainment world. Artie's noontime show lit up the place, though the Yard's newsletter acknowledged the industrial setting was a "far cry from the hotel rooftops, sophisticated clubs and mammoth ballrooms" that the musicians were used to. Thousands of welders, electricians, metal workers, and other tradesmen jammed shoulder to shoulder, climbed into the rafters, and squeezed together atop cranes. It was a welcome fit for music royalty; as one Navy Yard wit put it, "One way to detect a Jap spy: If he asks 'who's Artie Shaw,' nab him."[10]

"As a warmup, Shaw played 'Begin the Beguine,' always solid; 'Stardust,' mellow,'" a Navy Yard worker and jazz aficionado named Walter Primeau reported, "and then, with real cooperation from the rest of the band found the groove with 'Just Foolin' Around,' and 'Suite No. 8.'" Primeau was clued in enough to observe that Claude "did his stuff on a small upright, but despite the piano's limitations showed us why he's tops. . . . All in all," Primeau added, "the jiving Jacks and Jills are still jitting and await with enthusiasm the return of the Rangers."[11]

The Navy Yard performance reached thousands, and there were many more craving a taste. One defense worker, Walter Carvalho, wrote the *Honolulu Star-Bulletin* in late January to enthuse that Artie "certainly swings it in the groove" and to plead on behalf of others in his situation. "How's chances of having Artie Shaw play for us defense workers, especially at night, on some [radio] program?" Carvalho asked.[12]

Radio broadcasts of Artie Shaw's Navy Band in the Pacific could have been a sure hit, as Glenn Miller would show the next year with his Army Air Forces Band broadcasts from England, but with one brief exception the navy band stayed off the air. The exception occurred January 30 when Shaw's Rangers popped over to Ford Island in the middle of Pearl Harbor, the site of a modest Naval Air Station. Japanese dive bombers had battered it on December 7, 1941, damaging several hangars and other buildings as well as thirty-three navy patrol planes lined up outside like ducks in a row. Even a year later, Artie Shaw's men might have seen scars from the attack while they set up in a hangar.[13]

The Ford Island appearance was part of a broadcast show honoring President Franklin Delano Roosevelt on his 61st birthday. Artie knew the president a bit. In January 1939 he had joined actors John Garfield and Frances Farmer at the White House to urge support for the Federal Arts Project.[14] Now, some three years later, Artie was celebrating the president in an ambitious broadcasting feat. Clifton Fadiman, host of CBS radio's popular quiz show *Information, Please!* served as master of ceremonies from New York City's Waldorf-Astoria Hotel. The hour-long program included musical bits by Frank Sinatra, Bing Crosby, and a two-hundred-voice choir from the navy's Great Lakes Training Center, among others. On Ford Island band members set up in their rows, the brass and reed players each sitting behind the music stands that proclaimed "Artie" on one side and "Shaw" on the other. With Claude Thornhill at the piano, backup keyboard player Rocky Collucio wandered about, snapping photographs. When the radio show's baton was passed to Hawaii, Artie's band kicked off with the "Nightmare" theme song followed by Artie's personal happy birthday wishes for FDR and then a rendering of the inevitable "Begin the Beguine." Even some of the band's most road-weary musicians got a kick out of the show.[15] "Did you by any chance hear our air shot on the President's Birthday Ball?" Tough wrote relatives. "It was short-waved from here to the mainland. They announced 'drummer Dave Tough,' and I was at that very moment hoping that the gang [in Oak Park, Illinois] was listening in."[16]

Following the Navy Yard and Ford Island gigs, Shaw's Rangers settled into a bit of a routine. They interspersed shows throughout the islands with their twice-weekly performances at The Breakers, where one scribe enthused that "Shaw soon had the hepcats and jive artists from every ship and station turning up in large numbers."[17]

On Friday, April 16, the musicians boarded vehicles for the trip out to a remote facility known formally as Naval Ammunition Depot Oahu. The depot was spread across three locations, with its headquarters occupying some eight thousand acres in a deep valley thirty-five miles from Honolulu. Miles of tunnels had been dug into the mountainsides and underground railroad tracks laid down for the hauling and storage of ammo. The depot's workers were being presented with a morale-boosting star to the army and navy "E" pennant for proficiency they had first won the previous September, and Navy Band 501 was on hand to provide the celebratory music.[18]

By this time the musicians could handle a routine show like the ammunition depot job in their sleep. One Army Air Corps enlisted man who saw the band several times, Corporal Merrit Wetzler, reported in a letter to *Metronome* that he had "never heard anything like it." Wetzler added that in his "humble opinion, it is one of the best young bands out there," and he deftly recognized that Artie was also "doing himself a world of good in the way of publicity" with his musical service.[19] Another enlisted man recounted enthusiastically that "when Artie gets through, they have to get the boys and girls down out of the trees."[20]

At The Breakers business was brisk. By year's end managers of the enlisted men's recreational venue would report that attendance throughout 1943 had totaled approximately five hundred thousand.[21] Besides accomplishing its purpose of providing a place where servicemen can really enjoy themselves, The Breakers had "reduced attendance at less desirable bars in downtown Honolulu and cut in half the traffic jam in peak hours at the Army-Navy Y," the *Paradise of the Pacific* magazine reported in February 1943.[22] The joints in question included the legal brothels clustered around Honolulu's notorious Hotel Street neighborhood, where customers would wait their turn in line while the Honolulu Police Department's Vice Squad kept the working girls in their places and away from Waikiki Beach or anywhere else polite society might be found. Compared to such carnality, The Breakers did indeed offer a cleaner-cut entertainment alternative, although hot music, too, could rouse some passions.

One visitor to the enlisted men's club, an army musician named Jacob Kokinski, recounted throughout the spring of 1943 his mixed experiences at The Breakers. A multi-instrumentalist who could alternate between saxophone, trumpet, and clarinet, Kokinski advised his hometown newspaper in rural Virginia that one of his visits to the club was "believe me . . . the best time I have had since I am in the Army." But on another occasion, Kokinski described a chaotic scene that sounded closer to a rumble than a dance. Sweaty sailors and other men of war were jammed in together, shoulder to shoulder. Beer bottles clattered across the floor. Photographers, autograph hounds, and star stalkers crowded around the stage. Kokinski said it took him thirty minutes to push through the mob and reach the front, and he lost several buttons on his shirt along the way. He looked and felt, he said, like he had been tackled by the Notre Dame football team, and when he finally he got a close look at Artie, he saw a man who was recoiling from the chaos. "After taking one look at Shaw's face, I really couldn't blame him," Kokinski recounted. "Every guy there was bending over in every angle taking pictures and yelling 'Hiya Art' and shaking pencils and pens in his face and in general pestering him to death."[23]

Another audience member at The Breakers, a *DownBeat* contributor named Charlot Slotin, similarly recounted in early April that "one cat in Hawaii" had observed that at a performance of Navy Band 501, "most of the soldiers were greatly disappointed" in Artie's demeanor. "He looked like he just didn't give a darn," Slotin reported. "He walked onto the stage, took a bow without a smile, turned his back to the crowd and remained that way."[24]

However uncomfortable the relationship between bandleader and audience, these were the enlisted men Artie had committed to serving, the young soldiers, sailors, and Marines who manned the battle stations and pulled the triggers. In his later years, Artie would cast his Hawaii run as being strictly for the benefit of these common swabbies and GI Joes. "I was playing for enlisted men. I refused officers' dances. I wouldn't do that," Artie recalled four decades later, citing a particular incident in which he was asked to play at a soiree for officers and nurses. "I said, 'I'm not out here for that. The U.S. taxpayers are paying us, and we should play for the most men we can.'"[25]

His proclamation of principle was heartfelt, but inevitably Artie and his orchestra did cater to officers' country. In March the *Honolulu Star-Bulletin* carried an advertisement announcing that "Artie Shaw's Orchestra" would be playing at an April 1 midafternoon dance sponsored by the wives of Honolulu

Hospital doctors, the nurses' association, and the women's division of the USO. The program was held at the hospital's Mabel Smith Memorial Building on Punchbowl Street, and it was designed for a select audience. "Nurses, doctors and their officer friends are invited," the notice stated, adding that "refreshments will be served" by a hostess committee.[26]

The ad's highlighting of "Artie Shaw's Orchestra" underscored how the bandleader's singular status survived his enlistment into the ranks. In a similar vein, the *Honolulu Star-Advertiser* on February 22 noted that "Artie Shaw and his orchestra" would perform from 4:15 to 7:15 p.m. that day at the Honolulu Civic Auditorium in what was called a "tribute to the Father of America." The advertisement omitted the fact that the orchestra was a navy organization. The music stands that held the scores for the band members likewise associated the outfit with Artie Shaw rather than the navy. They would occasionally leave the music stands behind and assume yet other identities as small combos that could entertain the higher ranks at private parties. The young accordion player Harold Wax took part in some of these side gigs, as did arranger and piano player David Rose, trumpet player Max Kaminsky, and drummer Dave Tough. Pianist Claude Thornhill made a particular impression at some of these command performances, winning over high-ranking fans who would come in handy down the road as his relations with Artie soured.[27]

Artie, too, could charm like a champion when the occasion called for it. He had risen to the challenge the prior December, when his orchestra performed at the WAVES recruiting drive show in San Francisco. Catherine Nimitz, the wife of Admiral Chester Nimitz, had been there, and as he later recounted, she chatted with Artie afterward. "Mr. Shaw, I just want to tell you I'm eternally grateful for what you did. You did a great job for us. When you get to Pearl Harbor, you must tell my husband what I said and give him my love," Catherine Nimitz told the bandleader in San Francisco, according to Artie's subsequent account. Artie said he would, of course, but he figured he'd never get within a hundred miles of the admiral. Nimitz, after all, was formidable, a 59-year-old Texan serving as commander in chief of the US Pacific Fleet. His job was nothing less than the defeat of the Japanese Imperial Fleet. A bandleader was not on his radar.

Several months after that San Francisco encounter, though, Artie and his piano player Rocky Collucio came into the admiral's orbit when they were having lunch in the Halekulani. "All of a sudden, everybody in the place stands up to attention," Artie recalled. "So we got up, and here comes Nimitz, flanked by his braid officers, everybody in glitter and white, and they go to the end of the dining room, where there's a big table, the mayor of Honolulu and apparently some confab about Navy versus civilian business."

At their separate table, the two musicians commented on the arrival of the monarch and his courtiers. Collucio, either then or earlier, had heard of Mrs. Nimitz's message conveyed to Artie. He urged the bandleader to pass it on to the admiral.

"Rocky, I can't go over and interrupt the admiral in charge of the Navy," Artie said, by his recollection. "He said, 'Send him a note.' So I said, 'Yeah, maybe. Why not?'"

Artie recounted that he called the head waiter over and wrote a note, whose contents he recalled decades later: "While I was in San Francisco I had the pleasure of being of service to your wife in a recruiting drive for the WAVES, and she asked me to be sure and give you her love when I saw you. I told her there was little chance that I would, but as usual, the lady is right. Yours truly, Artie Shaw, Chief Bandmaster," Artie recalled the note as saying.

The head waiter took the note and conveyed it up to the admiral's head table. Nimitz looked, turned to a nearby officer, and handed him the piece of paper. That officer looked around the room, but nothing else came of it.

Until the next day, when two no-nonsense Marines came to pick up Shaw and deliver him without explanation to a navy headquarters building. Eventually, the bandleader was standing before one of the admiral's unhappy aides.

"Did you write this?" the officer asked.

"Yes, I did," Shaw said.

"Sir!" the officer sharply reminded the enlisted man.

"Yes, sir, I did," Shaw said.

"You've been in the Navy how long?" the officer asked.

"Almost a year, sir."

"Well, you do know that if you're going to approach a superior officer, you do it through channels?"

"Yes, sir, but this wasn't Navy business."

"Precisely," the officer said.[28]

The staff officer briskly dismissed the impudent musician. In hindsight, it made a story for Artie to tell, funny in a *Reader's Digest* "Humor in Uniform" kind of way, but in truth the upbraiding rankled. Artie was just doing a favor for an admiral's wife, and this was the thanks he got. The sting was an unwelcome reminder that officers could make the bandleader's life miserable in so many ways. Artie, a mere chief petty officer, was at the mercy of the chain of command. While Artie's celebrity status elevated him in the eyes of some, it also put a target on his back. The lash of navy discipline, moreover, came as Hawaii was losing some of its allure to the men of Navy Band 501.

"The sameness of the languid climate and the regular afternoon thunderstorms began to pall after a time," Max Kaminsky wrote.[29] Artie's leadership didn't help. He could shift from collegial jazz man to navy martinet in a moment. Harold S. Kaye, at the time an enlisted man in the Army Air Forces, recalled chancing upon trumpet player Conrad Gozzo, an old high school chum from Connecticut, at one of Navy Band 501's shows. Kaye expressed an interest in meeting the drummer Dave Tough, who he revered from his time with Benny Goodman's outfit. Gozzo gestured for the drummer to come over. "We had just started to talk when Shaw, without apology or excuse, barged into our group and began upbraiding Gozzo and Tough for sharing a can of beer on the bandstand," Kaye recalled. "I was embarrassed, not only for myself but for Gozzo and Tough. Dave muttered something under his breath and walked away with disdain."[30]

It was a telling moment. Artie was perfectly correct in maintaining bandstand discipline. It would not do for enlisted men under his command to be seen getting soused on the job. His public chastisement of the musicians, though, humiliated men whose loyalty he would need in the stressful months to come. Nor were Artie's barbs confined to members of his own band. A former army intelligence officer named Malcolm Aitken related to Kaye an incident when Shaw's Rangers had been cajoled to perform at the Pleasanton Hotel, a grand old estate located in one of Honolulu's idyllic residential neighborhoods. The beneficiaries were to be men assigned to an Army Corps of Engineers district headquarters based across the street at the Punahou School, a prestigious institution whose campus had been commandeered after Pearl Harbor. Aitken arranged for a piano to be delivered to the hotel ballroom. Artie tried out the instrument and deemed it lacking.

"He turned to me and shouted, 'Do you know who's going to play this?'" Aitken recalled.

The officer shook his head. No, he did not know who was going to play the second-rate Steinway.

"Well, for your information, my pianist is Claude Thornhill, and I'm not about to ask him to play this dinosaur,'" Artie reportedly told Aitken, who added that after Artie "stomped out" an adequate replacement was found that was played without complaint by the "genial" Thornhill.[31]

In this strange climate of both license and lash, band members sought out their own morale boosts. Kaminsky recalled that the musicians would "take off like a shot for Honolulu every chance they'd get [and] it wasn't long before they had a lot of romances going on."[32] Trombone player Tasso Harris would end up marrying a woman he met in Hawaii. Other attachments were less durable. Avid navy wives, Max Kaminsky said, would make a beeline straight for the handsome Chief Petty Officer Shaw. Artie had seen this phenomenon before in his civilian career. Young and maybe not-so-young women would assess the men on stage as if they were polished jewels displayed on a velvet swatch.

"I was famous," Artie said late in his life. "That attracts women like flies."[33]

Every musician who had been on the road grew accustomed to the ready, willing, and able young women who gathered in the bandstand's shadow. "The men didn't have to run after the girls," remembered Myla Taylor, vocalist with a Kansas City–based territory band. "The girls ran after the men."[34] Other sirens, the ones that live in a bottle, sang Dave Tough toward the rocks. In the futile hope of keeping his drummer clean, Artie set up a system of band members who would take turns watching over Dave while off duty. "I'd assign a man to him if we had an important concert coming up, say for the crew of an aircraft carrier, and that man would watch over him all day," Artie would recall. "This was so he wouldn't get drunk and fall off the bandstand, which he had done a couple of times."[35]

The chaperone system had mixed success. Some men who took liberty with Dave would watch him diligently. Others would not. When Gozzo was assigned Davey duty, Rocky Collucio recalled, the young trumpet player would shrug his shoulders and say, "What the hell, let him drink."[36]

Tough was not the only one to put back a few. Several band members recounted a soggy gig at the Royal Hawaiian, the famed pink stucco hotel that, along with its surrounding fifteen acres of gardens, had been commandeered by the US military for use as an R and R facility. Members of another military band welcomed Shaw's Rangers to the show with some formidable hootch. Known variously as pineapple swipe, torpedo juice, or some other moniker, these homemade concoctions followed different recipes but were typified by blending 180-proof grain alcohol with pineapple or grapefruit juice. Top shelf it was not. It did the trick, though, and then some. "The band never sounded so bad," trumpet player John Best said. "Nobody could play."[37]

Dave Tough's drinking accelerated. On one occasion he reportedly was so hammered that he kept dropping his drumsticks during a performance. Artie recalled a time when the Shore Patrol apparently picked up the intoxicated drummer hauled him to the brig. It humiliated the drummer and angered other band members when Artie told them he wasn't able to get Davey cut loose. "I went back to the guys and told them they were only going to keep him overnight, but they must have thought I was callous," Artie told Harold Kaye, pointedly adding that "these guys had to dislike somebody."[38]

As Artie saw it, he was doing what was necessary to keep Dave alive and in the service. The future of Navy Band 501 depended upon it. Broken down as he might have been, Dave Tough kept the band's heartbeat going. Lose him, and Shaw's Rangers would unravel. Other band members, though, did not appreciate Artie's position, and Davey's brief rehabilitative incarceration added to a growing bill of grievances.

But Artie, too, was feeling aggrieved. Once, in a latrine, a young navy officer thought he recognized the bandleader. "Are you Artie Shaw?" the officer asked.

Shaw said he was.

"Can I shake the hand that held Lana Turner's tit?" the officer reportedly asked.[39]

About the same time, Artie agreed to play for a charity event hosted by the wife of a big shot. She thanked him profusely, and Artie told her he was doing what he could for the common cause. Commander Hickey, the Pacific Fleet's morale and recreation officer, was there, as Artie sardonically put it, "to take bows."

"Sooner or later," Hickey assured the woman, "all the big shots come down here to work for me."

Artie looked at the glad-handing morale bureaucrat.

"Commander," he said, "I thought we were working for the same employer."[40]

# Chapter 11

# New Caledonia

Shaw's Rangers lost their first man before they left Hawaii.

Since disembarking from the *Lurline* in December of 1942, the musicians had grounded themselves in routine. They would play two afternoons a week at The Breakers on Waikiki Beach and then scoot about the islands for one-off gigs and small-group command performances. As military service went, it was pretty plush, and it would stay that way for about five months. Women, booze, and other distractions were plentiful, and the music itself was a snap. Soldiers, sailors, and Marines would holler while Navy Band 501 just kept hitting repeat on the juke box: "Nightmare," "Begin the Beguine," "St. Louis Blues." Over and over, ad—at least to Artie—nauseam.

Finally, Claude Thornhill couldn't take it anymore.

Their formative time together in Cleveland more than a decade before still bound Artie and Claude together, as did their mutual respect for each other's musical talents. Their reunion in uniform went smoothly at first, and Claude seemed to be adjusting to navy life. On February 1 he had been promoted to seaman first class. By mid-April he had been elevated to the rating of musician first class. A navy officer, apparently with a straight face, gave the musician a good professional qualification score for "seamanship."[1]

Claude's civilian band reportedly had a total income of up to $50,000 a month; now Claude had a common swabbie's monthly pay of $50 and still he seemed content.

"I don't mind," Thornhill told a reporter in January. "At least I'm still playing music and enjoying myself."[2]

Max Kaminsky recounted that one night he, Thornhill, and several other band members had split off to play for an officer's party. Admiral Nimitz was there, and the commander of the US Pacific Fleet turned out to be a fan. Reportedly charmed by Claude's rendering of "Rhapsody in Blue" and other classics, the warfighter spent the evening chatting with the 34-year-old musician. By Kaminsky's accounting Claude reportedly took the opportunity to say how much more he could do if he led his own band. He apparently was subtle enough that he got his point across without sounding mutinous. As Artie said of him, Claude was "more guileful than he appeared."

And the fact was, Claude wanted out.

"Thornhill couldn't stand Shaw's egomaniacal behavior anymore," trombone player Tasso Harris recalled. "I guess Shaw was the most disliked guy by that time by everybody, including the band."[3]

Harris had been a last-second addition to the navy band the previous November, after the sleepwalking Ray Heath had dropped out, and he and Artie never hit it off. But while Harris and others may have been ready to jump ship, only Claude had the musical stature to make something happen. His hit 1941 song "Snowfall" had put him on the map. Though a shy man and at times a strange one, he could lead a troupe. Over the months in Hawaii, just as Claude came to realize he could no longer play second fiddle, Artie, too, came to the conclusion that his old friend had to go. "He wouldn't show up, wouldn't work, he'd be late," Artie recalled. "Finally, I said, 'Look, I can't do this anymore. You have to show up at muster every morning. You know, it's the Navy.'"[4]

Artie explained years later to the *New Yorker* jazz critic Whitney Balliett that the two men "could never arrive at a modus vivendi." The split was probably inevitable, as there was only room for one leader on the bandstand. "After all, we had been friends a long time, and it wasn't easy being thrust into what amounted to a master-servant relationship," Artie said. "He would miss muster or rehearsals, and that would build resentments on both sides." Artie, wielding the blade, added that his longtime friend "was already a heavy drinker, and that didn't help."[5]

In his autobiography Artie recounted that "we arranged" for the unhappy Thornhill to obtain a transfer.[6] By this rendering Artie made it seem like he drove the decision, taking credit for introducing Claude to Admiral William Calhoun, the influential fleet support officer who would become Thornhill's protector. Max Kaminsky, in his own memoir, cast the move as closer to Claude jumping ship. By Kaminsky's account it was Thornhill who engineered his own transfer, starting with his cultivation of Admiral Nimitz.

However it happened, Claude departed Navy Band 501. The transfer was recorded in his personnel file on May 20 as a temporary reassignment to the commanding officer of a navy support unit, though Claude's actual exit happened several weeks earlier. Even before he was given command of his own outfit, Claude appeared on May 19 at The Breakers as featured soloist in a seventeen-piece orchestra led by Navy Bandmaster Max Carrick, an Iowa native who was a decade younger than Claude. The show targeted Navy Yard workers, who, it was reported, stuffed themselves with "thousands of hamburgers and sandwiches [and] with gallons of beer and soda pop and danced 'til their feet hollered for mercy." It was the start of a busy year for Claude, who would serve admirably in the war zone in his own time.[7]

Claude's former navy bandmates, meanwhile, had been introduced to the battleship USS *North Carolina* on Thursday, April 22. For the next two weeks, the musicians got a taste of real navy life as the *North Carolina* crew worked out the kinks.

Commissioned in 1941, the thirty-five-thousand-ton *North Carolina* was the navy's newest battleship, but it had already been bloodied. It had covered the US Marines' landing at Guadalcanal in August 1942, helping protect the navy's all-important aircraft carriers, and it had come under dive-bomber attack in the subsequent Battle of the Eastern Solomons in late August. On September 15 a Japanese torpedo tore a hole on the ship's port side and killed five crew members. The *North Carolina* had returned to Pearl Harbor for rest, repairs, and the installation of radars and other equipment, then had gone back to the fight and returned once more to Pearl Harbor in March 1943 for a refit.[8]

The Navy Band 501 musicians joined roughly ninety-nine officers and two thousand enlisted men along with some other hitchhikers, including several navy officers slated for staff duty in the South Pacific. The band members were ostensibly assigned collateral damage control duties, jobs they might be required to take on in combat. They were told where to go during general quarters, but unlike conventional military bands, Shaw's Rangers never really shouldered combat-support responsibilities. They were, however, shaken by the rumble from the battleship's big sixteen-inch guns that could propel a 2,700-pound projectile about twenty-one miles.

After returning to Pearl Harbor following the ship's work-up, the *North Carolina* and the men of Navy Band 501 set out on Saturday, May 8, 1943, for the world war that was advancing on all fronts. Kaminsky recounted that when the ship sailed off from Pearl Harbor, Thornhill was at the dock to bid farewell. Max wrote that he and Dave Tough, by then both equally disenchanted with Artie's leadership, watched their former bandmate glumly as the battleship sailed off. "I don't know where we are going or for how long or anything about it," Kaminsky wrote a friend. "But I know how serious this all is and I know my job."[9]

Five months of navy duty in Hawaii had been good medicine for the trumpet player. A healthy tropical tan had replaced the nightcrawler's pallor. He was keeping daylight hours, talking seriously of marriage and abstaining from cigarettes. Often casting himself as a jokester, the funny little guy, Max now seemed more focused on the task before him. "Of course, we have done good work here in Pearl Harbor," he wrote his friend, "but now we will have a chance to get to the real things of it all." And then, with a recruiting-poster pitch, Max declared that "the sooner everyone helps to do all they can, the sooner this war might end."[10]

Aboard the battleship, the men lived as bona fide sailors in conditions that made the Aiea barracks seem luxurious in comparison. Their sleeping racks were stacked two or three high atop one another. Air trickled in from topside but barely stirred the below-deck stink. With the other enlisted men, Shaw's Rangers made up their beds, folded their blankets, strapped everything down, and tilted the hammocks out of the way. If general quarters, or battle stations, were called, the men would rush up and down ladders and brave tight head-smacking hatches on their way to their assigned positions.

Strict discipline kept the ship's permanent crew in line. Shortly after the battleship's departure from Pearl Harbor, a *North Carolina* sailor was sentenced to two weeks restriction for disobeying an order. Another enlisted man was demoted for striking a shore patrol member while back at Pearl Harbor, several were punished for being absent without leave, and five were sentenced to one-month restriction for creating a disturbance while on shore.[11]

With its brig, its gun barrels, and its rough-edged boatswain's mates, the *North Carolina* was foreign turf to Artie and his fellow musician. He offered the briefest of fictionalized references to his experiences aboard the ship in a short story entitled, "A Nice Little Post-War Business." It's an off-beat scene, in which the narrator, a navy bandleader, and a trumpet player named Sammy chat idly while on deck. The narrator describes Sammy as a funny conversationalist, entertainingly offbeat.

"Like the time we were standing aboard the deck of a battleship pulling out of Pearl Harbor, watching hundreds of seagulls wheel and swoop in a dense swarm around the stern wash, some of them almost, but not quite colliding with one another," Artie wrote.

The two musicians-turned-sailors watched the gulls for a while in Artie's fictionalized account. Then, he wrote, Sammy "turned to me and, shaking his head in wonder, said, 'Boy, those birds sure got that flyin' down good.'"[12]

Artie's short story captured another recurring motif of his time in the Pacific, and that was the fog that shrouded everything, including their destination.

"As usual," Artie wrote, "the scuttlebutt was running wild all over the ship." He then elaborated with a wry little riff. "One day a rumor would get started that we were on our way to New Caledonia, the next day it would be the Aleutians, then a mess cook would say he overheard the navigation officer tell the gunnery officer about the climate on Espiritu Santo, so obviously we must be heading for the New Hebrides, or maybe even Guadalcanal."[13]

After five days at sea, the *North Carolina* and an accompanying destroyer, the USS *Pringle*, approached the equator. Aboard the battleship Kaminsky had been hanging out with crewmen. Always up for a kick, he asked one of his new bosun's mate buddies whether he could drive the thirty-five-thousand-ton behemoth. Handed the wheel and told they were crossing the equator, Max tightened his grip and said he felt a bump. "They all laughed, and I was only kidding, but the odd thing is, years later I read there really is a bump," Kaminsky recalled."[14]

To mark the occasion, the *Pringle* and the *North Carolina* maneuvered next to each other and tied together. The destroyer had a crew of about 330 officers and enlisted men, and as many of them as could squeeze together lined up along the ship's port side. Aboard the battleship Artie and his band arrayed themselves on makeshift risers flanked by the sixty-one-foot long, sixteen-inch diameter barrels of the battleship's main guns, the ones that delivered its punch.

"Soon that big band began to swing into Artie's theme, 'Nightmare,'" recalled Andrew Balog, a sailor aboard the *Pringle*. The band followed up with "Begin the Beguine" and "Stardust." Balog had seen Artie's outfit onshore at The Breakers, but this was a different world. Wind snatched away notes midair. The ship decks rose and fell. The whole setup conspired against musical competence, let alone excellence. And yet, on that day, Shaw's Rangers hit the mark that Artie had pitched to Undersecretary of the Navy Forrestal many months before. Shaw's Rangers were now a true fighting seaman's band.

"I glanced along the rail of the ship and saw reflected in my shipmates' faces the same thought I was having: 'How I wish the people at home were here to see this,'" Balog recounted. "The only other sounds were the sloshing of the waves between the ships and the shouts of the hose and line handlers. It was by far the most unique and spine-tingling band session I've ever had the pleasure to hear."[15]

The musicians paid a price for it. Years later retired Navy Rear Admiral James Grealish, who as a young officer had been aboard the *North Carolina*, recalled that "the refueling operation took about four hours under the South Pacific sun" and that afterward the band members "spent the next few days below deck being treated for severe sunburn."[16]

The *Pringle*, meanwhile, detached from the battleship and continued toward its own fate. The destroyer would earn ten battle stars by April 1945, when a Japanese kamikaze plane slammed into it off of the island of Okinawa and split the *Pringle* in half. Sixty-nine men died, seventy were wounded, and the broken remnants of what once was a warship settled beneath the surface. But that would be later. On Monday, May 17, 1943, the *Pringle* was still intact, and the *North Carolina* arrived safe and sound at New Caledonia's Noumea Harbor.

Located some nine hundred miles across the Coral Sea from Brisbane, Australia, New Caledonia encompasses an array of strategically located islands, the largest of which is about the size of New Jersey. Rugged in some parts, swampy in others, it was thinly populated before the war by about sixty thousand French settlers and indentured Asian servants. The Americans had first arrived in force in March 1942, with fifteen thousand soldiers coming to counter a feared Japanese thrust. The attack never came, but the Americans kept arriving as they transformed the harbor and the area around it into Naval Base Noumea. By December of 1942, Noumea was also the headquarters of the navy's South Pacific Force, under the command of Admiral Bill Halsey since November 1942.

Dispiriting confusion muddled Navy Band 501's arrival. Despite the outfit's celebrity, it could still fall through the cracks. A civilian band's road manager or agent would handle administrative and logistical matters like lodging and scheduling. As a civilian Artie was tended to by highly energetic, efficient booking companies who, as historian David W. Stowe noted, sent press releases, planted stories, arranged celebrity photographs, secured endorsement contracts, arranged commercial tie-ins, and, in ways large and small, took care of all the niggling details needed to get a band on stage and home again.[17] Artie had no such consistent support in the navy. He seemed to be left alone to deal with the bothersome details himself. "I was in a totally anomalous position," Artie recalled. "Nobody knew what to do with that band. Nobody knew what to do with me. I didn't know what to do. In effect, I had my own little platoon in the Pacific, going around."[18]

This created problems, particularly when the band moved from one command element to another. It could easily get lost in the shuffle, as it seemed to upon its arrival in Noumea. "All of us sat on our seabags for three or four hours while Artie reported in, made sure he had nice quarters and a jeep, then he said, 'by the way, members of my orchestra are sitting on the dock,'" arranger David Rose recounted. "By the time we were attended to, we had missed chow." The incident aggravated tensions within the band, a state of affairs for which Arte bore considerable responsibility. But Artie, too, was being whipsawed. "You never knew where you were, one place to another," Artie said. "One place, they'd say 'what do you need?' Another place, [they'd say] 'who do you think you are?'"

"I know who I am," Artie would recall retorting. "Who do you think I am?"[19]

Resentments contributed to Artie's recurring tensions with his superior officers. Some wanted to see the celebrity big-shot taken down a notch. Other officers had no personal animus but took seriously the necessity of maintaining military discipline. Artie tended to remember the worst of the lot. "There was one son-of-a-bitch out there who almost got us all killed," he recalled. "We were all set to ride on a transport plane when this officious bastard ran out and ordered us off, saying we had to travel like other Navy personnel, and made us take a ship. It not only threw us off schedule, it was particularly dangerous just then. Everyone knew a Japanese sub was waiting out there. Sure enough, the next ship in our little convoy got torpedoed and sank right there."[20]

In San Francisco Artie had joined his wife in a Mark Hopkins suite while his men bunked on Treasure Island. In Hawaii he nestled into the Halekulani while the rank-and-file crowded into barracks. Now, in Noumea, Artie seemed once again to be focused on taking care of himself. He wrangled a spot in a local official's house while his men were consigned to barracks. At that, though they hardly thought so, the musicians were lucky. A 1943 report found that of every 1,000 American serviceman on New Caledonia, 905 were sleeping in tents, 90 were in US-constructed buildings, and only a fortunate 5 managed to settle in French houses.[21]

Noumea was a study in contrasts, a busy military port planted in exotic terrain. Fuel tank farms, Quonset huts, warehouses, shop buildings, and barracks congested what once was a quiet French colonial town. Warships filled the Noumea harbor, everything from lordly aircraft carriers down to lowly tenders. Stevedores and teamsters manhandled more than 10,000 tons of supplies a day, up from the 1,500 tons a day managed the previous November. Among Pacific ports, Noumea was second only to San Francisco in tonnage handled. On the docks, Navy historian Samuel Eliot Morrison recounted, "Lights burned late [as] soldiers and sailors tried to relieve supply line congestion."[22]

Beyond the docks and the city's center, rolling foothills rose to mountains several thousand feet tall. Within Noumea, tree-lined boulevards and verandas gave the town a pleasing tropical feel, and the beautiful St. Joseph's Catholic Cathedral was a sight for sore eyes.

French authorities, accustomed to administering the remote colonial island with a free hand, resented the noisy Americans' presence. The French governor, Christian Laigret, would declare in December 1943 that the "population of New Caledonia has suffered greatly from the thoughtlessness of American troops on the island."[23] Low-cost canteens established for US military personnel undercut local business owners, the governor declared, while the Americans upset the local labor market by offering higher salaries with which French businesses could not compete. A US officer acknowledged the truth of some French complaints, conceding that "their cattle have been killed, their fences torn down, roads built over their property, their trees cut down and many other things done."[24]

It was certainly a colorful place. A reporter visiting the month before Shaw's Rangers arrived noted the Americans in khakis, whites, and green dungarees; the British in shorts and short sleeves; and the French civilian men in white pith helmets and their wives in white chiffon dresses. The native Kanakas, according to the reporter, were dark as midnight, their hair often reddish from their custom of rubbing lime into the roots.[25] "Graceful and fond of singing, they are a cheerful, happy-go-lucky lot," the US military's *Pocket Guide to New Caledonia* stated with more than a tinge of colonial stereotyping, adding to the demeaning characterization the assertion that "when you are dealing with a man, it is quite all right to call him 'boy' as this is a widely used term around the islands, and they are accustomed to it."[26]

But the influx of Black US troops had upset this seemingly convivial balance. Laigret declared that the Black soldiers and sailors were "the terror of the white women of New Caledonia." He asked that Black troops be prohibited from entering Noumea, to which an unnamed US official responded that "American negroes have full citizenship rights and can't be given treatment such as the French accord their blacks."[27]

The military's sixty-page guidebook advised soldiers that "New Caledonian mosquitos are very annoying" and that "the giant cockroaches might startle you," while the bite of the "giant centipedes" was said to be not lethal but "extremely painful." Man-eating sharks controlled some beach areas like thugs holding a street corner. Exotic snakes known as sea moccasins slithered about offshore, with the guidebook advising that "there is some argument about whether it is deadly, but no smart soldier will treat it as a buddy."[28] Venereal disease was rampant. Skin infections proliferated, and dysentery and other intestinal insurrections kept men on the run.

Max Kaminsky awoke one morning to find that mosquitos had infiltrated his mosquito netting and were drilling into his knee. Soon, he recounted, he was aching with dengue fever. The mosquito-borne disease also brought low other band members, including Dave Tough, guitarist Al Horesh, and arranger David Rose.[29]

Still, Noumea offered compensations as well, including relatively cool nights, dazzling sand beaches, and a picturesque coast. The navy's morale and recreation team augmented these natural features with touches of home that included baseball leagues, shooting ranges, and outdoor theaters. New Zealand brought in some of their female auxiliaries, described by a navy historian as "a fine, upstanding group of girls, efficient in work and merry at play."[30] There were also local women of note, as navy Petty Officer Second Class Keith Southwick of Kalona, Iowa, informed his hometown newspaper. "He will tell you that the best-looking girls in the world are the tall Free French beauties of Noumea, New Caledonia, with their long, black hair, blue eyes and flawless olive skin," the *Iowa City Press-Citizen* reported May 5, 1943.[31]

The war was just over the horizon; it could be reached in less than a day's flying. The town itself was more raw than Honolulu, combining the languor of a colonial outpost with the bustle of military industry and the buzz of the marketplace. Noumea shops were selling nickel bottles of soda for forty cents and dollops of ice cream for an extortionate twenty-five cents.[32] Decent liquor was hard to find but cheap trinkets and souvenirs abounded, with the military's guidebook noting the extensive trade in "New Caledonian curios in wood, shell, seed, fiber and leather." Prices were often "excessively high," the guidebook warned, adding that "natives as well as French know the value of a dollar."[33]

Shaw's Rangers scrounged and bartered and leveraged their celebrity status. One band member finagled a plentiful stock of tuna fish. Others bought freshly made French bread, fruits, and vegetables. When all else failed, trumpet player John Best would sometimes retire to his bunk with a precious, carefully hoarded candy bar.[34]

For officially sanctioned fun, Lieutenant Commander Arthur Noren served as the navy's morale and recreation officer in Noumea. A former recreation supervisor for the city of Elizabeth, New Jersey, Noren believed in the cause, telling one audience that "recreation is playing its part in helping the blue jackets do their job."[35] Some improvisation helped. Sailors from the aircraft carrier USS *Saratoga* and the cruiser USS *San Juan* had converted an unused slice of Noumea into a recreation area they dubbed Sanjuan Beach. Equipped with playing fields, barbecue pits, and rudimentary clubs for both officers and enlisted men, Sanjuan Beach offered the navy men one small piece of familiar territory.[36]

In town a place commonly known as Triangle Gardens offered space for every manner of entertainment. Later in the war, a US Army boxer named Joe Rodriguez would adopt the name Young Chino and take on challengers in weekly bouts held at the Triangle Gardens. Shortly after their own arrival in Noumea, Shaw's Rangers showed up for an evening show. Whether it was a boxing exhibition or an Artie Shaw performance, these outings were in keeping with Noren's observation that "the navy competes actively, positively and constructively to ensure the best use of off-time."[37] The band followed up with an unsurpassed performance aboard the aircraft carrier USS *Saratoga*.

The carrier was the heart of the Third Fleet's Task Force Fourteen, which also included eight destroyers, the cruisers USS *San Juan* and USS

*San Diego*, and the British aircraft carrier HMS *Victorious*. The *Saratoga* had been moored in the Noumea harbor for parts of early May, but even resting quietly, the big ship could be hazardous for friend and foe alike. Throughout the month two *Saratoga* sailors were burned while practicing firefighting skills, another lacerated his left shin when he dropped a packing case, another dislocated his shoulder when he fell down a ladder, and yet another fractured his left arm while gallivanting in town.[38]

On May 19 Task Force Fourteen had gotten back to the business at hand. Imperial Japanese Navy ships had recently departed from Truk, their advance base located 2,280 miles northwest of New Caledonia, and the *Saratoga*'s task force was directed to seek out the enemy. On the operation's first day, a Grumman Avenger torpedo bomber crashed on takeoff from the *Saratoga*. The pilot and two crew members survived. The search for enemy forces had other excitements, as well. The *San Juan* launched depth charges against a suspected submarine and another pilot was seriously injured while attempting a landing. Save for some additional suspected submarine detections, though, Task Force Fourteen came up dry, and the ships returned to Noumea on May 24.[39]

The *Saratoga*'s three thousand enlisted men and officers were ready for some relief, and on Monday night, May 31, they gathered in the aircraft carrier's cavernous 33,528-square-foot airplane hangar, said to be the largest enclosed space of its kind in the US Navy. On the deck above, Shaw's Rangers assembled on a makeshift stage constructed atop the ship's hydraulically powered plane elevator. Normally this elevator conveyed the *Saratoga*'s complement of approximately eighty Hellcat fighters, Avenger torpedo bombers, and Dauntless dive bombers to and from the deck. Loaded now with musicians instead of warplanes, the elevator slowly lowered down through the upper-half deck, the middle-half deck, and finally to the hangar deck. As the plane elevator moved down, the musicians slid into "Nightmare." It was a mirror image of the orchestral presentations at the famed Paramount Theater in New York City, where bands would arrive on a rising stage. When the *Saratoga*'s lights kicked on as the band descended, the aircraft carrier's men went wild. "Feeling the waves of homesickness flow out of them at the sound of the familiar songs, I began to fill up so much that when I stood up to take my solo on the 'St. Louis Blues,' I blew like a madman," Kaminsky recounted.[40]

The roars ricocheted around the hangar, rebounding off the steel walls as the band opened up the throttle. Dave Tough caught the moment and began to beat alongside Kaminsky. The trumpeter seized his plunger and growled away in a New Orleans voice. The sailors, Kaminsky recalled, "went stark, raving crazy [and] even the fellows in the band were shaken." The old chestnuts like "Begin the Beguine" came back alive. The band finished up with "The Star-Spangled Banner," the very kind of sentimental mush that Artie loathed. In that instant, though, it hit home. "It was really one of the most incredible experiences," Artie said. "I thought I was pretty inured to applause and all that, but as the saying goes, it really brought a lump to your throat. It really did. I mean, it was difficult to play. At that moment, for the first time it dawned on me that what we were doing musically had an enormous significance for the men who were out there."[41]

The revelation brought Artie to a lasting respect for "The Star-Spangled Banner" and the emotions it was intended to swell. At another point during the Pacific tour, Artie recalled, a band member handed him a jazzed-up arrangement for the patriotic song. It was the sort of orchestral innovation Artie and other bandleaders might have appreciated. About the same time, Glenn Miller was reported by *Time* to have had the "urge to touch up the late, great John Philip Sousa's scores with hot licks and modern dance hall harmonies." Miller reasoned that "we've got to keep pace with the soldiers. They want up-to-date music."[42] But Artie, so often the innovator, nixed the jazzed-up "Star Spangled Banner" arrangement. "I threw it out," Artie said. "I told them, 'Boys, we're going to play this tune and we're going to play it right.'"[43]

Following the *Saratoga* show, Shaw's Rangers roamed about. One day they loaded their instruments and gear aboard trucks for a bumpy ride to Tontouta, the island's chief air base located about thirty-two miles northwest of Noumea. Tontouta's two runways had been started by Australian and Free French forces and then expanded by the Seabees and US Army engineers. By the time Artie and his men arrived, the lead runway had been resurfaced and extended to five thousand feet, and the once-skeletal base had been fleshed out with shop facilities, a chapel, a post office, assorted barracks and administrative buildings, service roads, and hardstands where airplanes could park.[44]

Mountains rose around the base, picturesque and potentially deadly. One of the most prominent, rising about nine hundred feet roughly three miles from the end of the main Tontouta runway, was named Kimball Hill after a Marine Corps major whose transport plane had crashed into the hillside the previous October, killing all eight men aboard.

At Tontouta the band played for men of the 13th Air Depot Group, among others. The unit had arrived in Noumea the previous November, part of the support team that kept the so-called Cactus Air Force flying out of Guadalcanal's Henderson Field. "Cactus" was the US code name for Guadalcanal, but it also seemed an appropriately raw designation for the Marine Corps and other military aviators who had fought tenaciously while enduring primitive conditions. Also flying in and out of Tontouta were the C-47 carrier planes of the 13th Troop Carrier Squadron, whose work Shaw's Rangers would come to appreciate.[45]

The Tontouta show was enlivened by the presence of some women. A Marine Corps aviator, Rolf Pederson, had run into a navy nurse he had dated while training in Pensacola, Florida. Pederson sweet-talked her into recruiting some of her fellow nurses for a little socializing. Pederson's acquaintance recruited eight adventurous volunteers and a chaperone, while the resourceful Marine secured the use of two weapons carriers to convey the party guests from their base hospital to the Tontouta base. "Along with Artie Shaw and the orchestra, we had a night that many of us will never forget," Pederson said.[46]

Other mornings, the band members would make the shorter commute from their Noumea barracks to ships huddled in Noumea Harbor for onboard shows. One day the men played aboard the USS *Whitney*, a nineteen-year-old destroyer tender that trundled about as a seagoing warehouse and tool chest for the frontline warfighters, carrying fuel, provisions, and spare parts. It had been at Pearl Harbor on the morning of December 7, 1941, and it subsequently reached the South Pacific in May 1942, where it serviced the myriad US warships battling the Japanese fleet around the Solomon Islands.[47]

The band entertained newer, frontline brawlers, as well. Shaw's Rangers played a June 15 show on the *San Juan*, a light cruiser that was launched in September 1941 and subsequently bloodied in the October 1942 Battle of Santa Cruz Island. After surviving a hit from a Japanese dive bomber, it had since been patrolling the Coral Sea in concert with the *Saratoga*.[48] At Noumea, the *San Juan* was docked next to the light cruiser USS *San Diego*, which had likewise seen combat in the extended Guadalcanal campaign and associated battles around the Solomon Islands.[49] Both ships had spent the first weeks of June engaged in training exercises—zig-zagging, testing their five-inch guns, and firing torpedoes. It wasn't combat, but the long hours alone could wear men down. Day after day they had started at predawn battle stations, handled their daytime duties, and managed periodic four-hour watch responsibilities, and then returned to battle stations at day's end. "The effect of all this is you don't get much sleep, you're always getting interrupted, and this after several months gets to a battle fatigue situation, where you're too tired to do anything and you have continuous headaches," a *San Diego* radar officer named Charles Henry recalled.[50]

The *San Juan* had spent the morning of June 15 at sea, practicing torpedo runs, before returning to the harbor and its place alongside the *San Diego*. For the Shaw's Rangers show, sailors from both ships squeezed into every free space aboard the *San Juan*, while the musicians boarded an improvised bandstand constructed of potato crates. Instead of the standard navy whites, the band members wore distinctive khaki uniforms that set them apart from everyday seamen. They looked sharp and, to the young sailors, they sounded right on the money. Artie kicked off the performance with his take on "Nobody Knows the Trouble I've Seen," an old African American spiritual song. It was a sly nod to the combat-tested sailors, but soon enough, the joke would turn on Artie.[51]

# Chapter 12

# Beyond Noumea

On Wednesday night, June 23, Shaw's Rangers split up into three groups and boarded the destroyer-minelayers *Preble*, *Gamble*, and *Breese*. They were bound for the island of Efate on what would feel like one of the longest nights of their lives.

The three ships were not navy headliners, but they collaborated like seasoned sidemen who had their parts down cold. The previous month, rolling out mines at the rate of about one every twelve seconds, the trio of ships had blocked off a crucial maritime passageway near the Solomon Islands. Their mines reportedly sank one Japanese destroyer and mortally damaged two others. A few days later, on May 24, the *Preble* had rescued eighty-five survivors of a sunken US ship. The destroyer-minelayers were versatile instruments of war, though they had never before been called upon to ferry a famous bandleader, his orchestra, and all their instruments. Only 314 feet long, the ships offered neither privacy nor comfort.

The three ships cast off on the night of June 23 for a trip of about three hundred nautical miles north from Noumea to Efate. Save for hosting their special guests, the ships' enlisted men and officers had a routine transit. For most of the voyage, sea conditions were reported as being relatively calm, one or two on a scale of one to twelve. Even this, though, shook Shaw's Rangers. The musicians suffered through a miserable night in what felt to them like tumultuous waters.[1] "Although the Shaw men complained about rough seas, it wasn't really rough," a radioman aboard the *Breese* named Joe Bochner recalled. "They just weren't used to the sea, [they] had no sea legs."[2] The stacks of roughly eighty mines on the decks of each ship further discomfited the landlubbers. Each mine contained about 180 pounds of explosive material, enough to punch through steel. The musicians could only imagine what it would do to human flesh.

The three ships arrived the next morning at Port Vila, the harborside chief town of the island of Efate. The musicians staggered ashore and the ships moved on to their next assignment, mining waters to shield an American landing on Rendova Island in the Western Solomons.

Efate was the southernmost island in the chain then known by the colonial name of the New Hebrides, now called Vanuatu. It had been under joint French and British control before the war, but with the arrival of US Navy construction battalions starting in May 1942, Efate transformed. The Seabees built a six-thousand-foot runway as well as a six-hundred-bed hospital, fuel tank farms, administrative offices, warehouses, quarters, and everything else required by a bustling logistics base.[3] Still, beneath the military makeover, the capital city of Port Vila had retained some of its charms. One 1943 visitor recounted seeing "some beautiful homes and churches, a few places of business, a well-stocked post exchange, a gorgeous mulatto girl in a blue dress and two French girls in the window of a hairdresser's shop who looked good enough to eat."[4]

Lena Gelott had called the place home since January 1943. A native of Peabody, Massachusetts, Gelott had completed three years of college before enlisting in the Army Nurse Corps in 1942. The navy had rejected her for being too short, but she would not be deterred from following two of her siblings into the service. "Patriotism was strong," Gelott recalled, "and everyone felt it important to be part of this great war effort."

Assigned to the army's 48th Station Hospital, Gelott first arrived in Noumea and then, in January 1943, she and her team set out for Port Vila. There, the hospital unit established itself in the midst of a coconut grove near the colonial town. About five months later, she joined her fellow nurses and other hospital staffers for a performance by Shaw's Rangers. The band members hit their marks, though the show was, to them, nothing out of the ordinary. But for the audience, the show meant everything. The navy band's performance, Gelott recalled years later, "made us feel that we had not been forgotten."[5]

Gelott hit the nail on the head. For the thousands of young Americans scattered across the Pacific theater, the appearance way out in the boondocks of Artie Shaw, Bob Hope, Joe E. Brown, or some other name entertainer was more than a welcome distraction. It showed that higher-ups knew of them and kept them in mind. And, of course, the jokes themselves could be funny and the live music a blast. "Out here," a Marine named Charles A. Dean wrote in a letter published in mid-July 1943 in *DownBeat*, "music is all a fellow has for entertainment." His location identified only as "somewhere in the South Pacific," Dean added that "Artie Shaw and his band played in our camp and they were plenty all right. Boys came from all over when they heard that Artie and his crew were here, just to dig some good old-fashioned American music. Anybody who thinks it didn't lift the morale of everyone here is crazy."[6]

After several days of morale-lifting duty in Port Vila, Shaw's Rangers on June 29 boarded two army C-47 transport airplanes bound for Espiritu Santo, about 190 miles to the north.[7] Espiritu Santo was the northernmost island in the New Hebrides chain and thus closer to the front. As elsewhere through the South Pacific, wartime bustle had transformed what had been a quiet isle. The author and World Wat II navy veteran James Michener, in *Tales of the South Pacific*, recounted one version of how the transformation began. He narrated a scene in which Admiral John S. McCain Sr., the grandfather of a future US senator and presidential candidate, flew over a still-undeveloped Espiritu Santo early in the war. McCain's job as the navy's air commander in the South Pacific authorized him to conscript islands for service. On his aerial reconnaissance he could see the entirety of the island, thirty miles wide, forty-eight miles long, and endowed with a capacious harbor. "[He] pointed down at that island wilderness and said, 'that's where we'll build our base,'" Michener recounted. "And the base was built there, and millions of dollars were spent there, and everyone agreed Santo was the best base the Navy ever built in the region."[8]

Espiritu Santo was the Penn Station of the Pacific War, home to as many as forty thousand service members and passed through by tens of thousands more on their way to and from the fighting. Fighters, bombers and transport planes kept multiple airstrips hopping. Several large floating dry docks serviced every manner of navy warship. A thicket of Quonset huts squatted along the waterfront.[9] Although the nearest known Japanese air base was located some nine hundred miles away, Espiritu Santo remained subject to nuisance raids in the months prior to the arrival of Shaw's Rangers. One raid occurred just as Navy Secretary Frank Knox and Adm. Chester Nimitz were visiting the base in January 1943 as part of a two-week Pacific tour. The navy secretary, it was reported, "came through the experience without injury and with nothing but contempt for the inaccuracy of Japanese high-level bombing."[10]

From Espiritu Santo, as on Efate, Artie's outfit ventured out to play at several kinds of venues. "We'd set up shop in some eerie tropical setting, palm trees all around, board benches, Navy boys sitting on them or on the ground, and when we'd swing into one of the old favorites, you could see tears come into their eyes," Artie told *New Yorker* writer Robert Lewis Taylor.[11] For other performances the band would break up into smaller, more agile units to visit hospitals. These gigs, in particular, emotionally taxed the band members but also rewarded them as, Kaminsky recalled with wonder, "these broken men came to life again and banged their crutches and beat the arms of their wheelchairs or just yelled and shouted themselves hoarse if they were too smashed up or too weak to applaud."[12]

Any escape would do. One time, Kaminsky recalled, the surviving crew members of a sunken US Navy cruiser were brought ashore and settled into a makeshift theater for a showing of the cozy black comedy *Arsenic and Old Lace*. Seeing the revived sailors' faces soften under the flickering light of a motion picture was, for the trumpet player, an enduring lesson in the healing power of entertainment. Max recounted the moment, without naming the exact location, in his autobiography published twenty years later. On this matter, as on others, he may have misremembered or polished up some details. While director Frank Capra had originally planned on a September 1942 release for the film, the studio delayed its release until September 1944, a year after Max was touring the Pacific with the navy band. Still, his underlying moral of the story holds true: Entertainment eased men's suffering.

On July 1 Artie's wife Elizabeth gave birth to their son, Steven. Artie provided the inside story to syndicated *New York Post* columnist Leonard Lyons, who had been tracking the Pacific progress of Shaw's Rangers. As he related it to Lyons, Artie had heard by shortwave radio that his wife had given birth to a seven-pound baby girl. "Then came another news flash, telling me, correctly, that it was a boy not a girl," Artie reported to Lyons. "And this time, the announcer, bless him, referred to me as Lt. Shaw. Me, a bandmaster yet."[13]

By another account a navy chaplain took the stage during a performance by Shaw's Rangers to read the news of Steven's birth. Then and there, an Australian reporter would recount, thousands of soldiers and sailors "sang 'Happy birthday, little Steven' until the jungle re-echoed with their enthusiasm."[14] The happy news provided only a brief respite for little Steven's beleaguered father, as the band kept chugging along. On July 2 Shaw's Rangers performed at Espiritu Santo for the men of the 18th Combat Mapping Squadron. The next day the band played for the ground echelon of the Marine Fighter Squadron 122 of the First Marine Aircraft Wing. It was reported in the unit's war diary that "everyone enjoyed the show," although, in fact, not everyone could make it. While some support personnel were at Espiritu Santo, the squadron's warplanes operated out of Henderson Field on Guadalcanal, about 450 miles away. On the same day as Shaw's Rangers played for some of the men, the fighter squadron's war diary recorded that Marine Corps Captain Bertel Rasmussen was "critically burned when the Corsair he was starting blew up" at Henderson Field. The 23-year-old New Jersey native died later that night.[15]

Several days later, on July 5, the band made an onboard appearance on the USS *Curtiss*, a seaplane tender operating out of Espiritu Santo. Though the ship had previously served as the flagship for a navy air commander, the *Curtiss* and its four hundred enlisted men and officers that July were saddled with mundane supply and support duties. Still, in a touch of class, the crew had printed up a program commemorating the appearance of the Artie Shaw band. Two years later, in May 1945, while the ship was again serving as an air commander's flagship off of Okinawa, the *Curtiss* would be sundered by a kamikaze attack that killed thirty-five of its crewmen and wounded twenty-one.

Navy Band 501 was not the only musical outfit servicing the US forces in the Pacific, and the orchestras would sometimes cross paths. Several months into the tour, at a location not disclosed to the public, Navy Band 501 took on a Marine Corps band in an unlikely game of softball. The Marines were led by Master Sergeant Joe Sharfglass, a 27-year-old New York City native who as a civilian had played clarinet and saxophone with the likes of Woody Herman. His twenty-eight-member outfit was attached to the fabled First Marine Division and included seven men who had played professionally before entering the service, along with a ragtag roster that a Marine Corps correspondent described as "kids from high school bands, collegians who marched and counter-marched between the halves of Big 10 gridiron battles and old-line Marines who have seen service in Shanghai, Pearl Harbor and Midway."[16]

The Marine Corps musicians were jointly carried on the company rolls as headquarters' runners or ammunition bearers. Their Pacific service had put them into some alien circumstances, including an Easter-time performance the previous April before assembled Japanese POWs who had, so the reports went, enthusiastically joined their American captors in a version of "Auld Lang Syne."[17]

The Marine Corps and navy outfits took to an ad hoc softball field and battled it out in the tropical heat. Two of the navy band's outfielders, bass player Barney Spieler and trombone player Tak Takvorian, cramped up badly in the fourth inning and limped gingerly through the remainder of the game. Drummer Dave Tough, whose usual exercise regime was limited to hoisting bottles, muffed an easy fly ball but still "retained his cigarette and his dignity," according to the correspondent. The Marines won the game 6–5, and with it the heretofore unheard-of military band softball championship of the South Pacific. Good sports, the victorious Marines also shared with the navy men the beer that had been allotted to the victors.[18]

The Marine Corps correspondent who wrote up the game was a former *Tulsa Tribune* courts reporter named Jim Lucas. He did not elucidate what position, if any, Artie played in the game, an uncharacteristic omission of fact for the future Pulitzer Prize–winner who would compellingly detail the landing of Marines on Tarawa in November of 1943. "There was a brilliant moon," Lucas would write. "At home, I would have called it beautiful. We swore at it viciously. We were perfect targets."[19]

# Chapter 13

# Guadalcanal

G uadalcanal could have claimed Shaw's Rangers before they unpacked their instruments.

Ninety miles long and thirty miles wide, the island laid men low in countless ways. Fevers, infections, and exotic tropical diseases assailed everyone. There was no rear echelon. Centipedes and scorpions ambushed the unwary. Crocodiles owned the Tenaru River. Above all else, Guadalcanal's coastal swamps, lagoons, and meandering, sluggish streams bred malaria-carrying mosquitos. In the four months after their initial August 7, 1942, landing, half of the First Marine Division's total casualties were malaria cases. By the time the surviving Japanese slipped away from the island in February 1943, the American casualty total had reached some 1,600 killed and 4,200 wounded, with thousands knocked out of commission from malaria.[1] "It is safe to assume that almost every man who served on the island from 7 August 1942 to 9 February 1943 fell victim to the disease," the Navy Medical Department's official history reported.[2]

Some improvements had been made by July of 1943. Medics were making sure that men swallowed their antimalarial Atabrine tablets, initially shunned over rumors about the drug causing impotence and sterility.

Mosquito netting kept the disease vectors at bay, and sanitary conditions became more civilized as the military expanded its footprint and reclaimed swamp and jungle. Artie and his men apparently escaped the disease during their week on the island; still, it remained an ever-present threat. On July 10 the 61st Naval Construction Battalion suffered its first loss since coming ashore in May when malaria claimed the life of a Seabee enlisted man from Buzzards Bay, Massachusetts, named George Miller Hunter. The island, moreover, still teemed with toxic exotica. The Seabees of the 63rd Naval Construction Battalion quoted explorer Osa Johnson, who described Guadalcanal in 1917 as "a land of freaks inhabited by rats as big as cats, cockroaches a foot and a half long, lizards as large as small crocodiles, snakes that fly, toads that eat flesh and fish that climb trees."[3] Navy historian Samuel Eliot Morrison put it even more bluntly, summing up Guadalcanal as a "large and fecaloid island."[4]

Nor were human always a civilizing influence. A sign hanging over the main road at a US Army camp marked the spot where twenty wounded US soldiers had been clubbed and bayonetted by Japanese soldiers while they lay helpless. The sign memorialized the incident with a simple mandate: "Kill the Bastards!"[5]

All of this travail was the price to be paid for Henderson Field, the airstrip that in its half-completed state had been the original impetus for the US Marines coming ashore on August 7, 1942. By mid-1943 Henderson Field was host to army B-25 medium bombers, navy fighters and Marine Corps dive bombers, all supporting the American's advance up through the northern Solomon Islands and beyond. It had been from Henderson Field that US Army Lockheed P-38 Lightning fighters had taken off on an April 18, 1943, mission to kill Japanese Admiral Isoroku Yamamoto, the commander in chief of the combined Japanese naval forces.

A more typical Henderson Field mission occurred about three months later. On the early morning of July 25, dozens of warplanes started taking off at 0500. Once assembled they set out for Japanese positions on the southern coast of New Georgia. Two pilots turned back because of mechanical problems, but more than fifty others pressed onward through the approximately 150-mile flight. The Americans reported encountering serious flak above the target and two US planes were hit, but all survived and a subsequent intelligence assessment recorded that pilots had seen "all bombs falling in the area assigned." By 8:52 a.m. the last of the planes had landed safely back at Henderson Field.[6]

Guadalcanal was the place Artie Shaw and his navy band had been sailing to ever since their mission had been christened in the office of Undersecretary of the Navy James Forrestal. From New York to San Francisco, then to Pearl Harbor, then on to New Caledonia, and then to the New Hebrides, Navy Band 501 had been moving ever closer to the eye of the hurricane. Performing aboard the *North Carolina* and the *Saratoga* had put Shaw's Rangers close to the warfighters. They had stood on the same decks, climbed the same ladders, shared the same spaces. Their audience members had seen combat and would soon see more of it—sometimes within days of seeing the Shaw's Rangers perform. On Guadalcanal the musicians moved as close as they would ever get to war itself: the launching of planes, the sounding of sirens, the prayerful huddling of frightened men in foxholes.


On Sunday, July 11, the band boarded a warplane for the roughly six-hundred-mile flight from Espiritu Santo. The pilot looked like a kid to the band members, themselves mostly in their 20s. It was bad enough that every flight in the South Pacific could turn roller coaster at a moment's notice. A sudden atmospheric hiccup could rattle the plane. Lightning could strike, parts could fail, and pilots still too young to drink could lose their way. The ocean below could swallow a heavy bomber without belching. Somewhere out there among the clouds, Japanese fighters could be waiting to pounce. Still, the flight from Espiritu Santo was peaceful enough up until the final moments when the plane sought terra firma.

"Halfway down the runway, the pilot knew he had overshot [it], so he hit the throttle," Harold Wax recalled. The plane reportedly scraped the tops of the palm trees at the end of the roughly 3,800-foot runway as it rose, just in time, for another try. On the second chance, the pilot managed to wrestle the plane down before the runway ran out.

"Gozzo was shaking like a leaf," Mack Pitt recounted.[7]

Weak-kneed from the close call, Shaw's Rangers took their first steps onto Guadalcanal. The men were on Lunga Point, a promontory on the island's northern coast and the site of the unfinished Japanese airfield that had been the immediate focus of the untested Marines who landed on August 7, 1942. The first major US amphibious operation since 1898 "went off without a hitch," in Morrison's words.[8] Once the Marines had captured the airfield prize, engineers took over the work of completing the airfield. By August 20 the first US warplanes were using the airstrip that had been renamed Henderson Field for a downed Marine Corps pilot.[9]

Now, as Shaw's Rangers looked about them, they could see about six miles away the 1,514-foot-high Mount Austen, attended by a series of ridges and knolls that the Marines had seized at considerable cost from the Japanese. Closer at hand, planted amid palm trees, administration buildings, repair shops, and a post office bustled with everyday business like a frontier town. Foxholes covered with logs and layers of dirt reminded men of the hazards to come.[10]

Signs of civilization popped up like flowers through mud. A library and a playing field offered distractions. The Guadalcanal National Baseball League, as it was dubbed, had eight teams competing, with the Seabees from the 61st Naval Construction Battalion ultimately taking the crown one season. An outdoor theater constructed in a natural amphitheater and dubbed the Coral Bowl could seat four thousand men. It hosted performances by the Seabee's own pickup band, and recently an army division artillery band had become the first orchestra from off the island to play the Guadalcanal circuit. At other times movies were shown, albeit with the occasional ad hoc intermission not part of the Hollywood script.[11] "At times, air raids forced some [interruptions] to such an extent that, in some cases, it took three nights to see a complete single picture," one Seabee account recalled.[12]

An enlisted man, William O. Moylan, greeted Artie at Henderson Field and introduced himself as the band's escort. He had important information to convey to the newly arrived musicians as they stretched out the kinks in their legs and cast skeptical glances at their surroundings.[13] Speaking as the old hand, Moylan instructed the newcomers about air raid alarms and dugout protocols. He could also introduce the men to the island's alien menagerie. Snakes, rats, and spiders made reconnaissance forays into tents. Fungi, leeches, and crocodiles infested the freshwater streams. The scantily clad Melanesian Natives, their gums blackened and their teeth rotted from chewing betel nut, looked like practicing headhunters. Frequent downpours swelled the creeks and rivers and repeatedly washed out the Seabees' bridges.

Shaw's Rangers would encounter much of what the island had to offer. Artie, for instance, would recall a time that he was out in the wild. A fierce-looking Native appeared in loincloth and fancy headdress. The two men cautiously approached one another, aliens to one another. And then, Artie said, the islander asked in perfect English, "Would you please play 'Begin the Beguine?'"[14] It was a perfectly cute little anecdote, and it may even have happened, just as Artie said.

Nor were the Japanese themselves completely gone. Just a few weeks earlier, on June 27, a pair of unarmed Seabees returning from swimming in a river had encountered two desperate Japanese soldiers on a jungle trail. The Japanese bolted and one got away. The other was seized by a Seabee who bashed the enemy soldier's head in with a rifle.[15] The more serious threat came from above. The Japanese had kept plinking away at Guadalcanal by air even after their ground forces had been evacuated. The month before Shaw's Rangers arrived, Japanese warplanes had made their last concerted strike on the island. On June 16 an estimated 125 Japanese warplanes struck. It turned into a turkey shoot, as some 113 of the Japanese planes were shot down. The United States lost six planes, one landing ship tank (LST), and two barges. That would prove to be the last of the major air raids, but the Japanese kept jabbing with pinprick, nuisance raids conducted by solo planes known collectively by the US troops as Washing Machine Charlie.

"The throb of Charlie's motors was more fearsome than the thump of his bombs," recalled First Marine Division veteran Robert Leckie. "Once the bombs were dropped, we would be relieved, knowing he would be off and away. But the drone of Charlie's circling progress kept everyone awake and uneasy for so long as Charlie cared, or dared." The nightly raids, Leckie added, "did not kill many people, but, like Macbeth, he murdered sleep."[16] One Seabees unit, the 63rd Naval Construction Battalion, recorded that between July 5 and July 12, Guadalcanal was subject to "at least one condition red each day." Between July 16 and July 19 there were ten air raids.[17]

"The powers that be are still trying to decide exactly how the Nips get in to drop [their] bombs without getting picked up by any of the radars," a Marine intelligence officer with the Marine Fighter Squadron VMF 221 reported in his unit's July 12 War Diary.[18] The "invisible Jap," as the same intelligence officer described Washing Machine Charlie, wounded more Americans by panic than by shrapnel. The 63rd Naval Construction Battalion recorded that shortly before midnight on July 11, several Seabees suffered minor injuries "diving into foxholes" during an air raid that hit an adjacent Marine camp.[19] "Common casualties among the men were acquired by collisions in foxholes or track meets over rough ground," another Seabee outfit, the 61st Naval Construction Battalion, later recounted.[20] The real damage caused by Washing Machine Charlie's occasional lucky strike kept the fear churning. A July 20 air raid flattened two of the Seabees' Quonset huts. The Marine intelligence officer with the Marine Fighter Squadron 221 reported in his unit's War Diary for that date that there were "no bombs in our area, but rumors are rampant regarding hits on other parts of the island."[21]

"He made life miserable for our boys on Guadalcanal by a series of midnight raids, long after the Nips were driven out of that part of the Solomons," a reporter wrote not long after Artie's band arrived on the island.[22] Shaw's Rangers learned the drill. When the alarm sounded, men disentangled themselves from their mosquito netting and stumbled into log-covered trenches that could typically fit several men inside. One night, Artie would recount, bombs landed on either side of his foxhole. One night, and it might have been the same one, Artie recalled huddling in a foxhole along with eight other men. The ground, he said, shook with the bomb concussions.

"We really thought it had our name on it," Artie recounted.

In the shuddering darkness, he remembered, a packet of cigarettes and matches passed among the men. "I asked the kid next to me who they belonged to," Artie recalled. "He said, 'They're Bill's cigarettes, Jim's matches, and that quivering voice is mine.'"[23]

It's a funny little story, not least because matches and cigarettes would presumably have been as verboten as a bonfire among those praying the Japanese bomber pilot couldn't find his bearings in the dark. During one air raid, Dave Tough reportedly dismayed the other men by heedlessly striking a match for a cigarette. His bandmates shouted at him to put the damn thing out before he got them all killed.[24] Whether these episodes unfolded precisely as the musicians later recounted them is uncertain, at best. Still, the air raids undeniably shook the men who were increasingly fatigued and facing other, unfamiliar travails. While malaria control had improved, mosquitos still flew kamikaze runs against exposed skin. Guts churned with diarrhea. "Numerous rats, scorpions, spiders and centipedes refused to give ground," *Variety* subsequently recounted, adding that "in the raid-free hours the men lived in tents and the rats in foxholes; during raids, their positions reversed."[25] Against this Guadalcanal there was no inoculation, and some minds came altogether undone.

The previous year, the ground fighting was still intense when the destroyer USS *McFarland* had pulled alongside the island on October 16, 1942, to take aboard what one US Navy historian called "160 ambulatory hospital patients and 'war neurotics,' an emotionally inflammable cargo." In the late afternoon on that Friday, a Japanese dive-bomber showed up and scored a hit on the ship's depth-charge racks. The multiple explosions made "a shamble of the fantail and threw the poor neurotics into uncontrolled panic."[26]

Bombs and bullets weren't the only instigators of collapse. While direct ground combat had ended by the time Shaw's Rangers arrived, Guadalcanal remained a pressure cooker. "The profound jungle darkness, the unnerving night sounds of animals and birds, the tormenting attacks by insects and leeches, and the painful and distressing skin diseases all sapped the troops' energy and made them more susceptible to real and imaginary terrors," an army report on Guadalcanal medical conditions noted.[27]

The packed schedule ran Artie's men ragged. Tired from the nightly air-raid sirens, they were starting to jump in the daytime at the shades and shadows. The nights were worse. One night, about 11:00 p.m., the musicians were in their tents when the word spread that a Japanese infiltrator had been spotted skulking around camp. In the dark, their nerves stretched thin, the musicians could conjure the possibility; only a few weeks had passed since those two Japanese soldiers had emerged from the jungle, and one had gotten away. Perhaps he was returning, possibly in force. The alarm was finally rescinded when the men recognized the wandering stranger as Dave Tough, who might have been hitting the jungle juice.[28]

Doctors employed a variety of names such as "war neuroses," "traumatic neuroses," and "combat fatigue" to characterize the distraught. Common symptoms included repetitive nightmares and the "startle reflex" characterized by sweating, dilated pupils, heart palpitations, and other involuntary reactions triggered by sudden noises. The afflicted were often morose, sullen, withdrawn. Doctors catalogued the symptoms but had a harder time understanding susceptibility. Infantry platoons with comparable training and combat exposure diverged dramatically in the number of neurotic casualties. Fatigue, studies suggested, rendered men more vulnerable, as did insufficient training and lack of faith in the unit's leaders. Combat exposure thickened the skins of the survivors, seasoning them for a time. Then the inoculation lost its juice, and the soldier broke down for good.

The men on Guadalcanal in July 1943 were thus subject to both acute and chronic strains of war exhaustion. The nightly air raids, though far less than what they had once been, threatened them with the repeated possibility of obliteration. Make it through the night, and dreary days awaited. Donald Mangum, a Washington, DC, native, was a navy ordnance specialist based at Guadalcanal and the New Hebrides, where he saw Artie perform. The shows were a welcome but only temporary respite from debilitating conditions. "There were always mosquitos, rain that lasted for a week at a time, thick mud that covered the ankles, and not much of a variety of food. Mold would cover clothes in two weeks," Mangum reported. It might take days, weeks, or months, but in time the island would cut men down to size. "Some of the fellows began not to care if tomorrow never came," Mangum said. "Big strong healthy fellows lay in their bunks at night and you could hear them sobbing. It became dangerous to ask another fellow to do something. You never knew what was on his mind, and when he might turn on you."[29]

The men of Navy Band 501 could have been a case study in vulnerability. They had scant military training and no prior combat exposure. They were dog-tired, run down by fevers, and distrusted their leader. On Guadalcanal brass instruments rusted and reeds failed after only one performance. Artie's foxhole anxieties during air raids alarmed band members. Tensions latent since the band's earliest days intensified, sometimes expressed in prankish ways.

While on Guadalcanal, one of the band members received a cake from home. To protect it from rats, or so a band member later explained, it was placed on a helmet inside a pail of water. The helmet just happened to be Artie's, and when the next air raid siren sounded, he ran around in search of his protection. When he finally found the helmet, it was reported, "He was all for wrapping his clarinet around someone's neck."[30] Artie's men, chafing under his mercurial leadership, fancied other ways to dissent. Trumpeter Conrad Gozzo, another band member later recalled, "was one of the guys who signed a pact that whoever could get Shaw near the side of the ship would push him over."[31]

But in the end, it was Artie's own mind that cast him adrift.

# Chapter 14

# Nightmare

Artie was wound tight well before he went to war. His restless drive powered him up the charts and into fresh creative territory. It also kept him looking over his shoulder at his peers, who were likewise looking over their shoulders. The competitive spirit was pervasive.

"You have the *DownBeat* poll and the *Metronome* poll," trumpet player John Best explained. "So every year it might change, and one guy will come up, like Benny Goodman was the big guy, until Artie came up and went over the top. Artie was okay, and then Glenn [Miller] took over the top. And each time they'd do that, the leader, it would affect them a little."[1] Miller, Best elaborated, "was a tough loser. He took it hard, to lose things." In order to keep winning, he ran his men at least as hard as he ran himself. Myriad offenses could get a musician fired or disciplined, Best noted, including shortcomings in "your dress, your clothes, your appearance, and of course your drinking or whatever."[2] This could be grating, but it maintained standards and, Miller's biographer Dennis Spragg noted, the bandleader's "forceful and rigid management style" and "insistence on spit-and-polish" and "proper respect" for superiors also translated well to service in uniform for military rank.[3]

Benny Goodman, too, lashed his troops, albeit sometimes with ice rather than heat. His band members dreaded Goodman's glacial stare. As a civilian, Artie's own fire in the belly was second to none. It drove his search for perfection while leaving him with migraine headaches, gastrointestinal distress, and an unquenchable thirst for all he lacked. To this Artie's navy service added a toxic blend of crowding and isolation. Though he had secured special lodging in Newport, San Francisco, and Honolulu, Artie could not escape the common tents on Guadalcanal. He was stuck with the other men, oppressed by their sweat and stink. He could not get the space he craved. At the same time, he was isolated, with no peer he could confide in and no superior he could rely upon. Artie Shaw was both all alone and on display, with the spotlight that followed him wielded by Japanese and Americans alike.

After playing several shows during the day on Guadalcanal, Shaw's Rangers would gather around the radio in the evening and listen to Japanese shows intersperse rhetorical jabs with familiar music. Inevitably, the shows got around to "Begin the Beguine," the song Artie could not escape.[4] "One night we heard Jap propaganda announcers playing Shaw records and announcing in good English that Shaw and his men were playing at the St. Francis Hotel in San Francisco," Artie recalled. "The idea was to make American boys homesick." It was also a dirty dig at Shaw himself who was, after all, at that moment in a smelly Guadalcanal tent and not nestled in between the sheets of a luxurious St. Francis bed.[5]

An oddly parallel yarn was passed along by the *New York Post*'s columnist Leonard Lyons. Lyons, born Leonard Sucher and a one-time practicing lawyer, had been packing celebrity sightings, mini-scoops, PR morsels, and overheard witticisms into his syndicated column called "The Lyons Den" since 1934. He'd had many opportunities to cross paths with Artie before the war while popping in and out of New York City's nightspots like El Morocco and the Stork Club. Beyond that Lyons had an impressively wide, though not always entirely reliable, network of sources and tipsters. So it was that Lyons reported that Artie had "left his ship off New Guinea, to entertain some troops there." This was an unfortunate beginning for a column, as New Guinea was a good 860 miles from Guadalcanal. In any event, Lyons reported that after the show, "Japanese planes began to bomb the place, and the men leaped into the nearest foxholes." Artie, Lyons wrote, happened to land in a foxhole next to a tent where the radio had been left on. And so it was, readers of "The Lyons Den" learned Artie was able to hear the Japanese propaganda announcer declare, "You have just heard the orchestra conducted by Artie Shaw playing from the Mark Hopkins Hotel in San Francisco."[6]

On Guadalcanal the band played in a variety of locations and in a variety of configurations. The entire outfit played at the open-air Coral Bowl amphitheater that could hold several thousand men. The musicians could also break up into smaller, more mobile ensembles for performances elsewhere on the two-thousand-square-mile island, roughly the size of Delaware but much nastier.[7] The occupying US forces had spread themselves out. Fifteen miles east of Henderson Field, the Seabees had established a camp along a sandy beach at Koli Point. Six miles to the west of Henderson Field, docks were built at Point Cruz for the off-loading of the ceaseless stream of supplies needed to keep the whole operation going. Wherever they played, the island inhabitants pitched in with what Kaminsky recounted as the "chattering of monkeys, the screeching of parrots and the whistles of the bright-colored little parakeets, which were as common as our sparrows."[8]

The audience response was equally enthusiastic across the island. Marine Corps pilot Otto Keith Williams spoke for many when he recalled that "everyone was tickled to death" by Artie's appearance.[9] On July 17 the musicians traveled on several small boats twenty nautical miles across Iron Bottom Sound, so named for the warships sunk there during the early struggle for Guadalcanal. Their destination was the island of Tulagi.[10] Only three miles in circumference, Tulagi been seized from the Japanese in August 1942 after a short but vicious contest. It offered a suitable harbor that the Seabees had dredged and made cozy for seaplanes and motor torpedo boats, the so-called PT boats.

Arranger Dave Rose would recall years afterward that the skipper of one of the boats in Motor Torpedo Boat Squadron Two that transported Shaw's Rangers was a young navy lieutenant named John F. Kennedy. Several weeks later, in early August 1943, Kennedy would lose his PT-109 and nearly his life in a collision with a Japanese destroyer. That would have made Rose's trip across Iron Bottom Sound quite the war memory, but his recollection may have missed the mark. In fact, on July 15 PT-109 was detached from Motor Torpedo Boat Squadron Two and relocated to a captured base at Rendova, about two hundred miles away. This was two days before Shaw's Rangers were transported to Tulagi, casting doubt on, although not absolutely refuting, the notion that JFK and Artie Shaw's band crossed paths in South Pacific.

About Artie's nervous breakdown in the vicinity of Guadalcanal, too, some key details remain fuzzy. The gist of it was, he just took off one day. Where he was and where he was going, no one could quite say, not even him. The navy doctor who most thoroughly examined Artie during the Pacific band tour did not identify any one island as the location of a breaking point. Harold Kaye quoted Artie as saying that his definitive breakdown happened on Espiritu Santo.[11] The *New Yorker*'s Robert Taylor placed the episode on Guadalcanal. Artie does not mention the episode at all in his autobiography. Wherever it happened, Artie recalled a very specific moment in the midst of his Pacific tour when he simply split. He had had enough, and he started walking.

Away. He was going away.

An officer, who in some versions of the story was in a jeep, saw Artie looking lost.

"He says, 'where are you headed, sailor?'" Artie recalled in one version. Artie told the officer he didn't know.

"He just said, 'get in.' And I started to cry," Artie recounted.[12]

Artie told a somewhat different version of his breakdown in the award-winning documentary movie *Time Is All You've Got*. "At one point," Artie told the filmmaker, "I simply couldn't take it. I took a long walk, and I found myself almost blacked out. I [was] talking to a couple of corpsmen, and they said 'what's the matter?'

"I said, 'I don't know,'" Artie recalled. "'I really don't know what's going on.'"

Artie's nervous condition would be revisited by navy doctors. Meanwhile, Shaw's Rangers would continue their Pacific tour. The men were eager to escape the dreary island. They had been trucked on rough roads through jungles, across plains, and up and down hills that Marines and soldiers had fought for and died upon. They had set up at remote locales and reached men who welcomed the band like it was a postman delivering letters from home. For this service the musicians had paid a price. At least one other band member, baritone sax man Charlie Wade, would join Artie in reporting that the booming antiaircraft fire on Guadalcanal caused permanent ear damage and hearing loss. Shaw's Rangers had earned their stripes in a way they hadn't while playing at The Breakers back in Hawaii.

The band's eventful week on Guadalcanal that started with a close call during their landing at Henderson Field ended with some final frights and a little slapstick. One night before their scheduled departure from the island, their sleep-murdering nemesis Washing Machine Charlie made another unwelcome appearance. An Army Air Corps flight engineer named Joseph R. LaLonde, from the plane the Shaw's Rangers were scheduled to board the next day, recorded in his diary that the Japanese bomber was caught by spotlights in the night sky. "Ack-ack was shot all around the son-of-a-bitch and a couple came very close, but he was not brought down," LaLonde wrote. "A P-38 shot at him twice with no results. A new moon was out but it was very cloudy. It was [a] pretty show. The gun flashes on the ground and the red balls of fire in the sky went 'krumph.' I never saw such a sight before. . . . Everyone was quite scared, and most dove into the foxholes," LaLonde added.[13]

Having survived that night, Max Kaminsky recalled that the musicians were alerted the next night around 11:00 p.m. to get ready to leave the island. The men packed, Max recounted, and then they lugged their gear to a waiting truck, where Artie was itching to be on the way. Before they could leave, though, Max wrote that Dave Tough called out. "Hold it!" Tough shouted. "I've got to go back for the drums."

The other band members swore. It was an absurd oversight, a drummer nearly forgetting his kit. It would have been comical had the men not been so desperate to leave behind Washing Machine Charlie's hunting grounds. Davey and Max started back for the camp. They were two small men, weakened by fear and fatigue, and Kaminsky wondered how they were going to manhandle the cumbersome drum kit once they found it. On a shortcut through the jungle, the men stumbled into an answered prayer.

"I'll be a sonofabitch," Davey exclaimed. "It's a wheelbarrow."[14]

Problem solved. In Max's retelling the undersized drummer and trumpet player were able to hoist the drum kit into the wheelbarrow and make it back to the waiting truck that would haul them to the airfield. It's an amusing tale told by Kaminsky, but it's also a peculiar one—not least because of Max's recollection that the whole misadventure unfolded late at night. Flight records show that the planes of the 13th Troop Carrier Squadron, which handled much of the human and inanimate cargo going in and out of Guadalcanal, typically took off from Henderson Field in the early afternoon. On July 17, the date Shaw's Rangers departed from Guadalcanal, the squadron's flight records indicate the plane took off at 12:30 p.m., well before the late-night time recollected by Kaminsky.

However it happened, the band members did board the C-47 from the 13th Troop Carrier Squadron, an outfit that had anointed itself as the Thirsty Thirteenth. The squadron's C-47s were the military versions of the civilian DC-3, a versatile workhorse capable of carrying twenty-eight passengers or about ten thousand pounds of cargo. The plane and crew that pulled Shaw's Rangers off of Guadalcanal had flown in with one batch of cargo from Tontouta Air Base the previous day. Navy Band 501 would be the cargo on the return flight.

The aircraft's flight engineer, Joseph LaLonde, wrote his wife that Shaw's Rangers were "a regular looking bunch." A Traverse City, Michigan, native, LaLonde added that "we had a nice visit on the way back, as there were some fellows from Michigan." LaLonde also had better luck than some fans, as he reported that during the six-hour flight back he managed to get an autograph from Artie as well as from an unidentified navy commander. LaLonde affixed both signatures to a "short snorter," a fad at the time in which airmen strung together a collection of signed bank notes. Once back on the ground, the flight engineer recorded that "we had a Sunday supper together; tuna fish, bread and water. We really were a hungry mess after six hours flying, without a bite to eat."[15]

Compared to where Shaw's Rangers had just come from, Noumea was the lap of luxury. There was fresh fruit on their plates and the possibility of uninterrupted sleep at night. The men unwound, and sometime after the band's return, Artie popped into the navy headquarters' press hut. He borrowed a match and, once he had his cigarette going, he was ready to unburden himself. Artie was still deeply tanned, and in the words of veteran International News Service correspondent John R. Henry, he was "looking more like a salty seafarer than the king of swing."[16] An Ohio native, Henry had a reporter's knack for being in the right place at the right time. He had previously reported from Washington, DC, England, South America, and North Africa. He knew how to ask questions and how to listen, and so he got a pretty good feature story out of the bandleader that played in a number of US newspapers.

Artie told Henry how the band would play only during daytime hours, while impromptu audiences "perched atop jeeps and trucks and leaned against trees" and soaked up the moment. It was a great place to play, Artie confided, "because the fellows up there are hungry for music." He recounted that all of the performances were in the mornings or afternoons, never with any sort of advertisement, but the word was passed around informally. "They never seemed to get enough," Artie told Henry. "We played three and four times a day and visited every camp on the island." Artie was frank about the nuisance air raids, noting that "there'd only be one or two or maybe three Japanese planes, but that was enough to make us forget sleep a while and duck into a foxhole."[17]

Shaw's Rangers would never get so close to combat again. The island and the wounds it inflicted, though, would linger.

# Chapter 15

# The New Zealand Beat

Dave Tough, Max Kaminsky, and Conrad Gozzo went shopping in Noumea after their return from Guadalcanal.

Somehow, they sniffed out a precious bottle of 136-proof Pernod absinthe. Real, honest-to-God liquor was scarce and worth every penny the men had to shell out. Kaminsky was carrying his trumpet case, perhaps as a surrogate shopping cart for the outing, and he placed the high-octane treasure inside. He then quietly handed off the case to Gozzo when the trio got back to the barracks area, where a guard stood watch at the gate. Kaminsky kept on walking as the younger man got busted and apparently told no one about what happened when he got back to the band's barracks. "The next day, Gozzo was missed, so me and a couple of others went down to the guardhouse and saw Gozzo breaking rocks with a sledgehammer," tenor saxophone player Joe Aglora told writer Harold Kaye.[1]

The story as it was relayed by band members seems peculiar, as if it's missing a few key elements. However it happened, Shaw reportedly tried to free his wayward young horn man, but the guardhouse commander said Gozzo would have to stay locked up for five days. Artie finally sprang Gozzo after several days once the band received orders to ship out, but the incident, rather than being just another musicians' amusing caper, aggravated tensions in a band already stretched thin and ready to snap. Mack Pitt recalled that "everyone was pissed off at Max for sticking Goz with the bottle," and some band members reportedly shunned Kaminsky for weeks on end.[2] In his own autobiography, Kaminsky makes no mention of the incident. He was also largely silent about the other personality conflicts, though Kaye mapped them out decades later. Artie thought trombone player Tasso Harris was surly. Harris and saxophone player Mack Pitt came to blows. Pitt reportedly irritated fellow New Jersey natives David Rose and Harold Wax, and most everyone seemed to be fed up with Artie.[3]

"By then, our instruments were being held together by rubber bands and sheer will, having survived any number of air raids and damp foxholes," Artie recalled, "and the men were in a similar state of dilapidation." The navy, Artie added, "had a term for this sort of exhaustion. They called it combat fatigue, or operational fatigue, depending, I suppose, on the doctor who was doing the diagnosis. The men in my outfit had a far more descriptive phrase for this state—'I'm beat, man.'"[4]

Still, duty called. At 5:00 p.m. on July 27, Shaw's Rangers and other passengers aboard the SS *Mormacport* set out from Noumea Harbor. Originally launched as a freighter in March 1940, the vessel was converted to carry about two thousand passengers and provided with rudimentary firepower under the command of a young navy ensign and a few enlisted men. That first night at sea, Harold Wax was on deck when reportedly he saw something light up on the horizon. Gozzo caught word of the hubbub on deck and awoke Tasso Harris.

"Hey, there's something happening outside," Gozzo shouted.

"What's happening?" Harris asked.

"I don't know," Gozzo said. "But there are a lot of flares and things."[5]

The navy's crewmen, too, saw flashes off the starboard side starting at 9:40 p.m. They also heard gunfire, which they estimated to be coming from eight or nine miles away. Shortly afterward three white rockets lit the distant night sky. Over the next fifteen minutes, several more rockets flared, gunfire chattered, and spotlights stabbed at the dark. By radio the *Mormacport*'s officers heard a report that another ship had engaged with a submarine.

Eventually the evening's excitement petered out with no further evidence of an enemy presence. Ensign N. J. Davis, the overseer of the ship's small navy armed guard, subsequently reported that the *Mormacport* continued on its way, zigzagging along at about seventeen knots until it arrived, safe and sound, at Auckland, New Zealand, at 2:00 p.m.[6]

A ship in the convoy, the musicians later concluded, had been sunk. Following on the heels of the Guadalcanal air raids, a ship's sinking seemed further proof that Navy Band 501 was at war. Artie later related the incident to *Metronome* writer Mike Daniels, who elaborated on "a monstrous horrifying explosion" that sank one of the ships in a convoy. The vivid characterization, presumably echoing what Artie told him, aligned with Daniels's melodramatic tone in which he had also recounted Shaw "standing in front of his band, playing his clarinet, joking and kidding with a couple of hundred American kids on a tiny atoll plagued by insects, mud, the odor of death and more mud."[7]

Of mud, insects, and an odiferous Guadalcanal, Shaw's Rangers definitely had their fill. The business about a torpedoed ship and a massive explosion, though, was apparently blown out of proportion. No ship was recorded as having been sunk at that time while convoying from Noumea to New Zealand. The gunfire from US ships may well have been nervous sailors blasting away at shadows in the night.[8]

The first Americans soldiers had arrived in New Zealand a little more than a year earlier on an overcast day in June 1942, when a contingent of US troops reached Auckland. The city's mayor and four military bands greeted the Americans at the dock with serviceable renderings of the "Star-Spangled Banner" and "Colonel Bogey's March." A US Navy band, armed with sousaphones, countered with "Roll Out the Barrel." Two days later Marines arrived at Wellington, about three hundred miles to the south, where a local band took a well-intentioned stab at the "Marine Corps Hymn."[9] These initial US forces grew substantially over time as the island nation became a staging area for troops awaiting combat and a haven for those back from the front. By the time Shaw's Rangers arrived, there were upward of fifty thousand US troops lodged throughout New Zealand.

The Yanks found a largely welcoming population, a blend of both foreign and familiar customs, and a small but vibrant New Zealand jazz scene whose members revered the Americans as the originators of the art. Auckland's first large-scale cabaret had opened in 1922 under the aspirational name the Dixieland. The house musicians called themselves the Southern Dixieland Band, although their accents gave them away: They were, in fact, Australian.[10]

Conservative New Zealanders abhorred these new musical gyrations with the same knee-jerk fervor initially found in the United States, where the archbishop of Dubuque, Iowa, had once denounced jazz as "a communistic endeavor" and a "pretext for cannibalistic orgies."[11] So it was, too, in New Zealand, where the New Zealand periodical *Truth* in 1923 condemned the denizens of a Dixieland cabaret as "young jazz weeds, dashing sheikhs, effeminate nincompoops and frivolous flappers."[12] About the same time, an upstanding veteran of the New Zealand Medical Corps, Dr. Percival Clennell Fenwick, warned the New Zealand Board of Health's Committee on Venereal Disease that "jazz and other kinds of dancing in present vogue are . . . most unhealthy." If jazz and the dancing it spurred were "rendered unfashionable by public opinion," Fenwick declared, "a certain amount of sexual excitement would be avoided."[13]

Sexual excitement, though, has a habit of rearing its head under any circumstance, and the warnings could not inoculate New Zealanders from infection. In 1923, New Zealand music historian Chris Bourke recounted, a US Navy veteran named Dick Richards showed up in Wellington bearing fresh tune arrangements that he spread about like a jazzy Johnny Appleseed. Two years later the battleship USS *Mississippi* arrived with a ten-member band described by one New Zealand enthusiast as "the pick of Uncle Sam's syncopators." Bands from other ships likewise carried American tunes into town.[14] Technology accelerated this spread of American culture, as the number of radios in New Zealand households increased from 71,680 in 1932 to 345,682 in 1940. During the evenings, dial-twirling New Zealanders could find performances carried by West Coast US stations.[15] "How much of every weekday programme from [a station] is devoted to that ghastly croon-jazz-blare-baby doll American rubbish?" one disgruntled New Zealander asked in a 1936 letter to the editor of the *Christchurch Press*.[16]

New Zealand radio broadcasts carried Artie's prewar performances since at least 1938, when the country's newspapers carried notices of that evening's edition of "Swingtime with Artie Shaw and his New Music."[17] New Zealand's gossip columns also tracked his prewar personal adventures, as when the *Bay of Plenty Times* reported on June 12, 1940, that Artie's 19-year-old wife, Lana Turner, had suffered a nervous breakdown while the bandleader was said "to be dictatorial and to give his wife too much advice."

With the war came more American musicians in the flesh. In mid-November 1942 members of the Whangarei Patriotic Amusements Committee hosted a US Army band for three days' worth of performances in the town about a hundred miles north of Auckland. The regimental outfit performed for schoolchildren and hospital patients and saluted their New Zealand hosts with their rendition of a tune called "Maori Battalion."[18] In mid-1943, shortly before Shaw's Rangers arrived, men from a US Army infantry division established what New Zealand jazz historian Aleisha Ward described as a hard-swinging outfit that attracted audiences both through live performances and broadcasts over radio.[19]

The Americans played with an exhilarating verve that New Zealand trumpeter Bobby Griffith enthused "really blew" the heads off an audience accustomed to the "corny" and "Mickey Mouse" work of homegrown New Zealand bands.[20] A young singer named Pat McMinn echoed the sentiment, saying, "We were knocked out" by the Americans and that "the sound was just unbelievable."[21] The sheer volume of the American players stunned the New Zealanders, but that wasn't all. The arrangements were fresh, the solos were supple, and the swing was irresistible. "What a revelation!" exclaimed Bert Anderson, an Auckland columnist with the *Australian Music Maker and Dance Band News*. "That music went right to the hearts of dance musicians . . . I guarantee all hands tore home to put in a few hours practice on the strength of it."[22]

A New Zealand Broadcasting man named Jack Chignell guided Artie's navy band through the foreign terrain. As liaison Chignell would serve as cultural translator and concierge.[23] With his guidance the band's first nighttime performance in New Zealand was scheduled for August 1 at the St. James Theater in central Auckland. Opened in 1928 for vaudeville acts and eventually movies and music, the St. James was Auckland's closest approximation to the band members' prewar haunts like New York City's Paramount Theatre.

During a rehearsal for the St. James Theater gig, Chignell suggested the Americans might welcome an up-and-coming New Zealand vocalist named Esme Stephens to front a few songs. Artie knew nothing about this 19-year-old singer from a faraway land. He was, in truth, indifferent at best to most female vocalists. He admired Billie Holiday and respected the young singer who replaced her in 1938, Helen Forrest, but he dismissed some other female warblers as window dressing.[24] Artie knew they got the audience's attention, but that was the problem. "One little singer on the mike [and] you've got eighteen men back there blowing their hearts out [and] where are they?" Artie grumbled.[25]

So, unsurprisingly, his reaction to the guest-speaker proposal, historian Chris Bourke recounted, amounted to an unenthusiastic "sure, why not."[26] Artie would not stand in the New Zealand singer's way, but neither would he actively support the teenager. That night, while Stephens trilled "White Christmas" and "This Love of Mine," Artie sat out both songs. "I guess Esme was nervous, but it didn't affect her," New Zealand trombone player Sal Alderton recalled. "She sang well."[27]

For the bulk of the St. James show, Shaw's Rangers relied on their well-worn arrangements of "Begin the Beguine," "You'd Be So Nice to Come Home To," and Jerome Kern's "Dearly Beloved." Artie also broke out a small piece for a trio in which he was joined by Rocky Collucio on piano and Dave Tough on drums. The audience ate it all up. "Looking down the rows between the seats, long rows of single feet could be seen," a writer for the *New Zealand Observer* reported. "The feet were all tap-tap-tapping in time with the music. Swing, they say, has that effect."[28]

Following the St. James show, trucks on August 2 carried the band about twenty miles south of Auckland to the Papakura Military Camp. The men assembled for training there had their own home-grown Papakura Camp Band for routine entertainment, but Shaw's Rangers delivered fresh American zip with a ninety-minute performance at the camp theater followed by an appearance at the Papakura Officers' Mess. The band satisfied the audiences musically, though some fans hoped for more. While he could turn on the charm when needed, Artie could just as easily turn his back on the clamoring public. Marjorie Watson, a nurse with the New Zealand Women's Auxiliary Army Corps, learned this essential truth about the elusive Artie Shaw at Papakura.

Watson was in her early 20s, a somewhat sheltered country girl raised in a South Island farming community of about seventy-five residents called Ruapuna. She had joined the Women's Army Auxiliary Corps in January 1943, trained as a nurse, and was working at the New Zealand Army's Ravensthorpe convalescent hospital while awaiting orders to go overseas when she learned that Artie Shaw's Navy Band was coming to the area.[29] Watson and several fellow nurses shed their distinctive white organza veils and large red capes and ventured to the Papakura Military Camp, about twelve miles away. The young nurses had Artie in their sights, "We were to meet him," Watson recalled, "but he took off back to Auckland, having borrowed someone's car."[30]

Artie's men next took the stage at the Auckland Town Hall on Friday, August 6. The show was designed to honor men from the New Zealand Expeditionary Force who had returned after more than two years in the Middle East. By war's end well over one hundred thousand New Zealand men would serve overseas.[31] The first round of officers and other ranks who had been granted three-month furloughs began to see how their country had changed. Some hardly recognized it. Americans had seemingly overrun the island nation. "Men returned to Auckland or Wellington have had their eyes opened to sights they thought they had left behind in Cairo, girls peddling their bodies from darkened doorways and cheap dance halls, so-called 'socialites' dining and drinking at fashionable hotels with visiting servicemen and displaying an unrefined technique veering from . . . banditry to . . . harlotry," the *New Zealand Observer* declared.[32]

The soldiers home from war found themselves displaced, their wives, girlfriends, and sisters fallen prey to the Americans with their big grins and open wallets. Several months prior to the arrival in New Zealand of Shaw's Rangers, the built-up tensions exploded in the so-called Battle of Manners Street.

On the late afternoon of Saturday, April 3, 1943, soldiers from both nations swarmed the streets of central Wellington. At the United Servicemen's Club,

Maori men encountered Americans. By some accounts racist Southerners among the US troops took offense at the dark-skinned Maoris' presence. Push came to shove and the fighting soon spread, aggravated rather than deterred by the arrival of baton-swinging military police. The serial brawls kept reigniting, on and off, for about four hours before dwindling. With newspaper coverage of the incident censored, word-of-mouth spread the most dramatic accounts: hundreds injured, several dead. Though the actual casualty figures were far less dramatic, the exaggerated accounts accurately captured the tensions.[33] "Fueled by alcohol and jealously at the Yanks for 'stealing their women,' fights between New Zealanders and Americans regularly broke out at dances," jazz historian Aleisha Ward noted.[34]

The circumstances required a diplomatic touch, a fact appreciated by Navy Commander Edwin V. Raines, executive officer of the US Navy Operating Base, and Lieutenant Commander Brooks Gifford, a Pasadena, California, attorney in his early 40s serving as a navy public relations officer on Admiral Halsey's staff. As cohosts for the August 6 performance by Shaw's Rangers, they arranged for free admittance for the New Zealand soldiers. In the same peacekeeping spirit, a New Zealand Army colonel suggested that an additional one hundred US sailors be admitted.[35]

At the earlier August 1 show, Artie had unenthusiastically assented to the young singer Esme Stephens fronting a few numbers. He received a similar request for the August 6 show, on behalf of a Maori singer named Molly Te Meihana. His first instinct might have been resistance. Still, as with Stephens, Artie could appreciate the strategic considerations in having his US Navy band accommodate a New Zealand singer. And, unlike the white teenager Stephens, Molly Te Meihana brought maturity to the stage. The talented mezzo-soprano had been recorded as early as 1927 as a member of the Rotorua Maori Choir. Sometimes known as Guide Molly, she felt herself transported by music. "When I sing any Maori song, I am far, far away from anything that is 'pakeha,'" Molly said, using a term that refers to things of European descent. "I am back in the old Maori forest, where no foot has trodden, save that of the Maori."[36]

This sounded plenty soulful. For the August 6 show, Artie's arrangers worked up a version of what was variously known both as the "Maori

Farewell Song" and as "Now Is the Hour." The piece had an ambiguous history, though its poignancy was undeniable when it was sung to Maori soldiers going off to war. For an America military band to play it was a certain crowd-pleaser.

"Po atarau," Molly sang. "E moea iho nei / E haera ana / Ko ki pamamao."

In 1948 Bing Crosby would sing it in a lush and languidly paced take, the song's eternally recurring image illuminated in its English translation: "Now is the hour / when we must say goodbye," Crosby would croon. "Soon I'll be sailing / far across the sea."[37]

# Chapter 16

# "The Ladies Were Wonderful"

S ome New Zealanders resisted Artie's siren song.

Early in Navy Band 501's tour of the country, Ashburton Patriotic Committee members dismissed the horn-tooting Americans as unworthy of attention. True-blue residents of the nation's rural South Island, 320 miles from Auckland, the Ashburton patriots preferred the likes of the Royal New Zealand Air Force Orchestra. That military band's "bright, modern dance music" sounded just the right note in an August 1943 performance that included an arrangement of "The Skaters' Waltz," readers of the *Ashburton Guardian* were advised.[1] Shaw's Rangers, on the other hand, were denounced at an August 30 meeting of the town's patriotic committee. " 'Don't invite that swing band we have heard so much about,' said one speaker," the *Ashburton Guardian* reported. " 'That's not a band at all,' remarked another.' "[2]

But the old guard's lamentations could not restrain the new wave. One defender of Shaw's Rangers advised the Ashburton patriots that "if the persons concerned would deign 'lower' themselves to spend a half-hour or so listening to Artie Shaw . . . they would hear some of the best clarinet playing in the world."[3] Another noted, somewhat acerbically, that "there are more swing fans in Ashburton than the Ashburton Borough Patriotic Committee realizes."[4]

In the larger cities, enthusiasts outnumbered or at least outshouted the naysayers. On Tuesday, August 10, following a show several days earlier at Auckland's Town Hall, the band appeared at the city's resplendent Civic Wintergarden. This had opened in 1929 as a movie theater, dance hall, and all-around pleasure palace. It had a rising stage, like the Paramount Theatre in New York City, and it topped that with a ceiling that depicted the starry night sky. The establishment's Lucky Lovelies chorus line gals flashed their gams, and a star attraction named Freda Stark performed her Balloon Dance, a bawdy audience-participation number punctuated by the popping of Miss Stark's strategically placed balloons.[5] "The Civic Theater and Wintergarden was luxurious, elegant, sophisticated and incredibly exotic, with its mix of Indian, Middle Eastern and Asian decorations," New Zealand jazz historian Aleisha Ward observed.[6]

Since the earliest days at The Breakers in Hawaii, Navy Band 501 had often limited their performances to daytime. In locations like Guadalcanal, it wasn't prudent to be out in the evening. For the August 10 show at the Civic Wintergarden, though, the band kicked off at the jazz-appropriate hour of 10:35 p.m. The audience was jumping from the start, with some leading members of the country's professional music community among the enthusiasts. Saxophonist Ted "Chips" Healy, who once led the Civic Wintergarden orchestra and had since joined the Royal New Zealand Air Force band, showed up. So did another Civic Wintergarden veteran, Freddie Gore, described as "New Zealand's hippest bandleader" and as a man who "could apparently make a piano do everything but climb stairs."[7]

One night about this time, Gore joined with Pete Sellers, an astute jazz enthusiast who wrote for *Australian Music Maker*, at a post-performance party convened at a mansion in a neighborhood called Lyall Bay. Artie never made the scene, but saxophonist Sam Donahue and other navy band members did, and the evening turned into a good old-fashioned jam session.[8] Artie's absence from that particular get-together could have been coincidental. He might have been feeling tired. He might have had other plans. Or his absence may have reflected his isolation from the band and his habitual withdrawal from the hubbub. It was about this time that a reporter for the *NZ Listener* sought an interview with Artie and was told bluntly that the bandleader had "neither the inclination nor the permission" to speak.[9]

The former seemed the more likely explanation. As one day followed the next in New Zealand, individual shows began to bleed together into one endless march. Artie could feel himself going through the motions as the band performed a few more shows in Auckland, at one of which the redecorated town hall was described as a "gay scene."[10] The band on August 12 then traveled by train the three hundred miles from Auckland south to Wellington, a city whose rolling hills and atmosphere reminded some Americans of San Francisco. There, the outfit kept up a breathless pace, performing at camps and hospitals during the day and at dances and concerts at night.

In Wellington, a city of about one hundred thousand residents, most of the musicians stayed at navy barracks, while Max Kaminsky managed to join Artie and the New Zealand liaison Jack Chignell in finagling rooms at the Midland Hotel, a five-story, Spanish Mission–style establishment built in 1915. Female fans quickly learned of the accommodations and gathered outside for a shot at meeting the stars. By this time in the tour, Kaminsky recounted, Artie had reverted to form with regards to women. Though his wife Elizabeth had given birth to their son just several weeks before, she was six thousand miles away. More than time zones and the months apart separated them. New Zealand offered steak, milk, and bottomless glasses of Waitemata beer, and those were just the appetizers.[11] "The people in Auckland were unusually warm and wonderful," piano player Rocky Collucio said. "The ladies were wonderful [and] after the New Hebrides, Solomons and New Caledonia, the food was manna from heaven."[12]

A mid-August performance at Wellington's Majestic Theatre brought the band to another one of the country's modern cultural landmarks. Opened in 1929 as a combination of movie theater and performance hall, the Majestic strove to live up to its name with its grand staircase, elaborate flourishes, and king-sized dance floor.[13] The venue was made to order for Shaw's Rangers, and as word spread about the upcoming show, some die-hard fans took desperate measures. Jazz historian Dennis O. Huggard recounted how a young New Zealand Army private named David Commin abandoned his guard post in hopes of seeing the Majestic Theatre show. When he arrived, he learned the performance was sold out.

"I turned to leave the theater, no doubt looking extremely downcast, when a U.S. officer approached me," Commin later recalled. The officer asked him if he wanted to attend the concert. Most definitely, Commin assured the officer. "He responded by presenting me with a ticket," Commin said. "That ticket entitled me to a seat in the centre of the first row of the dress circle. For the next two hours, I was in seventh heaven."[14]

It was, Commin added, well worth the fourteen days of punishment duty he received when caught sneaking back into the army camp. The show was an eye-and-ear opener even for those who didn't go AWOL to attend. For many of the New Zealanders, it marked an inauguration into what one reporter earnestly described both as "jive" and "hotted-up jazz, super jazz." This reporter added that "some of the guests were thrilled over it, some did not like it so well, but everyone was certainly surprised at the vigor and rhythm and electrical 'go' of this type of music."[15] Some did know what to expect. While the band was still backstage, a Canadian expatriate musician named Art Rosoman greeted Sam Donahue. Thirteen years earlier the two men had shared a stage in Sunburst, Montana, at a time when Rosoman was leading a Canadian orchestra. After catching up, Rosoman invited Sam and the other navy band members to an aftershow party.[16]

While in Wellington, Max Kaminsky and Dave Tough accepted an invitation from Chignell to meet the jazz aficionado Arthur Pearce. The 39-year-old Pearce, the Americans discovered, was a colleague of Chignell's from New Zealand 1ZB radio station. More than that, Pearce was the country's leading jazz broadcaster. He could hold forth on jazz history and minutiae for hours on end. He was a champion talker, a match for Artie in his propensity to lecture. He was also a solicitous host, and for his American guests he brought out a bottle of rare whiskey. "Asked what they would like with it," jazz historian Chris Bourke recounted, "Tough replied 'glasses.'"[17]

Several days later, the band performed for men of the Second Marine Division stationed at Camp MacKay, located about thirty-five miles north of Wellington. Saxophone player Mack Pitt recalled how a small subset of the band played for a hospital audience that remained eerily silent. Artie, accustomed to adulation, asked an orderly what the problem was. It's an amputee ward, the orderly said. The men were preoccupied. Artie, Pitt recalled, started to cry.

"It's a bitch," Artie said. "It's a bitch."[18]

The hospital patients were both a reminder of past combat and a fore-shadowing of what lay ahead for the Camp MacKay men. On November 20 they would be going ashore at Tarawa and Betio atolls at the start of a four-day battle that would kill 1,009 Marines and wound another 2,000.[19]

At a lavishly decorated Centennial Exhibition Hall in the Wellington suburb of Rongotai, the band played at an August 21 Welcome Home Ball for New Zealand troops. The Wellington City Council footed the bill, and the organizers put themselves out to make the occasion special. With a quaint if misplaced sense of formality, the tickets identified Shaw as "Arthur," the name he had dropped years before. Sandwiches, cakes, and assorted savory treats were laid out in great quantities, and a reporter described the hall as "ablaze with flags, and it was one of the gayest and most satisfying scenes that anyone could wish to see in these wartime days."[20] Some one thousand audience members took in the show, including the likes of Wellington's mayor, the region's governor-general, the prime minister's wife, and a slew of high-ranking military officers. "Artie Shaw's music was strange to many; it was alternately soft and then came with resounding volume," a reporter recounted, "but no one could escape the rhythm of a master melody-maker's combination."[21]

The New Zealand leg of the tour climaxed September 1 at the Auckland Town Hall in an event organized by the American Red Cross in honor of First Lady Eleanor Roosevelt. She was visiting the South Pacific on a three-week long tour and sharing her experiences with the American public through a published "My Day" diary. The first lady's September 1 diary entry recounted a particularly busy day that started with a reception at the town hall, followed by visits to a Red Cross Service Club. She then dropped by two rest homes where, Mrs. Roosevelt reported, "Fliers come to rest in great numbers." The visits were followed by a late afternoon tea and supper with high-ranking officers.[22] At about 8:30 p.m., wearing her gray Red Cross uniform, Mrs. Roosevelt arrived at the town hall and made her entrance through a lane of US and New Zealand servicemembers and their dates.

The first lady watched the dancers for about fifteen minutes and then was introduced by the senior US Navy officer in New Zealand, Captain Stanley Dexter Jupp, a 48-year-old Naval Academy graduate. Mrs. Roosevelt informed the crowd of some 1,500 that, alas, she would not be joining the dancers. The 57-year-old former debutante explained she was "too old," adding that the dances she knew didn't quite fit the moment. "The floor is too crowded for the waltz, and I doubt whether anyone here remembers the Virginia Reel," Mrs. Roosevelt said.[23]

The crowd ate it up, and the music that followed had the snap that came when Shaw's Rangers were playing for the big brass. "Artie Shaw's orchestra," Mrs. Roosevelt reported, "gave everyone much pleasure."[24]

She stayed for about an hour, enjoying both the music and the energetic young dancers. When she finally called it a night, the first lady departed amid rounds of cheers. Artie stayed in character throughout. Accordion player Harold Wax recounted that Artie at first resisted a navy admiral's urging that he chat up the commander in chief's wife and adviser. Finally, the admiral insisted that Chief Petty Officer Shaw perform his duty. "Artie acquiesced and spent the next intermission with her," Wax recalled. "Then he came over to me and commented, 'she said just what I thought she'd say, "chawmed, I'm sure." ' "[25]

Notwithstanding Artie's world-weary cynicism, his band's New Zealand tour was a seminal moment for the country, as jazz historians Aleisha Ward and Chris Bourke both recounted. Jazz writer Bert Peterson noticed this as it was happening at the time, observing in the September 1943 issue of the *Australian Music Maker* that "the arrangements the band played put new life into every musician present." Exaggerating only slightly, Peterson added that "all hands tore home to put in a few hours practice on the strength of it [and] long-forgotten tutors, textbooks and studiers were rescued from the attic and studied anew."

Next stop: Australia.

Artie Shaw was a man of many parts: a demanding bandleader, a brilliant clarinet player, a genuine celebrity and a World War II Navy veteran. William P. Gottlieb Collection, Library of Congress, Washington, DC.

Piano player and composer Claude Thornhill joined the navy band led by his old friend Artie Shaw but soon had second thoughts. William P. Gottlieb Collection, Library of Congress.

Dave Tough earned a reputation as a top-notch drummer with a curious mind and a serious drinking problem. William P. Gottlieb Collection, Library of Congress.

Saxophone player Sam Donahue led his own prewar band and again rose to the occasion when the navy band needed new direction. William P. Gottlieb Collection, Library of Congress.

The diminutive and talented trumpet player Max Kaminsky was a veteran of Shaw's civilian outfits and an entertaining teller of tales. William P. Gottlieb Collection, Library of Congress.

Artie leads his band, still looking fresh, in a performance onshore, with accordion player Harvey Wax and saxophone player Sam Donahue poised for action to his right.

Max Kaminsky, Dave Tough, and a third man were still lighthearted in Hawaii as they horsed around on a bicycle. Courtesy of Danny Levin, Harold S. Kaye Collection.

Max Kaminsky, Dave Tough, and a third man before the Pacific tour turned arduous. Courtesy of Danny Levin, Harold S. Kaye Collection.

Trumpet player Max Kaminsky, closely watched by bass player Barney Spieler, blasts out a solo aboard a warship. Naval School of Music Library, Virginia Beach, VA.

Artie Shaw leads his navy band in a performance aboard a US warship. Naval School of Music Library.

The band performs for US troops stationed in New Caledonia. National Archives at College Park, MD.

Artie solos in a nighttime performance for troops in New Caledonia. National Archives at College Park.

The band performs outdoors in the area around Espiritu Santo, a major navy base built from scratch in the New Hebrides. National Archives at College Park.

The band plays on a makeshift stage near the major navy base at Espiritu Santo in the New Hebrides. National Archives at College Park.

Sailors hungry for entertainment jammed into every available space to hear the band play in tight quarters. Naval School of Music Library.

US Army Technical Sergeant Carroll "Chuck" Hathorn took this picture of Shaw with fans in the area of Townsville, Australia, near the end of the band's Pacific tour. Courtesy of Peter Dunn, Australia@War.

The navy musicians were exhausted and at the end of their tether when they performed for patients and staff at the 13th General Hospital in Australia. Courtesy of Peter Dunn, Australia@War.

With Shaw no longer in charge, the navy band went head-to-head with Glenn Miller's Army Air Forces band in a September 1944 show in London. Courtesy of Dennis Spragg, Glenn Miller Collections.

Artie and his men, in happy days. Courtesy of Danny Levin, Harold S. Kaye Collection.

Shaw's Rangers, looking worn under the Pacific sun. Courtesy of Danny Levin, Harold S. Kaye Collection.

Sam Donahue, having taken over leadership of the former Navy Band 501, meets with Major Glenn Miller of the Army Air Forces. Courtesy of Dennis Spragg, Glenn Miller Collections, American Music Research Center, University of Colorado, Boulder.

Accordion player Harvey Wax was one of the youngest and least-known band members when he stood to take this battleship solo. Naval School of Music Library.

Artie, home from the Pacific with a war souvenir. Photo by Michael Ochs Archives/Getty Images.

Artie shows off a Japanese sword. Photo by Bettman/Getty Images.

Artie plays for sailors aboard a US warship. Photo by Bettman/Getty Images.

# Chapter 17

# Down Under

Machine-gunner Robert Leckie reached Australia in February 1943 with his run-ragged First Marine Division mates following five debilitating months of combat on Guadalcanal. Once among the civilians, they were ready to maraud.

"A happily blaring band played us on to the docks at Melbourne," Leckie recalled. "It was our first sight of the land Down Under, for we had been below decks since leaving Espiritu. We grinned at the band, and suddenly every one of us knew it was going to be all right." Quite specifically, Leckie added that he "passed a red-haired WAAF and exchanged smiles with her, detecting in her gladsome eye a second hint of the good times to come."[1] The good times would, in fact, roll on for months, and not solely with obliging members of the Women's Auxiliary Air Force. Welcomed with open arms in a country whose healthiest young men had been dispatched to the Middle East, the young US Marines had a ball until the war reclaimed them several months later for a job that needed doing on the island of Peleliu.

On September 3 the men of Navy Band 501 boarded a transport plane in Auckland. The musicians' duty was infinitely safer than battling for Peleliu, a fight in which an estimated 2,000 Americans died and another 8,500 were wounded. Still, the 1,400-mile flight to Brisbane had its own frights. Relegated to the status of cargo in the noisy, unheated plane, the musicians endured seven or so hours aloft over open ocean. Confronted by a midflight electrical storm, as potentially lethal a surprise as a Japanese sniper, the pilot abruptly plummeted the aircraft to a safer altitude, rattling bandmembers' stomachs and nerves alike.[2]

They landed, at last, in a country that, like New Zealand, had been transformed if not overwhelmed by a significant US military presence. By the end of the war, upward of one million Americans would pass through Australia, itself a nation of only about seven million residents. Comparatively well paid, combining both innocence and swagger, the Americans impressed without even trying. They were polite and generous, bringing with them bouquets and gifts of chocolate. They liked to dance. "When all's said and done, they were interesting and good-looking, especially the first lot that came out," recalled Estelle Funcie, a photographer's assistant who lived in Brisbane. "They had beautiful teeth, that's what you noticed, their beautiful teeth, whereas a lot of our fellows had their teeth pulled out when they went into the Army and had dentures."[3] Inevitably, as in New Zealand, the grinning Americans provoked jealousy and resentments.

On the night of November 26, 1942, at the corner of Creek and Adelaide streets in Brisbane, US military policemen reportedly attempted to take a US soldier into custody for lack of a proper pass. Australians who had been drinking with the GI attempted to interfere. An MP struck one with a baton, and a crowd gathered. Soldiers spoiling for a fight jostled about and urged each other on. It got unruly and an American opened fire with a shotgun, killing one Australian soldier and wounding nine others. The fracas carried on for about three hours, calming for a while and then reigniting at some new friction. One constable subsequently testified that he saw an Australian signalman named Owens stirring up the crowd.

"What is the matter?" the constable asked him. "Why do you not go away and be sensible?"

"One of our chaps has been hit by an American baton," Owens replied. "Tell them to put their batons down, and we'll have a go at them."[4]

The go became known as the Battle of Brisbane, not unlike the Battle of Manners Street that would follow in New Zealand the next year. Nor was it the only clash between the Australian and American allies. They had been nipping at each other for some time. In just the week before the clash in Brisbane, an American sailor had been thrown from a train and seriously injured. An Australian soldier reported that while walking near the Palace Hotel in South Brisbane, a Black soldier had stabbed him in the right arm after he refused to hand over some money. The altercation brought additional injury when, it was reported, a "farmer tried to watch the fight from a passing train and hit his head against the buttress of Victoria Bridge, sustaining a compound fracture of the skull."[5]

But if the Americans were threats, they were also objects of fascination. Although Australia was ten thousand miles from New York City, its residents had come to know of Artie well before his navy band days. Some of his prewar shows had been aired by the Australian Broadcasting Commission, and the Commission's *ABC Weekly* periodical had kept readers abreast of Artie's prewar musical forays. Writer Jim Davidson in particular had observed the American bandleader, predicting in April 1940 that Artie would benefit from shrinking in half a planned sixty-three-member orchestra. The larger group was "too expensive," Davidson opined, adding that the public was "clamoring for a change" from what he called the "large and repetitive diet of swing and near-jazz the bands have given them the past five years."[6] The Australian celebrity-chasing photo magazine *Pix* also put the spotlight on the bandleader, running in 1940 a picture of Artie gallivanting in Hollywood with his then squeeze, actress Betty Grable. "He flared that jitterbuggers were nitwits, business of making their music was bunk," *Pix* snapped in a full-page spread.[7]

Artie's arrival thrilled the Australian media. *Australian Women's Weekly* writer Peg McCartney led the reporting pack. She approvingly described Artie as "dark-haired, tanned and athletic-looking" and recounted that he took what she called "a small boy's delight" in collecting a "bewildering array" of war mementos. The souvenirs included a Japanese battle flag and a bracelet that a US soldier had fashioned from a piece of a downed Japanese bomber. Artie further charmed the writer by confiding that he had cabled his wife Elizabeth asking her to wire some more money into his account. "Knowing my passion for souvenir hunting, she cabled back, 'money deposited as requested. Please don't buy an island,'" Artie told McCartney.[8]

McCartney seemed quite taken by the American bandleader. She noted how Artie spoke "deliberately, decisively and fluently," and she credulously recounted his story that he had broken up his civilian band after Pearl Harbor and considered organizing orchestras to visit military bases but then decided that "it might look like it was evading service." He further told McCartney that he had joined a class of navy men "with experience of small craft for such work as mine-laying and coastal patrolling," an early example of Artie's puffing up his navy experience.

The band took the stage on Thursday, September 9, at Brisbane City Hall, a venue more theatrical than its name suggests. Opened in 1930 following nearly a decade of construction that made it one of the country's most expensive public works projects, the civic headquarters featured massive Corinthian columns, an expansive auditorium, and a 285-foot-tall clock tower that was at the time the city's tallest structure. On the day of Navy Band 501's show, crowds began lining up outside at 5:30 p.m. Two hours later the line standers were six abreast and stretched around the building. These eager beavers included "100 demure young women lined up near the entrance steps," a reporter observed, adding that "they were some of the 1,500 girls invited to the dance."[9]

Girls—young women demure and otherwise—made all the difference. They changed the essential atmosphere. Playing for sailors aboard a warship or for Marines in a jungle amphitheater was one thing. The music marched along but it could remain stuck up in the head. Add women, though, and bodies began to sway. The room softened. Hips rolled. Now the military band became Shaw's Rangers, a kick in the head that got dancers moving. "Inside the hall, swing and string, Harlem and Hawaii, rumba and rah-rah melody had dancers melting into one big soulful, swaying crowd," the *Brisbane Courier-Mail* reporter recounted.[10]

Shaw's Rangers recovered from that evening romp and next flew about 850 miles to Melbourne for shows at both the city's town hall and its Red Cross building. Leading members of the Australian jazz community awaited them. While some members of the navy ensemble—including Conrad Gozzo, John Best, San Donahue, Dave Tough, and Max Kaminsky—were already admired by clued-in Australians, orchestra leader Graeme Bell noted that prior to the arrival of Navy Band 501, "None of us had heard or spoken to one single genuine American jazz musician in the flesh."[11] Consequently, Bell recalled, the news of the American band's arrival "spread like wildfire and the excitement among the musicians was at a fever pitch." To their dismay the Australians learned that the show was billed for Americans only. Bell recounted that several university students snuck in and managed to sidle up to Kaminsky, who invited them to visit him at his hotel.

The next morning two of the die-hard Australian fans showed up at room 412 of the Victoria Coffee Palace, an ornate hotel located next to the town hall. On entering they found Kaminsky lounging on one bed and piano player Rocky Collucio sprawled out on another. The Americans proved friendly, and they all went to lunch, where they were joined by Bill Miller, the Oxford-educated founder of the Australian periodical *Jazz Notes*. The ideas started bouncing back and forth, and soon the musicians hatched the idea of recording some sides. On September 19, Bell recounted, Kaminsky joined with half a dozen Australian players at the city's Legionnaire Recording Studios to lay down four tracks that would launch Miller's Ampersand record label.[12]

On September 23 the band took off again for a 1,600-mile flight to a coastal US military base at Townsville, located in the remote northeast province of Queensland. It was about this time that Artie recalled an eerie midair encounter. The musicians were crowded into a troop carrier. With the plane's cruising speed of about two hundred miles an hour, the trip north from Melbourne to Townsville took eight or nine hours. Below them the drab and featureless Queensland expanse was an empty quarter, with a population density of barely one person per four square miles. It offered few distractions until, Artie recalled, the pilot alerted him to the radio traffic coming from a nearby plane. "I heard a Jap-accented voice say, 'I see you, DC. I ain't got time for you now. I'll get you on the way back,'" Artie recounted, adding that he looked out the window and "there he was, a Japanese fighter."

"I lived through that one," Artie added.[13]

The close call in the skies above the northern Australia wasteland was not an incident recalled by any other band member in any published account. It may or may not have transpired just as Artie recounted it for a 2003 BBC documentary. It sounds improbable; enemy planes passing so close, the Japanese pilot's English fluency, the common radio channel. Still, this war story can't be ruled out. Navy Band 501 had experienced enough unlikely encounters that one more is not out of the question.

Finally landing at Townsville, the men found a town that, like so many others they had passed through had been transformed by US forces. Early on the American brass had pinpointed the small coastal city, located about 1,100 miles southeast of the city of Darwin, as suitable for a maintenance and supply facility as well as for training and other support operations. It had a decent harbor, though it needed improving to accommodate the largest warships.[14] Thus anointed, Townsville had grown from twenty-five thousand to one hundred thousand inhabitants between 1942 and 1943. A ring of pill boxes protected the old downtown. Warehouses, quarters, and a 120-bed hospital sprawled outward. In Cleveland Bay as many as forty ships a day awaited loading or convoy service.[15]

However remote, Townsville was a significant enough navy base that, just about two weeks prior to the scheduled arrival of Navy Band 501, First Lady Eleanor Roosevelt had paid a visit. Other Americans had likewise swung by. The month before Shaw's Rangers showed up, Jack Benny head-lined a performance at Townsville, and movie stars John Wayne and Gary Cooper would likewise pay their respects. Shortly before Artie and his men arrived, five US senators, led by the influential Georgia Democrat Richard Russell, came as part of an inspection tour. The solons spent one night in tents and then, it was reported, they "mounted jeeps and went in search of kangaroos." Finding a large pack, the expeditioners gave chase and, it was reported, they "ran down one big kangaroo at twenty miles per hour."[16]

Other than the beleaguered local 'roos, Townsville's residents were not living in a combat zone. Still, simply coming and going could get dicey. On August 7, 1943, about seven weeks prior to the arrival of Shaw's Rangers, a C-47 transport plane carrying men bound for R and R crashed into Cleveland Bay shortly after its early morning takeoff from Townsville's

Garbutt Airfield. Twenty-three American passengers and four Australian crewmen died.[17]

The band played on September 24 for the patients and staff of the US 13th Station Hospital in Townsville. Opened in 1942, the hospital had by the time Shaw's Rangers arrived some 450 beds along with a recreation facility, administrative buildings, and assorted secondary structures. The daytime concert was held outdoors, with Artie and some of the other men wearing sunglasses against the glare. Patients in white hospital bathrobes occupied the front row in wheelchairs. Khaki-clad nurses stood in clusters in the back behind a waist-high fence, as did male orderlies. A writer for the *Music Maker*, Eric Ambler, subsequently described a show from about this time that started off quietly but then began to accelerate with the ever-popular "Begin the Beguine." As the band's energy picked up with songs including "Stardust," "Night and Day," "Everything's Jumpin'," and "Frenesi," Ambler reported, the "enthusiasm of the boys and girls knew no earthly bounds."[18]

The band on September 26 traveled about two hundred miles north of Townsville to the provincial capital city of Cairns, home to a harbor conveniently close to a passageway through the Great Barrier Reef. At about 8:00 p.m. the next day, in the town of Parramatta Park, a navy chaplain introduced the band to an audience estimated at upward of ten thousand. It was among the largest crowds of any during Navy Band 501's entire tour, and, as the *Cairns Post* put it the next day, "To say that [it] was successful is putting it mildly." The ninety-minute performance concluded with a crowd-pleasing take on the US and Australian national anthems.

The band flew on September 28 the 450 miles south to the coastal city of Rockhampton. They again followed the stout heels of First Lady Eleanor Roosevelt, who had recently stopped by the city's theater and cajoled women to perform their patriotic duties. Multiple hospitals were arrayed throughout the area to handle casualties from the gruesome slog through New Guinea that would claim about 12,400 American dead, two-thirds of whom died from disease or other nonbattle causes, and another 7,900 wounded.[19]

Shaw's Rangers pitched in where they could. Sometimes this meant splitting up into small units so they could move bedside to bedside in hospitals. The close quarters validated Artie's prescience in hiring the young accordion player Harvey Wax, who could lug his portable keyboard throughout the wards. On one occasion Wax might have been the key to answering a dying soldier's wish. While swinging through one of the Rockhampton military hospitals, the small band of musicians reportedly came upon a young soldier who was receiving a blood transfusion though his cause was, apparently, all but lost.

"He asked us to play 'Pennsylvania Polka,'" Artie recounted. "We had heard it only once or twice before, and I had never played it." The song had been written the year before and had been covered by Sam Donahue's civilian band as well as by the Andrews Sisters, among others. It was pure kitsch, not part of Arie's standard library, but the musicians kick-started it as best they could. Artie recalled that "in the middle, we got mixed up with 'Beer Barrel Polka'" but still, he said "the boy seemed to enjoy it."[20]

"While they're dancing all around / Everyone's cares are quickly gone / Sweet romancing. / This goes on and on and on 'til dawn / Ha, ha, ha, ha, ha / Gay with laughter, they're as happy as they can be."[21]

# Chapter 18

# "Wake Up Screaming"

Musicianship had its privileges, but the privileges had a price.

Since their start, even before they had adopted Shaw's Rangers as their nom de guerre, Artie's handpicked band members had one foot on the stage and one foot on the parade grounds. As celebrated stage performers, they enjoyed special treatment: a dedicated train car that took them cross-country, roomier cabins and better eats on their ship to Hawaii, freedom from KP-like duties at the Aiea barracks. They weren't entirely free from navy discipline, as both Dave Tough and Conrad Gozzi had learned, but when they departed Rockhampton in an army transport plane and arrived in Sydney on Thursday, September 20, they went not to conventional barracks but to a hotel. This apparently aggravated sailors who had already been swapping scuttlebutt about Artie's band. Myriad rumors circulated, some rooted in fact and others spun from pure imagination: The band members were paid more than other enlisted men. They cut in line at mess halls. In Sydney, they broke the hotel's toilet seats—or so some other sailors claimed.

It was a peculiar allegation, but serious enough to get the musicians summoned one morning to the office of a navy captain who attempted to plumb the allegations. After a chief petty officer laid out the toilet-seat charges, Max Kaminsky, as he later recalled it, took upon himself the role of band defense attorney. The diminutive trumpet player stood up to the accusers and assured the navy captain that, as road-tested musicians, the members of Navy Band 501 knew what was expected of them. "We've played in the best places and in the worst places, but if there's one thing that we've learned it's how to behave ourselves," Kaminsky earnestly assured the captain. The self-assessment would amuse anyone with first-hand knowledge of a jazz musician's road life. Toilet seats could be the least of a hotel's casualties following a band's overnight revelries. Still, the officer seemed to take Kaminsky's point. Finally, he announced his decision: charge dismissed.[1]

As with other Kaminsky recollections, this one is both amusing and quite possibly a stretch. Arranger Dave Rose recalled that though the men were indeed summoned before a navy commanding office, the bit about Kaminsky's inspired defense "never happened." Instead, the captain seemed from the start to see the absurdity of the incident before he summarily dismissed the charges.[2] However it happened, Shaw's Rangers emerged from the Case of the Broken Toilet Seat with their records still clean. They would not be confined or otherwise restricted in their ongoing exploration of Sydney's nightlife, a venturing out that inevitably brought them into the arms of a remarkable after-dark operator who answered to the name Sammy Lee.

Born Samuel Levi, he was a Winnipeg native who had first arrived in Australia in the late 1930s as the leader of a band named the Americanadians. Over the course of eighteen months, the band impressed audiences in Wellington and Auckland and recorded a take on the popular song "Jeepers Creepers" before disbanding. In about 1940 Levi-turned-Lee came back to Australia and opened the Roosevelt Club on Sydney's Orwell Street. It was described as the country's first theater restaurant, though that didn't quite capture the essence of the place. "We gave them a long line of chorus girls, a couple of overseas artists and we were a big hit," Sammy told a reporter.[3]

Since opening the Roosevelt Club, the go-getter had branched out. He ran a wartime establishment called the Yankee Doodle Club, as well as what was rebranded as the King's Cross Roosevelt Club for Allied Officers. Lee was only about 30 years old when he met Shaw's Rangers, but he could seem older, weightier. He was a hefty, prematurely balding cigar smoker with a thin mustache and a thick wad of connections. When he got hold of money, he said, he was prone to "bet big and gamble" He allowed that he had "gone broke and borrowed money many times," although he stressed that he always paid back the loans.[4] He favored garish clothes and was described as "generous, excitable and as hard as nails."[5]

In short, Sammy Lee was just the kind of wised-up character the band members had known their entire professional lives. He was the connection, the guy with a glad hand out front and some shady business out back in the alley. Ever since they arrived in Australia, Max Kaminsky and Dave Tough had repeatedly heard of him as someone to hook up with. Dave had written down Lee's name and the address of his club, and one night a thoroughly lubricated quartet of band members directed a skeptical cab driver to take them to this supposed hot spot.

"Shove off, you coves," the nightclub's doorman told the disheveled Americans. But, as later recounted by Kaminsky, Lee happened to be standing nearby, and he came over to check out the commotion.

"When Dave introduced himself, Lee couldn't believe it," Kaminsky wrote. Lee enthusiastically welcomed the musicians, and for the remainder of their time in Sydney he treated them to steak dinners, top-shelf liquor, and whatever other pleasures a nightclub owner might command. The hospitality would help sustain Shaw's Rangers through a hectic performance schedule.[6]

On the night of October 2, the band played at Sydney's David Jones Auditorium. It was a good venue, with warm, well-designed acoustics, though for many audience members, celebrity viewing replaced dancing as the activity of choice. Couples jostled for position and pressed toward the stage when Artie picked up his clarinet. When Artie wasn't playing, he stood to the side of the stage and let the others blow. Rocky Collucio, the piano player, "sits and chews gum incessantly while playing in a nonchalant style," an Australian reporter observed.[7] A high-ranking army officer present, Brigadier General Thomas Edward Rilea, was heard to tell Chief Petty Officer Shaw that he admired his sharp-looking uniform but he wished the army had had the sense to grab him before the navy. The audience was equally impressed and didn't want to leave until, it was reported, "they were reminded by a sharp blast from a saxophone that the dance had ended."[8]

The next day, a Sunday, the band was lined up for two shows at the city's Trocadero nightclub. An afternoon performance was intended for Australian service members and an 8:00 p.m. show targeted US personnel.[9] Opened in 1936, the Trocadero was popularly known as the Troc by Sydney's dance music fans. Its Art Deco murals depicted dancers from around the world. Multicolored lights illuminated its revolving, shell-shaped bandstand. A broad marble foyer, polished granite walls, and potted palm trees welcomed customers. Once through the double-glass doors into the auditorium, dancers delighted in a fourteen-thousand-square foot floor set atop rubber that yielded just so. The space could accommodate about two thousand people, and it had been drawing crowds for months.

"After the Americans came, we all used to wear makeup—that puce color, very purply, and lip gloss, rouge and lipstick, tons of it," recalled Lola Taylor, a one fetching Trocadero regular. "I used to put it on very thickly indeed."[10]

Artie's navy band took the Troc's stage in their uniforms. The musicians were arrayed in three rows, the saxophone players up front and the physically imposing stand-up bass player, Barney Spieler, anchoring stage right. Behind the stage two representations of the American flag augmented the Art Deco lighting design. In front of the stage, the audience at one point pressed together so tightly, shoulder to shoulder, that there was hardly room to move, let alone dance. "I could stand this kind of music all day and night," an army sergeant told a reporter that week. "It's perfect."[11]

Crowded around the stage, audience members beseeched Artie for autographs during the few seconds he spared between songs. He granted his fans a smile but declined all autograph requests, while members of the band obligingly signed their names on whatever was thrust their way: slips of paper, the backs of train tickets, leave passes. When the musicians picked up their instruments and played, a reporter tried desperately to capture the raw energy in the room:

"Naked thighs and legs are straight and slim beneath the swirling skirts. A dusky brunette, wearing a scarlet brassiere bolero and separate chews and waggles and smiles bewitchingly.

"A youthful Veronica Lake and a coal-black sailor show a spell-bound crowd how Artie Shaw's music should be interpreted. More dancers crowd the floor. Feet stamp. Hands slap and clap. Hips huddle.

"The dancers are gayer, madder, crazier, abandoned.

The music louder, hotter, louder."[12]

The crowd's admiration for the dancing of the "coal-black sailor" and the "Veronica Lake" look-alike, and the reporter's equally casual acceptance of the biracial couple, hinted at a significant wartime social development. At the time Australia had a long-established practice of racial exclusion that was known as the White Australia Policy and was rooted in a set of immigration restrictions imposed starting in 1901. Somewhat akin to the literacy tests employed in Southern US states to impede Black voters, Australia required would-be immigrants to pass a dictation test in which they would have to correctly write down fifty or more words dictated to them. Under the guise of a seemingly neutral test, the intention was to deter Asian immigrants. More broadly it reflected an official animus toward all nonwhites that was amplified by fears of allegedly rapacious Black men.

In early 1928 a ten-member Black American outfit led by a slightly built but dynamic drummer and pianist named Sonny Clay arrived Down Under. Sonny Clay's Plantation Orchestra delivered the goods, with one satisfied Australian reviewer in February 1928 describing one member of the troupe as a "rotund negro of liberal proportions" who "sings, dances and announces items in an amusing and inimitable negro style."[13] The next month, though, Melbourne police burst in on orchestra members who were sporting about in what the rabblerousing periodical *Truth* described as an "atmosphere poisonous with cigarette smoke and fumes of liquor." More to the point, former Australian Prime Minister William Hughes thundered that the Black musicians had been "been too familiar with the white women since their arrival."[14] Australian authorities expelled the orchestra.

The White Australia Policy was entrenched enough that even when the Japanese threat seemed its strongest, Australian officials at first rejected the inclusion of Black troops among the US reinforcements. This outright nay-saying later softened to conceding to the arrival of Black troops but, whenever possible, keeping them in remote locations. Tensions periodically flared, particularly around the issue of white women consorting with Black servicemen. Sydney's popular Trocadero nightclub, initially open to all races, was reportedly limited to whites only following an interracial brawl.[15] Still, while Australian leaders propounded a segregationist policy, the biracial couple dancing to Artie Shaw's music exemplified how everyday citizens proved more accepting of racial diversity.[16]

Even with the crowds going wild and Sammy Lee tending to their appetites, Shaw's Rangers were wiped out. Civilian bands working in peacetime would likewise burn out on the road. Musicians could lose track of where they were, night after night. For Navy Band 501, the customary road grind was aggravated by tropical fevers, rolling ships, plunging airplanes, and sporadic air raids. Five months since departing Pearl Harbor, the band's gas tank was empty. Artie confided to one Australian reporter that he was "muzzy in the head and too tired to think," and he was not alone.[17] "I could hardly play and began to have nightmares and would wake up screaming. The whole band started to fall apart," Kaminsky said.[18]

Navy medical personnel examined the men in early October and found them depleted by their service. Conrad Gozzo had weighed 180 pounds on a compact five-foot, six-inch frame at the time of his 1940 draft physical. He had shed so many pounds that he now looked almost gaunt. His fellow trumpet player John Best, arranger Dick Jones, and others had likewise been drained.[19] The physical deterioration reflected their dire emotional straits. In his short story "A Nice Little Post-War Business," Artie conveyed the exhaustion through the voice of a weary navy bandleader. "We were about a week out of Brisbane, heading for God knows what destination," Artie's narrator recounts. "And as usual, the scuttlebutt was running all over the place. One day, a rumor would get started that we were on our way to New Caledonia, next day it would be the Aleutians.

"By that time," the bandleader added, "I couldn't have cared less."[20]

It was likely about the time of the band's October check-up that navy psychiatrist and neurologist Dr. Mark Gerstle Jr. saw Artie. His was a name Artie would recall, albeit in contradictory ways.

Born in 1897 into a prominent West Coast family, Gerstle had first entered the navy in 1918 while a senior at Harvard. He served for several months at the navy's Mare Island Hospital near San Francisco until he was discharged that December.[21] Gerstle went on to graduate from Stanford and Stanford Medical School. He still had an itch to serve, and he joined the Army Reserves as a medical officer in 1925. He kept his commission until 1934, when he transferred to the Naval Reserve. All the while he was advancing his civilian career, with stints as an assistant clinical professor of neurology at the University of California Medical School. He had worked in New York City between 1933 and 1938, much the same time as Artie was making his own name in the city.[22]

Gerstle, like Artie, was many times wed. His first marriage was in 1917. Divorced in 1926, the young doctor waited two months before marrying a young lady described by the *San Francisco Examiner* as "one of the most beautiful women in San Francisco society." Four years later she filed for divorce, charging "cruelty and humiliation."[23] He found a new wife. They divorced in 1937, with Gerstle this time being the one to complain, about how while the couple was living in New York City, his wife had "created a public scene" at the swank El Morocco nightclub.[24]

For all of his misbegotten marriages, Gerstle was an energetic physician. Early in his career, he authored a slim volume of advice entitled *The Doctor Answers Your Questions*, in which he had tackled topics from sex and social diseases to diet and cancer.[25] Later, after joining the Naval Reserve, he focused on weeding out the mentally unfit or fixing them so they might get back into the fight. In August of 1942, Gerstle and two other navy medical officers had laid out their findings from evaluating recruits at the Naval Training Station in San Diego.[26] Proper testing, the doctors reported, could help keep the unfit out in the first place and thereby avoid the costs associated with their later attrition. For the fundamentally fit, the navy doctors determined that the psychologically infirm could be eased back to their proper fighting positions in their tanks or battleships.[27]

Ambitious and resourceful, Gerstle was promoted in July of 1943 to what amounted to the position of chief medical officer for the Seventh Fleet's Service Force. Gerstle learned more about the subject of the neuropsychiatric costs of war once he deployed to the Pacific theater. In a February 1943 letter to his father, reprinted in the journal *California and Western Medicine*, Gerstle wrote that he "can't say much" about his current location and circumstances except that "it's all pretty grim, vague and disorganized." He described his previous experience of Australia as "a cross between Coney Island, Greenwich Village and Sacramento," and he added that "I'm trying to do what I can to bolster my morale and combat the ennui and nostalgia."[28]

Gerstle had more to worry about than individual patient assessments. Chief Petty Officer Shaw, though, was not a typical patient. He was arguably the navy's highest-profile enlisted man, and Gerstle might have thought it prudent to assume direct responsibility for his evaluation. The doctor, with his own high-society background, might also have simply been intrigued by the celebrity bandleader. However their encounter came about, Gerstle reported that he spent "several days" with Artie in October of 1943, when the band was in Australia.

"He was suffering from insomnia, loss of appetite and appeared to be under tremendous tension, overcome with countless fears and worries," Gerstle subsequently recounted in a brief memo. The doctor observed that Artie was "excitable and depressed" and had suffered similar symptoms on "numerous occasions" throughout his life. The long-standing anxiety and nervousness had rendered him susceptible to the shocks of war. It was clear, Gerstle stated, that the patient had a "basically unstable emotional makeup," and all things considered, Gerstle recounted, "it was, therefore, considered advisable to recommend his return to the United States." [29]

Artie offered several conflicting accounts of his experience with Gerstle. One version cast the doctor as severe and unreasonably demanding.

"We're going to ask you to play a concert for the entire fleet tomorrow," Gerstle said, according to this account. "Can you do it?"

Gerstle presented the case "briskly," Artie recalled. Rest time was over. Artie said he told the doctor he was by no means capable of playing.

"You're a goldbricking son-of-a-bitch," Gerstle said, in this version of Artie's retelling. If this was a mind game, it struck a nerve. Artie might have had a habit of checking out, but he had an even more powerful urge to prevail.

"I had always been driven by an overpowering desire to vindicate myself, to prove myself, to assert myself, in my dealings with people," Artie said.

"Life had always seemed to me a kind of race, between me and the rest of the world."[30]

It was this Artie that sprang up at Gerstle's reported provocation. "I'll show you, and, by God, you're no friend of mine," Artie declared.

The next day, Artie recalled, he played before an audience he estimated as being upward of twenty thousand men. The whole band, wiped out as they were, really cooked.[31]

"Oh, boy, how we hit it!" Artie recalled.[32]

It's not clear which show Artie was referring to. The descriptions of the audience as the "entire fleet" and characterizing its size as "twenty thousand" does not readily match Shaw's Rangers known shows. According to published reports at the time, the largest audience among the band's Australia shows appeared at Parramatta Park and numbered ten thousand. This version of Gerstle as a goad also conflicted with another version that Artie himself offered in an interview with Harold Kaye. The military doctor, Artie told Kaye, "saved my life," and he attributed to Gerstle the consoling wisdom that " 'Look, we are in a lunatic war. All wars are crazy [and] you have to take a certain perspective.' "[33]

Gerstle's relatively brief patient assessment notes included in Artie's navy medical file make no reference to either scenario. Artie's inconsistent recollections of Gerstle as both a goad and a good guy echoed other contradictions in the bandleader's recounting of his military service. In later years, for instance, Artie would attribute hearing loss in his left ear to bomb explosions from Japanese air raids. "Ended up in Guadalcanal, where we were being bombed," Artie told interviewer Bruce Talbot in 1992. "Lost my left ear there."[34] But in May 4, 1953, testimony before a House subcommittee investigating communist activities, Artie stated that "my left ear has not functioned very well since I was about 24." That would have been about 1934.

"Actually, I must be guilty of a deception to the United States government," Artie told lawmakers. "I ordinarily would not have been allowed to enlist in the Navy had I told them of this information when I went down."[35] A prewar examination had, indeed, found he had lost 40 percent of his hearing in his left ear, long before he reached Guadalcanal, according to Artie's medical file. By 1944 that had progressed to a 94 percent left-ear hearing loss.

While the deterioration could have been accelerated by proximity to an explosion, the root causes of the hearing loss preceded his wartime service. Artie, in any event, wasn't the only musician breaking down. The men were fed up with their bandleader, their music, and each other. Several band members recalled that, one time, Dave Tough was too smashed to play in Brisbane. A sound engineer named Jack Towers recounted one show at a converted racetrack named Camp Doomben, five miles northeast of the Australian city. "I went out early while the band was setting up," Towers said. "Dave was lurching around backstage and he was drunk."[36]

The drummer was so plastered, Towers recalled, that Artie recruited someone to handle some rudimentary beats for the Camp Doomben show. It was clear that Davey had reached the end of the line. Kaye talked to multiple band members who recalled Davey sprawled out on his bunk, incapacitated and incontinent. "I was only two bunks away and Dave was lying in his bunk amid shit and pass," band arranger David Rose recounted. "It was pathetic."[37]

Max Kaminsky, meanwhile, had decided he needed to check out of general quarters altogether during the band's downtime. He telephoned Graeme Bell, the Australian jazzman, and asked if there was a spare room someplace. Bell invited him over, and for a few nights Kaminsky collapsed on a spare single bed. "Max was still having nightmares and I bought him some [sedatives] over the counter at the chemists," Bell recalled. "I would come home each night [from work] and find him sitting up in bed with a book and a bottle of gin." The two men would talk for hours, with Bell soaking up the stories about the American jazz scene. The trumpet player, Bell observed, seemed to "find it therapeutic to talk about his civilian days."[38]

The entire band was out of sorts. The drummer was incapacitated. A trumpet player was shacked up with a bottle in bed. Morale had reached rock-bottom. Even as Melbourne's *Sun-News Pictorial* was pleading in its October 19 edition for Artie to make an appearance in the city, it was clear that Navy Band 501 had reached the end of the road. The decision was made to return Shaw's Rangers to the United States, though it's unclear who the actual decision-maker was and whether this was cutting short previous plans for an extended tour. There was always something a little ad hoc about the band's day-to-day operations; in any event, the men on October 26 boarded a transport ship for the trip back to the United States.

The vessel was manned by a civilian crew, save for a handful of navy men assigned to work the ship's paltry guns. The ship's captain believed in running a tight ship. Roy Goedeke, an enlisted man being transported back to the States aboard the same ship, recounted in a 2007 oral history that the captain told Artie he wanted the musicians to stand watch. Artie said no.

"You've got a choice," the captain told the bandleader, according to Goedeke. "You can either stand watch or put on a performance." Artie still said no. He was through with all that.

"Sure enough," Goedeke recalled, "the captain put them on watch. He had one about every ten feet around the main deck." The stand-to finally ended when the bandsmen were so badly sunburned from their time on deck that Artie agreed to put on a show in exchange for an end to watch duties.[39]

Max Kaminsky and Dave Tough were, at one point during the return voyage home, assigned to night watch duty in a gun turret. They were ill-suited for the task. Between them they could hardly lift the shells. They also had no idea of how to actually fire the gun. Kaminsky would pass the time by opening the intercom to the other gun turrets and playing his muted trumpet.[40] One night, while Max and Dave were together, staring out into the darkness, their worst nightmare surfaced. It was apparently a Japanese submarine, and it was coming for them. Frantic, the two fatigued, ill-trained musicians sought the order to fire.

" 'It's a Jap!' shouted Kaminsky, as the sub came closer," the *Capitol News from Hollywood* subsequently reported. " 'Let's go!'"

The scare passed without a shot being fired, or even a confirmation that it was, in fact, a submarine that the two men saw. Still, trombone player Dick LeFave said it was enough that "Dave and Max shook for a week."[41]

Not long afterward, the ship arrived in San Francisco and the men disembarked. It was November 11, 1943—Armistice Day. Artie knelt down and kissed the dock. He thought he was home.

# Chapter 19

# "Shaw Is Not Well"

As usual, the navy brass didn't know what to do with Artie or his men. A passing suggestion popped up in the press that the band might next be heading to Africa. The European theater seemed another option. Artie had previously talked of performing stateside at bond rallies. The band's future was all quite vague, beyond the thirty-day leave granted the musicians once they cleared a medical examination. A number of the musicians reportedly were still underweight, despite several months of fattening up after Guadalcanal. Some ached mentally, including Artie. On November 18, a week after the band arrived in San Francisco, he sat down with two navy doctors who specialized in matters of the mind. Commander Emory L. Dravo was in his mid-40s, a Kentucky native and former professor of neurology at the University of Louisville.[1] He and his fellow physician, Lieutenant Commander T. P. Rogers, recorded their assessment of Chief Petty Officer Shaw. While the two doctors were careful not to write him off altogether, they noted the bandleader seemed to be unstable and suffering from a "situational psychoneuroses." "He displays many evidences of a frustration complex which appear to be a normal result of various positions in which he was placed during his service in this country and overseas," the doctors wrote, adding that "a series of misunderstandings and unfortunate circumstances has accentuated his fundamental instability." Nonetheless, the doctors maintained that Artie could remain useful to the navy so long as his situation was changed. "The thirty days leave granted should enable him to readjust satisfactorily, provided extrinsic [factors] are adjusted," Dravo and Rogers stated.[2]

With their characterization of Artie's condition being a "normal result" brought about by "extrinsic" factors, "unfortunate circumstances," and a "series of misunderstandings," the two navy doctors implied that anyone else might have responded similarly to such external pressures. But with the reference to Artie's "fundamental instability," the doctors were also noting something deeper, a preexisting condition shaken from its slumber by stress, sleepless nights, and the sounds of Washing Machine Charlie. Artie's wartime experiences may not have been the worst anyone had seen, but they were sufficient to knock him out of the saddle. The doctors could only wonder whether Artie had it in him to rejoin the fight.[3]

Released from duty in San Francisco, Artie headed for Los Angeles to join his wife Elizabeth and young son, Steven, born the previous July. Their little family reunion was awkward. It had been a long and eventful eleven months since the *Lurline* set out from San Francisco the previous December. Artie had traveled, by some accounting, roughly some sixty-eight thousand miles throughout the Pacific. He had ducked into foxholes and hidden from bombs. He had felt his stomach lurch at sea and in the turbulent air. He had been bedside with the dying and he had entertained admirals, generals, and foreign dignitaries. He had been cheered by thousands and he had charmed the president's wife. All the while, Elizabeth had been raising their son. She had written Artie letters; it's not clear how much he might have written her back.

Every returning soldier, sailor, airman, and Marine faced their own adaptation challenges, poignantly depicted in director William Wyler's 1946 classic *The Best Years of Our Lives*. In the movie a hard-drinking infantryman, an emotionally shattered bombardier, and a dismembered navy petty officer struggle to reenter civilian life. Artie struggled too, and unlike most veterans, he would be finding his way while under the spotlight. An industry publication called the *Capitol News from Hollywood* reported that during his thirty-day leave, the bandleader was "preferring to spend virtually all of his time with his wife and son," adding that "like Glenn Miller, Shaw takes his military responsibilities seriously." This was pure spin from the publicists at Capitol Records. Artie did, in fact, hit the town.[4] One night not long after his return to Los Angeles, Artie made it to the Palladium nightclub to check out Les Brown's orchestra. Another night he dropped into a Wilshire Boulevard club called Slapsy Maxie's, owned by an ex-boxer named Max Rosenbloom, for a get-together with bandleader Phil Harris.

While Artie was in Los Angeles, he left the other navy band members to their own devices, apparently without a hint about when, where, and why they might reassemble. The bandleader simply split without ceremony, the way he had so often before with his civilian orchestras. The men took off on their own while the "foremost thought in several minds seemed to be marriage," *DownBeat* reported.[5]

Saxophonist Sam Donahue headed for Detroit, where he was, in fact, awaiting the arrival of his fiancée. Max Kaminsky ended up in Boston, where marriage was likewise reportedly in the works. Conrad Gozzo, already married, reunited with his wife in San Francisco. Trombone player Tasso Harris, too, was already hitched; he had secured a marriage license in Stockton, California, the previous November 22, just about a week before he joined the navy. He was said to be with his wife on the West Coast. The other musicians scattered, their reported destinations a cross-section of the United States: Tak Takvorian and Charlie Wade to Boston, Mack Pierce Pitt to Brooklyn, Ralph LaPolla to Providence, Harold Wax to Newark, Al Horesh to Cleveland, and Rocky Collucio to the small upstate New York city of Rome, among others.

Music journalists applauded the return of Navy Band 501. *DownBeat*'s headline in the December 15, 1943, issue set the boosterish tone, touting the "amazing saga" of the band's war-zone adventures under fire. The article expounded on how the band had been "traveling for a year through battle-scarred Pacific islands" and how the band members "were all trained for battle stations [and] they all spent watch duty as the huge boats ploughed their way through the dangerous, submarine-infested Pacific waters."[6] The story conjured an image straight out of Hollywood, Artie wielding a clarinet in one hand and a tommy gun in another. Some factual exaggerations and plot simplifications were inevitable; they came with the celebrity territory. Still, the flourishes attending the Shaw saga struck a sour note among those in the know. Copies of the December 15 *DownBeat* article eventually reached the Pacific theater, where it was read by men who knew better. Two readers with firsthand experience wrote to correct the false impression conveyed by the article about Shaw's Rangers. "When Artie and the boys got to Guadalcanal, it was as peaceful as Central Park," one soldier wrote *DownBeat*. "Maybe they did get a scare air raid, and maybe they did have to crawl into a dugout once in a while, but the ineffectiveness of 'Maytag Charlies' bombing is now history."[7]

Another soldier, identified only as a former bandleader, likewise questioned what was so "amazing" about the "saga" of Artie's band. Other military bands, this soldier noted, routinely took on support duties like stretcher bearing. When called upon they put down their instruments and pitched in on the front lines. They were true combat-tested soldiers, sailors, and Marines. Shaw's so-called Rangers might have the star power, but they didn't know about war—real war. "How about the musicians who have been in tropic combat zones for 26 long months and who really know what it is to be shelled and bombed day and night," this soldier wrote. "By comparison, the tour of the Shaw band was a complete ball."[8]

Chastened, *DownBeat*'s editors in April 1944 offered a remarkable apology for the "amazing saga" account. In their lavish mea culpa, the editors declared they did not have any "intention to glorify Artie and his musicians while ignoring the true heroism of soldiers such as in these letter writers."[9] But adulation was the norm, and *Metronome* magazine, too, welcomed Artie home with the journalistic equivalent of a parade down Main Street. Reporter Mike Daniels and a photographer met the musician at his father-in-law Jerome Kern's house, where Elizabeth had been staying to get help with little Steven. The resulting article was the magazine's January 1944 cover story that announced Artie as "Musician of the Year."[10]

The article, which was noted to have been "approved by Navy censors," matched *DownBeat*'s in its melodramatic strivings. Artie's account of his band's Pacific tour was described as "graphic and thrilling," and the story immediately grabbed readers with the recollection of the "seventeen times he and his musicians took their battle stations to fight Jap bombers." Artie, the article said in a somber hush, "has seen men killed." Torpedo attacks were "numerous." The entire tour was "danger-studded." The ships the band traveled on were targeted by "high-level precision" Japanese bombers. And, the writer took pains to add, "don't get the idea that Shaw and his boys were carted around the Pacific like a chauffeur wheels a banker." No, Daniels wrote, Shaw's Rangers hitchhiked their way across the Pacific on battlewagons and other warships.[11]

On this last point, the *Metronome* article got it right. Navy Band 501 had, in fact, island-hopped on a cross section of the fleet that included a battleship, destroyer-minelayers, and PT boats. They had performed aboard an aircraft carrier, light cruisers, and assorted support ships. The story also got another point right, though it was buried in the middle, where it might easily be missed. "Shaw is not well," the article abruptly declared.[12]

The assertion appears suddenly, without preface or evidence other than Daniels's acute observation elsewhere in the three-page spread that "Shaw is nervous" and that "he apologized for being so fidgety while posing for *Metronome*'s photographer Charley Mihn."[13] Beyond this, the author did not delve, leaving the story a mixed bag of well-reported detail and press release purple prose.

The accompanying photographs, too, blended fact and fancy. Two photos taken during the Pacific tour showed Shaw and several of his men visiting patients at unidentified military hospitals. These pictures conveyed some of the best moments of Artie's wartime service, how he reached traumatized men far from home. But the cover photograph is strange, and foreshadows the mythmaking that would characterize Artie's retelling of his World War II service. The photo shows Artie in his chief petty officer's uniform. He's hatless and sitting at a piano. All that is accurate enough. Two service ribbons adorn his left breast, both of them earned. But then, over the ribbons, there is what appears to be an inexplicable set of army jump wings, the sign of a qualified paratrooper.

The story offered no explanation, nor did it address the incongruity at all. One possibility is that a bona fide paratrooper, moved by a performance by Artie's band, had presented them as a sign of thanks. Artie had, in fact, performed for some elite airborne troops. In one of his postwar accounts, Artie recalled his band performing "out in the pouring rain with only a tarpaulin over us, before several thousand paratroopers spread out on a hill, wrapped in their ponchos."[14] The pioneering 1st Marine Parachute Regiment had been organized during the summer of 1943 and was based in New Caledonia while the men prepared for action. The 2nd Marine Parachute Battalion was based for a time in 1943 at a camp about fifteen miles north of Wellington. Artie, who combined an eye for style with a blithe indifference to military protocol, might simply have pinned on a pair of gift jump wings as if they had been earned—which, Artie might have convinced himself, they had been.

Another disconcerting photo in the *Metronome* piece showed Artie in a tough-guy's pose straight out of a B-movie poster. A cigarette dangling from his lips and a jungle campaign hat on his head, Artie is depicted examining a Japanese rifle that had been captured by Marines and then found its way into Artie's hands. The rifle seemed a bit much for a man who fought the war with his clarinet.

While *Metronome*'s cover story anointed Artie as Musician of the Year, the magazine's readers selected Benny Goodman as the nation's top clarinetist, with 342 votes to Artie's distant second-place showing of 42 votes. Drummer Dave Tough was the only other member of Navy Band 501 to rank in the readers' poll, placing fifth among drummers. That same month, Goodman's outfit was ranked the nation's best swing band by *DownBeat* readers, scoring 5,952 votes to swamp Artie's eighteenth-place finish with 144 votes.

As the home leave clock ran down foe Shaw's Rangers, rumors circulated about both the band's future destination and Artie's own ongoing role. *DownBeat* in January 1944 noted the "mystery surrounding Artie Shaw's rumored Navy discharge." That same month the magazine cited a source "close to the Jerome Kern household" as indicating that Shaw "was in San Francisco undergoing treatment for sinus trouble and was awaiting his next assignment."[15] This was a ruse. Artie was, indeed, "undergoing treatment" in early 1944, but his underlying malady was emotional, not otolaryngological. "I was shell-shocked," Artie said. "I was really in shock. I couldn't get out of bed in the morning. It was a mess, because I was useless."[16]

Artie returned to San Francisco following his thirty-day leave and was again assessed by Lieutenant Commander Rogers, one of the doctors who had checked him out in November. The time away, Rogers realized, had not cured the patient. The bandleader said he was now suffering from near-constant headaches so severe that pain relievers provided no respite. Artie described the headaches as dull, often beginning in a tooth or his left eye before eventually spreading. They lasted for six or more hours. At Rogers's suggestion, Artie was checked in to the US Naval Hospital Oakland, also known as Oak Knoll.[17]

Opened in July 1942 on what had formerly been the site of the Oak Knoll Golf and Country Club, the navy medical facility sprawled across more than 190 acres in the low foothills east of Oakland. By 1945 a staff of three thousand military and civilian workers would be caring for upward of eight thousand patients at a time.[18] The hospital addressed all manner of ailments. There were the physically diseased, like a 29-year-old navy lieutenant commander named Thomas Hart who had taken ill while commanding a destroyer. Hart's father, a former admiral and at the time a Republican senator from Connecticut, arrived at Oak Knoll just in time to be with his son before he passed away in mid-1945 from leukemia.[19]

The sick shared space with the combat-wounded. In early 1943 First Lady Eleanor Roosevelt had visited the hospital complex. She signed casts, asked questions, and offered reassurances. She told one triple amputee who had lost both arms and a leg in Guadalcanal combat, Marine Sergeant Ted Jones of Lake Mills, Wisconsin, that she knew of a craftsman in Wisconsin who could fashion very fine prosthetics. It might have seemed cold comfort, but Sergeant Jones's spirit was strong enough to take advice. He would, in fact, go on to get his prosthetics, find postwar work as an insurance agent, and eventually win election to the Wisconsin state assembly.[20]

Besides the disease-ridden and the overtly wounded, Oak Knoll treated those suffering from what was variously called shell shock, battle fatigue, or neuroses. These patients would include a psychologically fragile navy officer with a fevered imagination named L. Ron Hubbard, who would move on from writing mammoth science fiction tomes to conjuring into existence the Church of Scientology. Hubbard's extended stay at Oak Knoll did not overlap with Artie's, though the two men might have shared some symptoms of emotional exhaustion.

"At that point I wanted nothing more than to lie down in a deep hole and have someone shovel enough dirt over me to cover me," Artie recounted in his memoir. "I was really beat, not only physically, but completely." He added, "I couldn't make it, that's all."[21]

On this point, Artie's recollections are consistent with what physicians reported at the time. "He states he hates his work," a navy doctor wrote, adding that Artie "has had terrific difficulty adjusting to navy life with a CPO rating as he is frequently called upon to fraternize with very high-ranking officers, only to be dashed down the next day by reprimands."[22]

Still, Artie was in better shape than some of his Oak Knoll psychiatric wardmates. He was not delusional, manic, or schizophrenic. Even in his doldrums, he retained his customary edge.

"Do you hear voices?" one Oak Knoll doctor asked, Artie later recalled.

"Yeah, I do," Artie responded.

"Whose?"

"Mine, yours, kids out there in the yard hollering at each other. I hear all those voices. What do you expect? You mean like Joan of Arc?" Artie snapped.

The shrink perked up.

"You hear Joan of Arc?" the eager doctor queried.[23]

On January 17, 1944, Oakland newspaper readers learned that Army General Omar Bradley had been selected as senior ground commander of the US forces preparing for the long-awaited Allied invasion of Europe. In the Pacific military progress was being measured by the meter, as Marine veterans of the fight for Guadalcanal were reported to have finally taken Hill 660 on the island of Cape Gloucester. In Italy elements of the US Fifth Army had reached the Rapido River and were at the start of what would become a four-month long battle for the high ground of Monte Casino.

That day a panel of three navy officers reached a conclusion about Chief Petty Officer Artie Shaw's state of mind. In addition to their own observations, they had in hand a brief diagnostic summary written by Doctor Gerstle, the Seventh Fleet's Service Force chief physician who had assessed

Artie back in Australia. All agreed Artie was medically unfit for further service: "The psychiatric findings are those of a deep-seated anxiety state of long-standing with insecurity, tremulousness, restlessness and excessive perspiration," the navy medical board reported.[24] Artie did not dispute the doctors' conclusion that he suffered from a disability characterized as "anxiety neurosis," nor did he challenge their determination that this disabling anxiety preexisted his navy service and was aggravated by his wartime experiences. He signed the medical form with his long-since abandoned name of "Arthur Shaw," and with that the bandleader was on his way out of the navy.

"I rented a car and drove around California for a while," Artie recounted later. "I was sort of at loose ends. I didn't know quite what I was going to do with myself."[25]

Some other band members were similarly cut loose. Max Kaminsky headed for the East Coast during his thirty-day leave and ran into Milt Gabler, the entrepreneurial brains behind New York City's jazz-oriented Commodore Music Shop and the founder in 1938 of Commodore Records. Gabler had guts as well as a great ear. In 1939 his Commodore label had made a splash with its release of Billie Holiday's anti-lynching protest song "Strange Fruit." After sizing up Max and his battered, brine-encrusted horn that had endured eleven months in the Pacific, Gabler bought him what Max described as a "gleaming new golden Selmer trumpet." Gabler then set up a recording session that included Max and trombone ace Jack Teagarden venturing a fresh take on "Basin Street Blues."[26]

With the furlough over, Max returned to an uncertain future. The navy bureaucracy shuffled him off to a base on Long Island and from there to Washington, DC, where he ended up in Bethesda Naval Hospital. He was clearly spent, and the navy discharged him in March. For the next few months, Max could barely rouse himself to leave his apartment. He would awaken each night from the same nightmare in which he was choking on a black cloth stuffed into his throat. "It was all mixed up in my mind with the bombing," Kaminsky wrote," adding that "the nightmares of those first six or seven months were the worst."[27]

Dave Tough, too, was completely wrung out. The day after Shaw's Rangers docked in San Francisco, he joined his bandmates in a raucous seventy-two-hour liberty romp through the city. Once he was good and sloshed, Davey stumbled into a fracas with other sailors. The instigation was unclear, but however it started, it ended badly for slightly built drummer. "Somebody clobbered him," band arranger Dick Jones recalled.[28]

Even without the barroom beat-down, Davey was no longer fit for service. In truth, he was never suitable in the first place. He had only slipped into uniform because Artie had vouched for his world-class talent. Now, though, Artie wasn't around to vouch for the drummer, and doctors could see Davey as he was: underweight, overtaxed, and severely alcoholic. Doctors held on to him at the navy's Mare Island base in the San Francisco Bay Area for a few weeks before he was discharged from the service on January 24. The base newspaper reported that he was headed for New York City to join Tommy Dorsey's band.

# Chapter 20

# A "Dying Duck"

Artie's 1942 marriage to Elizabeth Kern was always a divorce waiting to happen. War simply accelerated the inevitable.

The reunited couple moved into a Tudor-style house in Beverly Hills. Always restless, Artie couldn't settle into the overstuffed nest. He'd get the urge and just go, anyplace other than where he was. On the occasion of their son, Steven's, first birthday, July 1, 1944, Elizabeth planned a get-together at their house and invited assorted friends and acquaintances. They included 61-year-old actress Marjorie Wood, a veteran of the stage who had landed bit parts in movies, including the 1940 version of *Pride and Prejudice*. Wood's exact connection to the Shaw family is unclear, but she later recalled how the partygoers had waited until after 2:00 a.m. for the father of the birthday boy to show up. When Artie finally did, he reportedly explained only that he had been "driving around."[1]

Even when he was physically present, Elizabeth said, Artie was emotionally elsewhere. He would not speak to her for days at a time. He froze her out, like she didn't exist. They shared the same space, at least when he wasn't driving around, but in every other respect Artie had, once again, walked away. He finally put his cards on the table on the night of July 10, nine days after his son's birthday. "We just don't make sense together anymore," Artie told her, Elizabeth later recounted.[2]

Artie moved out to the Garden of Allah Hotel, a West Hollywood hideaway that had been accommodating celebrities and scoundrels since the 1930s. Elizabeth and young Steven retained the Shaw house. The marriage was all over but for the negotiating. Elizabeth brought her case to attorneys David Tannenbaum and Ralph Wilson, who ran a small but socially connected law firm. It was to Tannenbaum that actress Lucille Ball had turned when she sought a divorce in 1944 from her philandering husband Desi Arnaz.[3] In mid-August Elizabeth and Artie reached an agreement on Artie's alimony obligations, and on August 22 Elizabeth formally sued for divorce. The brief filing in Los Angeles Superior Court was both blunt and rudimentary. It alleged that "Arthur Shaw, also known as Artie Shaw" had treated Elizabeth with "extreme cruelty and caused grievous mental suffering" during the marriage.[4] There were no affidavits or statements itemizing Artie's alleged abuses. There was no need for them.

Artie retained the small Los Angeles firm of Bachrack and Keilsohn to represent him, though there was not much for them to do, at least at first. Artie did not contest the divorce and filed no formal response, content to lose the case by default. The couple's divorce transpired much like their quickie civil marriage back in Yuma, Arizona. Asked in one court document how long would be needed for trial, Elizabeth's attorneys wrote "15 minutes."[5]

On Thursday, September 28, Elizabeth and her attorneys appeared before Los Angeles Superior Court Judge Stanley Mosk, a young up-and-comer in the judicial world. In later years Mosk would serve as the state's attorney general and then as an influential judge on the California Supreme Court. For the uncontested 1944 divorce case of *Shaw v. Shaw*, Mosk had relatively little to do. The divorce was precooked. Elizabeth and the actress Marjorie Wood were the sole witnesses. Elizabeth described the anguish she said Artie put her through, and Wood mentioned Artie ignoring little Steven's birthday party. In almost no time at all, Mosk approved the divorce. Under the settlement Artie agreed to pay Elizabeth alimony of $2,000 a month for five years if his annual income exceeded $70,000. If his income was lower, he would pay Elizabeth less. Artie also had to procure a $75,000 life-insurance policy with Steven as beneficiary.[6] Elizabeth won full custody of Steven until his sixth birthday. Artie did not contest the custody decision. It certainly made sense, given Artie's professional life on the road and in studios for late-night sessions. Once he got over the first wrench of separation, Artie stayed cold toward his issue. "When my brother first went to visit him," Jonathan Shaw, Artie's subsequent son from his seventh marriage to actress Doris Dowling, recounted, "my father said, 'what do you want? You're nothing but a biological happenstance to me.'"[7]

Artie seemed similarly indifferent toward his alimony obligations, eventually compelling Elizabeth to go to court and secure the help of the Los Angeles Sheriff's Department in garnishing Artie's funds. He laid low in Hollywood in the months surrounding his discharge from the navy and his subsequent divorce. In the living room of his house, visitors noticed a painting by the American artist Dan Lutz that captured his drift. The watercolor depicted, *Metronome* writer Barry Ulanov observed, a "knocked-out colored trombonist, sitting, bedraggled, in an almost shapeless lump, astride a chair, horn held loosely in hand."[8]

Slowly, at first, Artie started to get a grip. There was talk of his getting a new band together, with *Metronome* in its September 1944 edition declaring that the bandleader was "back in action" and recruiting a new civilian outfit after recovering from "an illness which he contracted more than a year ago while touring the South Pacific as leader of a U.S. Navy band."[9] Artie's reputation preceded him, though, and hindered his recruiting effort. "Reluctance of men to throw in with Shaw is based, according to the conversation of musicians who have been approached by him, on his notorious habit of disbanding quickly," *Variety* reported, adding suggestively that "there are other factors, too, stemming from his days in the Navy as head of a uniformed combo."[10]

Artie road tested an outfit with a series of one-nighters in November 1944 and a recording session the same month and then returned with his new ensemble on December 1 at the Orpheum Theater in Minneapolis. In an otherwise positive review, *Billboard*'s Paul Socone observed in the periodical's February 10, 1945, issue that Artie was "not exhibiting much enthusiasm for what's going on," adding that "he's obviously a more subdued guy than he once was." In the liner notes to an album, Artie acknowledged that "I didn't feel terribly dedicated during this period in my life, because I was busy putting myself back together" after the war.[11]

Artie was as uncompromising as ever, both as a leader and as a critic. In an early 1945 interview, Artie proclaimed the nation's other bandleaders were "incompetents who have found a market for mediocrity in the wartime appetite for popular music." American jazz, he added, was "a dying duck that needs artificial respiration," and he railed, as he had before the war, that "all this hysteria, screaming and swooning will kill jazz as effectively as the mediocre bandleaders and songwriters are killing it today."[12] Once again, as with his prewar excoriations of moronic jitterbuggers, Artie and his team had to do some clean-up work. Screaming and swooning could be perfectly acceptable behaviors, it was subsequently explained on Artie's behalf, so long as these were natural reactions to the music itself and not a celebrity-driven contrivance.

Artie had more success, albeit briefly, with the actress Ava Gardner. He met the 21-year-old North Carolina knockout in the summer of 1944 at a Hollywood party, introduced by the wife of actor Van Heflin. Ava knew Artie's music; he knew nothing of her, save for the fact that she was, as he later put it, "the most beautiful creature you ever saw." They went out for a drink after the party and then met again, and again. Artie talked and talked, a fount of erudition and confession. One of Gardner's biographers, Lee Server, paraphrased what Artie apparently told Ava about his navy experience. "They were," Server wrote fancifully, "on Guadalcanal during some of the worst fighting. People were wounded and killed all around them."[13] Whether this was how Artie recounted it to the impressionable young actress, or how Ava misremembered what he told her, or simply how the biographer spun it, is not entirely clear, but it seems likely that Artie left Ava with some erroneous ideas about his war experience.

On Wednesday, October 17, 1945, Artie and Ava were married in a civil ceremony at the Beverly Hills home of Judge Stanley Mosk, the same judge who had presided the previous year over Artie's divorce from Elizabeth Kern."[14]

In November 1945 Artie once again broke up his orchestra. His future was uncertain.

# Chapter 21

# England

Artie's old navy crew, or what remained of it, started swinging under new management.

Though Dave Tough and Max Kaminsky had gone civilian, the other Navy Band 501 members remained in uniform. The thirty-days' homecoming leave had refreshed their spirits, and their release from Artie's dictates opened their eyes to new possibilities. For all his flaws, Artie had recruited stellar musicians and had drilled them well. The Pacific tour had frayed them, but it had also knit them together. They shared a history and a common tongue. They could follow each other's lead and finish each other's jokes. Ironically, it may have taken Artie's departure for Shaw's Rangers to realize their orchestral potential. All they needed now was someone to step into Artie's big shoes.

Sam Donahue was that man.

On January 18, 1944, one day after the Oak Knoll doctors declared Artie medically unfit for military service, Donahue reported to the Naval School of Music in Washington, DC. The 25-year-old sax player was already plenty streetwise, having started his own first professional band at the age of 15. He had fronted this outfit for five formative years before joining drummer

Gene Krupa's group in 1938. Described by *DownBeat* as a "tenor ace" during a brief stint with Benny Goodman in 1940, Donahue had again been leading his own band when he broke it up on November 1, 1942, to join the ranks of Navy Band 501.

This background made Donahue the only member of Navy Band 501, other than the long-since departed Claude Thornhill, who had led his own professional band. He was a natural fit to take over, though it took a little while for the dime to drop. After the band members had returned from leave, they had laid about in Lido Beach, Long Island, the site of the Naval Personnel Redistribution Center. The musicians were said to be "totally inactive, much to their chagrin and boredom," but their lassitude was tinged with alarm over what "redistribution" might mean for them.[1] Some in the navy were considering breaking up the band into components, selling it for parts. Trumpet player John Best, for one, had been given the option of joining Saxie Dowell aboard the aircraft carrier USS *Franklin*.[2] But as Best and the other musicians thought more about it, Navy Band 501 seemed to be a pretty good gig now that Artie was gone. "We chipped in the train fare for Sam Donahue and [arranger] Dick Jones to go down to the Bureau of Navy Personnel in Washington, and they talked to a captain there, and asked for permission to allow the band to stay together," Best recounted.[3]

Jones was known as an affable diplomat amid the intramural band politics, and he and Donahue apparently managed to persuade Capt. Albert Bledsoe, head of the Bureau of Enlisted Personnel. Two years earlier Bledsoe had been the officer credited with implementing Undersecretary of the Navy James Forrestal's directive authorizing Artie to establish Navy Band 501. Now, with Bledsoe's reported go-ahead, the band could reconstitute itself. From the highly regarded orchestra at the Great Lakes Naval Training Center in Illinois came 23-year-old trumpet player Don Jacoby, a veteran of the Les Brown and Teddy Powell bands. Jacoby had been plugging away at the navy base along Lake Michigan since 1942 and was ready for a change. On drums, filling in for Dave Tough, the band added Bob "Buzz" Sithens; they also added a singer, Bill Bassford.

The musicians flourished under Donahue's leadership. He'd had the opportunity to learn from Artie's mistakes and he had a more congenial temperament. He could be just one of the guys, an equal rather than a superior. Though not a public sensation, Donahue had earned the respect of his peers. In April 1944 he and the reformed navy band shipped out from the East Coast on a plodder called an LST, for landing ship tank. The 330-feet long LST was half the length and one one-hundredth of the status of the USS *North Carolina*, the battleship that had conveyed Navy Band 501 across the Pacific.

The LST could carry troops as well as several dozen tanks, but it lacked all creature comforts. Sailors bleakly joked that the initials stood for "Large Slow Target," as it labored to reach speeds of ten knots, one-third of a battleship's pace. The LST led with its chin, punching its way across the Atlantic Ocean one swell at a time. Unlike the *Lurline*, the converted passenger liner that had conveyed the original Shaw's Rangers to Hawaii, there was no jazz-loving purser on board to serve up fresh fruit and lemon meringue pie. Not that the pie would have stayed down for long. Smacked about by every wave, the LSTs were brutally efficient seasickness machines. They stank, one navy veteran recalled, "of diesel oil, backed-up toilets and vomit."[4]

Typical LST Atlantic crossings lasted about twelve days. Trombone player Tak Takvorian recalled that "it took 30 days to make the trip to England, and it was awful."[5] Somehow the band members survived the ocean crossing and staggered ashore at Plymouth near the southern tip of England. They later squeezed an upbeat four-minute-and-twenty-second song out of the miserable ocean-crossing ordeal, jauntily entitled "LST Party." It was released in January 1945 as a V-Disc, one of some eight hundred records produced between 1943 and 1949 under nonprofit program overseen by the Army's Special Services Division.

The band had arrived in England still commonly labeled as Artie Shaw's Navy Band. Soon enough, though, the rejiggered orchestra gained the title of the Band of the US Navy Liberation Forces. The men played with power and finesse, while Donahue appeared to be comfortably in command. The band's library was redone. Artie's moody "Nightmare" theme song was replaced by an up-and-jumping piece called "Convoy." The difference between the two themes was night and day, a perfectly on-the-nose representation of the change in both leadership and atmosphere, but the band's mission remained the same as it had been in the Pacific. They played at an assortment of military bases and also broke up into smaller units to visit hospitals. As in New Zealand and Australia, the band also carried the true flame of jazz into a land populated by fans and would-be emulators. The Brits would do their best to talk jive, an amused Donahue said. They'd sling words and phrases like "solid" and "send me," and they'd field their own bands that played pieces note-for-note just like they'd heard them on a platter or over the BBC. "It knocks them out," Donahue said. "But somehow, they don't get with it the way boys and girls do here in the states. Maybe it's because the music isn't quite natural to the English."[6]

Back in the States, Artie was slowly venturing into public. That September he joined pianist Calvin Jackson and songwriter Jimmy Van Heusen in discussing the "sociological and psychological implications" of swing music as part of a four-day conference held by a new Institute of Music in Contemporary Life. The conference attracted to the University of California at Los Angeles campus big thinkers like Hollywood director Orson Welles and music bureaucrats like Colonel Howard Bronson, the army's music administrator. The forum's lofty ambitions appealed to Artie's intellectual aspirations with panels on such topics as "Music under Fascism" and "Music and its Allied Arts in a Democratic Civilization."[7]

The FBI thought the whole thing was a leftist crock. In a December 15, 1948, memo compiled by a special agent in the bureau's Los Angeles office, an informant identified as "Source G-13" described the overall UCLA event as one "dominated by the expression of pro-Russian and pro-Communist sympathies." The same informant recounted that Artie had chaired a panel on jazz and swing music in which Artie "in his capacity as chairman very definitely followed the interests of the Communists present who presented their material."[8]

Artie's former navy bandmates left the theorizing to others as they jumped from gig to gig. On the southern tip of England, about thirty-eight miles from Plymouth, a US Navy training base at Fowey had been converted into a rest-and-rehabilitation center. It was a safe space, out of range of German buzz bombs and offering a recreation hall and movie nights as well as horseback rides, softball games, and swimming parties. Better yet, young women from the area and with the Auxiliary Territorial Service sashayed in for dances. A wowed critic with Great Britain's *Melody Maker* raved about Donahue and the navy band as being "easily as good as any civilian outfit playing right now," adding that "it plays fresh, exciting modern jump arrangements [with] guts, power and finesse."[9] The musicians, too, sensed they were riding something special. Newcomer Don Jacoby, who had joined fellow trumpet players Conrad Gozzo, John Best, and Frank Beach, called it "one of the greatest bands I ever worked with." "What a gas that was, even if we were in the Navy," Jacoby added.[10]

The growing self-confidence prepared the navy men to take on the reigning champions among US military bands in England, Major Glenn Miller's Army Air Forces outfit. With his officer's commission and his proximity to headquarters, Miller seemed untouchably supreme. While Shaw's Rangers were island-hopping through the Pacific, Miller's band had been recording and performing on radio. First appearing on CBS in June of 1943 as the Army Air Forces Training Command Orchestra, the Miller-led band also did broadcasts for the Armed Forces Radio Service and recorded so-called V-Discs. Miller kept his men in line. Biographer Dennis Spragg in his definitive account *Glenn Miller Declassified* recounted that "Miller's forceful and often rigid management style was arguably quite necessary to ensure the existence of his organization," even though the band members sometimes "bristled" at the bandleader's orders. Miller made progress, Spragg recounted, in teaching his "boys how to swing the military classics" as he embarked on his "earnest crusade to put swing on the U.S. parade ground."[11]

Still, some jazz fans had grown weary of Miller's acutely disciplined performances. Army PFC. David Bittan, for one, wrote that he was looking forward to hearing "some real musical kicks" from Sam Donahue and the boys rather than the "repetition of arrangements that have been played and replayed, all in the same precise, spiritless manner that has characterized (Glenn) Miller's bands since he first attained commercial success."[12] The sniping became persistent enough that Miller retorted that his audiences "know and appreciate only the tunes popular before they left the states. For their sake, we only play the old tunes."[13]

Miller invited Donahue to an old-fashioned battle of the bands, set for September 21 at the Queensberry All-Services Club in London. The venue was a former cabaret restaurant in London's rather gamey Soho neighborhood, opened in 1930 and acquired in 1935 by a syndicate that owned casinos in Miami and New York City. Since the war began, the refashioned club had been the venue for Sunday broadcast performances. It could accommodate three thousand people and it was often packed. The navy outfit had played in the venue before, including at a three-way battle of the bands with a Canadian military orchestra and a British group called the Squadronaires. At that performance Miller had been in the audience, visibly impressed by the Navy band's pepped-up versions of "One O'clock Jump" and "C Jam Blues."[14]

For the September 21 contest, the Army Air Forces and navy bands were arrayed side by side on the stage, the Army Air Forces musicians on stage right in khaki and the outnumbered navy musicians on stage left in their blue sailor outfits. Miller began the show by introducing the musicians, as a reporter for *Melody Maker* put it, "without relaxing one iota that stern, militaristic manner which so many of us have come to know so well." Miller also paid tribute to the navy band's prior service in the Pacific, which, Miller said, "completely puts our own record to shame."[15] He then led his men through a solid set, capped by a number belted out by singer Johnny Desmond, a veteran of the prewar Bob Crosby and Gene Krupa organizations. When Miller's set was done, the navy band kicked off with a "Caravan" that sounded a bit rough. The group found its groove on the next few tunes, and the two bands capped the evening with an exuberantly joint rendition of "One O'clock Jump." When the applause died down, the Marquis of Queensberry himself thanked the US combatants for fighting by the rules.[16]

The winners by general acclaim: Sam Donahue and his navy men.

"Well, sir, when the show was over, Miller walked out to the microphone and said 'Sam Donahue has the best band in the service,'" Donahue recalled several decades later. "My boys walked in the clouds for quite some time after that."[17]

Trumpet player Bernie Privin acknowledged that "the Navy band really cut us up that evening, and Glenn knew it." But while Miller "wanted a rematch," Privin added, "it never came off."[18]

London was dangerous.

The German bombing known as the Blitz had long since passed. The Allied troops that had landed in France on June 6 had since broken out of Normandy and were on a roll. But even as the Germans gave up ground, they launched across the English Channel swarms of so-called buzz bombs and later V-2 rockets that fell indiscriminately on English cities. The aerial assaults put Donahue and his navy band at risk in a way they had not been since enduring Washing Machine Charlie's nighttime visits to Guadalcanal. The Soho neighborhood in which they sometimes stayed was both convenient for their London performances and hazardous for their health. "That part of London was known as 'Buzz Bomb Alley,'" Donahue recalled. "It got even worse when the V-2 rockets came over."[19]

Starting in June 1944, Germany launched more than eight thousand of the buzz bombs, also known as the V-1. The crude weapons primarily hit London over the course of about three months. By the end of the first week in July, British authorities had reported that the buzz bombs had killed 2,752 civilians and sent another 8,000 to the hospital. The buzz bombs were succeeded starting in September by the more technologically advanced V-2 rockets, more than 1,300 of which were launched. Close calls were everywhere, and some became the stuff of legend.

On August 16 Glenn Miller's men were performing at a British RAF fighter base and just kicking into "In the Mood" when they heard the distinctive buzzing of a V-1 engine overhead. The flying bomb continued on its way and exploded, perhaps harmlessly, elsewhere. Hollywood would later goose the incident in the movie version of *The Glenn Miller Story*, ratcheting up the drama so that the bomb exploded close to the boys in the band.[20]

One day in mid-December, navy band trumpet player John Best, a veteran of Miller's prewar orchestra, went to London to visit his old colleagues. On Wednesday night, December 13, Best had quite a time of it. At one point in the evening, Miller pulled Best aside to show off a model of his fancy new California home. The musicians rolled on from there in the company of newspaper heir William Randolph Hearst Jr. and his wife, Doris. Miller, scheduled to travel to France on band business early the next morning, eventually peeled off from the troupe. When Best awoke about 11:00 a.m. on

December 14 and went to say good-bye to his former boss, he found Miller sprawled across the bed, asleep in his uniform. "I figured if I woke him he'd only get mad," Best recalled, "so I didn't disturb him."[21]

Best returned to the rest of the navy band, while Miller awoke to find himself grounded by bad weather. It wasn't clear when he would board a plane to get to France where he intended to finalize plans for his orchestra's upcoming tour. Finally, Lieutenant Colonel Norman Frances Baessell of the Eighth Air Force Service Command offered Miller a lift. Shortly before 2:00 p.m. on December 15, a Norseman C-64 plane piloted by 22-year-old Flying Officer Stuart Morgan and carrying Miller and Baessell took off into deteriorating conditions.[22]

Miller's subsequent failure to arrive in France did not fully register for some time. The Allied high command was overwhelmed by a surprise German offensive that would become known as the Battle of the Bulge. Transport officers were scrambling to return army field commanders back to their units. One complication piled upon another, and although reporters picked up rumors earlier, it wasn't until December 23 that army officers informed Miller's wife, Helen, that he was missing and presumed dead.[23] In the United States, the first word of Miller's disappearance was published December 24. Without the bandleader's body, though, speculation ran wild. "It is thought that while he was arranging for a troops' concert he may have been captured," the *Birmingham Post* declared on December 27.

Eventually, the inevitable sank in. Major Glenn Miller was dead. Artie took a characteristically pungent view of the news. Although in public he bit his tongue, Artie all but blamed Miller himself for what happened. "Hubris," Artie explained decades later. "If he'd stayed with the band, he wouldn't have died. If he'd been an enlisted man, he wouldn't have flown with that general."[24]

The navy band under Donahue caried on, in England for a time and then in France. In February 1945, nearly one year after arriving in England, they were tapped to return home. Musically triumphant, though nowhere near as high-profile as they had been while led by Artie, the band after arriving back in the United States performed at a broadcast homecoming of sorts at the US Navy Receiving Station in Washington, DC. In an amusing salute to the service, the orchestra ran through a sassy selection that included "A Drunken Sailor" and "Farewell to Grog."[25]

After a month-long leave, the navy orchestra reconvened and, over a two-day period in mid-June at the CBS Playhouse in New York City, they accomplished something that had eluded the group when it was Shaw's Rangers. Under Donahue's leadership, the band recorded some pieces, including a languid take on "My Melancholy Baby" and their own, hopping "LST Party."[26] By November 1945 half of the band members had accumulated enough points of service to earn their honorable discharge. Donahue, though, was deemed still to be short of the magic number of forty-four points and so, along with some others, was packed off to Los Angeles to finish up with the Armed Forces Radio Service.[27] "It was a real kick playing for those kids overseas," Donahue said. "Most of them hadn't heard a swing band since they left this country and they really got a boot out of hearing live jump tunes again."[28]

Claude Thornhill, too, musically prospered outside of Artie's orbit.

After ditching Navy Band 501 at Pearl Harbor, Thornhill landed with another outfit conducted by John "Ike" Carey. Though a newcomer to the band, Thornhill was its immediate standout. The lettering on the band members' stands read "Ike Carey's Mustangs," but the newspaper ads soon added "featuring Claude Thornhill." It was Claude who ran the rigorous and occasionally eccentric daily rehearsals. He also became, trombone player O. B. Masingill reported, "a great favorite" of Admiral William Calhoun, the commander of Service Force, US Fleet Pacific. The admiral, a former submariner then in his late 50s, would "cry like a baby" at Thornhill's rendering of "Somewhere over the Rainbow," Masingill recounted. Calhoun was a good ally to have. In July, several weeks after performing at a war bond rally held in Honolulu's International Theater, Claude was transferred into Calhoun's command. The move was accompanied by an advancement in rating that came, one navy personnel administrator explained, at the "direct verbal orders of Vice Admiral Calhoun."[29]

The admiral thought even that was insufficient for a man of Claude Thornhill's reputation, and he pressed for a further promotion to the rank of bandmaster. "Thornhill, in civilian life, is at the top of his profession [and] to subordinate him to bandmasters far less skillful is an obvious waster of his established and well-known talents," Calhoun declared.[30]

The admiral's request nonetheless unsettled navy personnel officers, who noted stiffly that Thornhill's promotion could not be approved "in view of his extremely short Naval service and the present excess of bandmasters in the Navy as a whole."[31] The personnel office bureaucrats held their ground. On December 31, 1943, Calhoun's shop waived certain requirements and authorized Thornhill's advancement to the acting rate of chief musician. Six weeks later, a commander in the Bureau of Navy Personnel objected that unless the advancement was for "meritorious performance in action," it should not proceed.[32]

For a solid year after leaving Navy Band 501, Claude repeated the Hawaiian show circuit as he cycled through enlisted men's clubs, military installations, officer's parties, and anyplace else where morale needed lifting. He played at the opening of a new theater at the Bellows Field air base on Oahu, at the opening of a USO Victory Club in downtown Honolulu, and at Honolulu's baseball stadium. His outfit competed in a battle of the bands at one theater, and then at the Honolulu Armory they enlivened a "Lei Day Dance" that a newspaper ad described as a semiformal affair to which ladies were "cordially invited."[33]

Touring the Pacific theater, Thornhill would later recount, resembled his civilian band-leading work only, instead of playing four conventional theaters in a day, he said, his outfit was playing "four ships a day."[34] *DownBeat*'s recitation, equally melodramatic, had it that Thornhill's "outfit moved out in small craft to entertain the men in big battle wagons at sea and now and then [their] concerts were broken up by air raids."[35]

Claude's first foray into the war zone took place in May 1944. He was accompanied only by Navy Yeoman Second Class Rex Emrick, an Ohio native in his mid-20s who sang and played piano, and Musician Second Class Earle Parchman, a former Lansing, Michigan, nightclub entertainer whose set of skills ranged from playing piano to impersonating comic dialects. Parchman was sometimes described as a radio star, which was a generous accounting of his entertainment stature, but he could handle duties as a master of ceremonies.[36] This initial tour included, one navy officer recounted, shows on some thirty ships that included "every battleship, practically every carrier and eight of the cruisers" in addition to "many of the destroyers by means of performances on tenders. . . . To reach this number of ships, they presented three shows a day most days, and considering the amount of traveling necessary to go from ship to ship, this has not been easy for them," an impressed navy officer reported, adding that "they have made a real contribution to the morale of crews in this anchorage."[37]

Thornhill, Parchman, and Emrick were an unusual trio, and available records don't illuminate much about their shows. They were certainly mobile, however, able to pick up their minimal gear and go at a moment's notice. On June 3 the men boarded the USS *Ajax*, a repair ship whose handymen maintained radar systems, antiaircraft guns, and other components needed by frontline fighters. Claude's trio started skipping across the atolls that US forces had seized from the Japanese and converted into stepping stones for the march across the Pacific. Majuro, for one, had been more or less abandoned by the Japanese and taken by US troops in January 1944. By the time of Thornhill's visit, Majuro been bulked up with several airstrips and a garrison of some 7,100 soldiers, and its fortified lagoon harbored dozens of warships at a time.[38]

From Majuro the trio hopped to Eniwetok and then to Kwajalein. The world's largest coral atoll, spanning some sixty-six miles and encompassing nearly one hundred islands and islets, Kwajalein had been a key Japanese base. The Fourth Marine Division had seized it in early February 1944 after fighting that left one isle, Namur, a "stinking mess of debris and dead Japanese," a navy historian recounted. In the months since, the indefatigable Seabees had worked their magic and salvaged the airbase on Roi, another isle.[39]

Claude, Emrick, and Parchman were ready for R and R when the June run of shows ended. Claude received a thirty-day leave that sent him back home to his parents in Terra Haute, Indiana. He then bounced around a bit after that and spent time between September 19 and October 11 in the Los Angeles area, where he was said in navy orders to be "scouting for show talent."[40]

The pickings were slim. Two-and-a-half years into the war, conscription and preemptive enlistments had already harvested many of those men who weren't 4-F or otherwise exempt. Still, there was a talent pool of sorts. Singer Dennis Day, for one, had joined the navy as an instant ensign in early 1944. Born Dennis McNulty, he had sung in the St. Patrick's Cathedral boys' choir while growing up in New York City. He trained to be a lawyer but made it into radio, with his last name changed to Day and his singing voice pitched as a tenor. He landed a spot on Jack Benny's radio show, and for the five years preceding his navy enlistment, he combined singing with comic turns as a high-pitched foil variously described as in newspaper profiles as "brow-beaten" and as "Jack Benny's stooge."[41] Ensign Day was appointed putative head of a new musical outfit on January 15, 1945, joining acting Chief Musician Thornhill and about a dozen other seamen and musicians. Reputation-wise, the group was no match for the original Shaw's Rangers, but it included the capable trombone player Ted Vesely, a Benny Goodman veteran, as well as clarinet player Rollie Morehouse, formerly with Red Nichols's outfit. A dance team known as the Graziano Brothers added toe-tapping talent that Artie's band somehow did without, while Jackie Cooper, a one-time Hollywood child star and now a 21-year-old seaman third class, joined as a teller of jokes and Tinseltown stories. He was also a capable swing-style percussionist with unfulfilled aspirations. "I would have liked to have been the regular drummer," Cooper wrote in his autobiography, "but Thornhill had asked a kid from Coffeyville, Kansas before he asked me, and he couldn't go back on his word."[42]

In a crucial support position, the group included as its manager Quartermaster Leonard Vannerson, a former Los Angeles–based agent and manager for actors and bandleaders including Tommy Dorsey and Benny Goodman. With Vannerson on board, Claude could concentrate on the band's music and personnel without worrying about securing barracks space and wrangling transportation from point A to point B.[43]

A *Honolulu Star-Bulletin* reporter caught up with Claude in December 1944, when he appeared to be in a chipper mood. Claude told the reporter that, come peacetime, he'd like to vacation in the islands. The bandleader who two years before had recorded a poignant version of the 1936 Rodgers and Hart tune "There's a Small Hotel" now fancied himself in a little grass shack, mellowing out and writing music. "The only trouble with that dream," Claude acknowledged, "is that I probably couldn't earn enough money to make ends meet."[44]

After some preliminary shows in Hawaii, Claude and his new troupe headed out on tour in February 1945, the same month as the Marines landed on the island of Iwo Jima. Among the navy musicians' first shows was a return to Kwajalein, where they performed two shows for an estimated seven thousand soldiers, sailors, and Marines at the Richardson Theater, a venue completed the previous July just in time to host Bob Hope and a USO show. Army Brigadier General Ogden Ross reported that Claude's troupe was "very well received by the servicemen here" and that "the performers worked hard and put on an excellent show."[45] The morale-building continued offstage. One time Cooper was doing his hospital walk-around when he came to the bed of a soldier blinded in battle. What could the 21-year-old former child actor from the Our Gang flicks do for such a man? "They told him that Jackie Cooper was standing next to him," Cooper wrote, "and he felt around on his bed for a pen and paper so he could get my autograph."[46]

Some big-shot USO entertainers would set up on a central stage and let the audience come to them. Claude approached his job more assertively. He would lead his troupe to the men, wherever they might be, and he would stick it out whatever the circumstances. Cooper recalled one outdoor show during a torrential tropical downpour. Cooper began packing up his waterlogged drum kit, deeming it impossible to proceed. "Thornhill wouldn't hear of it," Cooper recalled. "We played on. Claude said that if the men would sit in the rain to hear us, we'd play."[47]

Claude's will kept his men driving forward through myriad Pacific island hardships, and with a nod to Shaw's Rangers, they took to calling themselves Thornhill's Raiders. They dressed in green fatigues and had the name stenciled on their bags and equipment. It might have seemed a bit of a put-on, but the fact was that Claude took his assignment seriously, and his effort was much appreciated. The commander of the US forces on the Tarawa atoll wrote that the work of the "Thornhill Entertainment Group" was "very desirable and contributes greatly to the morale of the officers and men assigned to advanced bases."[48]

The band likewise received praise for its work on the island of Saipan, captured the previous July following a gruesome three-week struggle that left approximately 3,100 Americans dead and another 13,000 wounded. In the succeeding months, the US forces had built up the island's Isely Field to serve as the launch point for B-29 bombers striking the Japanese homeland now only 1,300 miles away. When the band played, both that past and the bloody business at hand faded away for a precious moment. Navy Pharmacist's Mate Second Class Jack Wade saw a nine-piece ensemble version of Thornhill's Raiders on the Pacific tour, and though the piano was out of tune, he reported that trombone player Ted Vesely performed a divine solo on "Body and Soul."

"I went away that evening feeling there was something still right with the world. That something I associated with the past was still the same, and was destined to improve through the years," Wade informed *DownBeat* readers in the June 1, 1945, edition. In a letter cited as coming from the "South Pacific Area," Wade added the prediction that "when I am home again, and once more 'Snowfall' drifts across the airlanes, I'll remember that little band and how they played it 'on the way to Tokyo.'"[49]

All told, between May 4 and May 27, Claude's outfit was reported to have staged twenty-eight shows for army, Marine, and navy units, as well as in hospitals.[50] He couldn't, though, seem to get away from leadership problems. In Hawaii his issues with Artie had led to his departure from Navy Band 501. With Thornhill's Raiders Claude's problems were with his putative superior, the baby-faced Ensign Dennis Day. Serious musicians recognized Claude as the genuine article while Day was more of a novelty item. Nonetheless, it was Day who had the higher rank, and over time he began to swell into his role. Cooper recalled that Day developed "officer-itis," a malady characterized by excessive self-regard and insistence on protocol. "On every island we visited there was an officers' club, and Day would head directly for that," Cooper recalled. Soon, he added, "He began trying to tell Thornhill what to do."[51]

While Day took his rank too seriously, Cooper said the singer was a "rotten" conductor and a poor leader of men. The group splintered into cliques and factions. Musicians clashed. They were physically and emotionally taxed. Day wanted to change the order of the show. In some smaller shows, he didn't want to sing at all. He wanted to have Thornhill, the enlisted man, follow orders. The tensions boiled over on Tarawa, where it seemed to Cooper that Claude "just had it with the hassling with Day and decided he couldn't take it anymore." Claude escaped into sick bay with an earache that Cooper suggested was more or less contrived, and he stayed there until his troupe flew off under Ensign Day's command.

On July 15, 1945, *DownBeat* reported that Thornhill was "ill on Tarawa with an ear and sinus infection and has had 125 shots of penicillin." In the same issue, Bob Crosby, Bing's pleasant-voiced brother and front man for a Marine Corps band, reported that he "saw Claude Thornhill the other day" in the hospital and that he was "not seriously ill" but rather was feeling "fatigue" from having been on tour for six months.[52] As with Artie, the music trade press and the daily newspapers amplified Thornhill's exposure to combat during his Pacific tours, with *DownBeat* asserting that he had been "under fire for a considerable portion" of his time in the navy.[53]

Thornhill, meanwhile, was ordered back to the States on August 10, and on August 30 he ended up at the Great Lakes Naval Training Center Hospital in Illinois. He was complaining of sneezing, itching, and wheezing. In mid-September the Great Lakes doctors recorded that the symptoms had been increasing in severity since their onset about a year prior. They did not respond to treatment, and the navy doctors concluded on September 18 that Claude should be discharged as medically unfit for further duty.[54]

As in Hawaii, where Admiral Calhoun had championed his cause, Claude once again secured the help of a well-placed ally. On September 4 a fellow Terra Haute native, Republican Rep. Noble Johnson of Indiana, wrote the Navy Bureau of Enlisted Personnel on Thornhill's behalf. Johnson advised that he'd been told that Thornhill's mother "has a cancer and probably cannot live long" and asked about the possibility of securing a discharge for the musician.[55] The navy got the message and answered in the affirmative, and on October 4 navy musician Claude Thornhill received his honorable discharge.

# Chapter 22

# Rearrangements

Shaw's Rangers scattered after the war. Some would visit or stay in touch, but there was never a grand reunion. The men were back on their own.

Dave Tough landed in Charlie Spivak's band before Woody Herman reeled him in to a rollicking outfit that Herman would dub his First Herd. Initially Herman's choice was a tough sell among the other musicians. "They felt Dave wasn't a modern enough player," Herman recalled, noting that "also, they were all in their 20s and Tough was older." But Herman knew the drummer was much more than some Dixieland has-been, and during the summer of 1944, the younger musicians began to appreciate Dave Tough as the real deal. Bass player Chubby Jackson acknowledged that his initial dismissal of the drummer was "the biggest mistake in the world" and he called Tough "totally brilliant."[1] For a good while, the streetwise drummer held it together and drove the Herman band onward and upward. *DownBeat* readers voted him the top choice in the magazine's 1945 All-Star Band.

The accolades could not sustain him. Tough collapsed on stage while performing in Minneapolis in mid-1945. His subsequent departure from the band was made official in late September 1945, with Herman vaguely explaining that the drummer had become too ill to work regularly. It was downhill from there, though Dave's reputation carried him for a while. He joined his old navy colleague Max Kaminsky in a Dixieland-style outfit at a jazz club in New York City's Greenwich Village newly opened by bandleader Eddie Condon. In 1947 his book *Dave Tough's Advanced Paradiddle Exercises* was published. His comings, goings, and occasional musings were chronicled in *DownBeat* and *Metronome*, where his penchant for acidic wisecracks drew rebukes that were no longer restrained by the diminished respect for his musicianship. "Why doesn't SOMEBODY hire him?" cornet player Bill Davison asked, sarcastically, in the March 26, 1947, issue of *DownBeat*. "He's the greatest drummer in the world, isn't he? So why isn't he working? The last I heard he was on his way to Brazil to fill in for a bass player."[2]

In early 1948 Dave abruptly abandoned Muggsy Spanier's outfit when the band still had three weeks to go at New York City's famed Blue Note nightclub. He left so quickly that he abandoned his drum set back at the club, and according to *DownBeat* his sister "got them out of hock [and] had to produce a written appeal from Davey before being able to send them on."[3] He was hitting friends up for money. One night, at New York City's Cirque Club, drummer Buddy Rich peeled off some bills for the bedraggled legend he had once looked up to. About the same time, a music store employee found Dave one morning lying, "bleeding and dirty," near the doorway.[4]

In mid- to late 1948, Tough's condition worsened and he entered the Veterans Administration Hospital in Lyons, New Jersey, apparently for treatment for malnutrition and alcoholism. He found a little escape by playing in the VA hospital's band, and he also received passes to spend time outside of the hospital, but by this time he was too far gone to stay dry for long. Early in December, jazz writer Leonard Feather would recall later, he saw Dave with "his mood quietly desperate, his speech thick" at the apartment of a friend.[5]

On Wednesday, December 8, 1948, Dave took his final tumble. Shortly after 5:00 p.m., he was making his way along downtown Newark's Market Street. He was several blocks from the city's Penn Station and close to the Novelty Bar and Grill, from which he reportedly had been ejected. At about 5:15 p.m., Dave apparently fell and struck his head. Passersby could not rouse him, and they summoned an ambulance. He was taken to the Newark

City Hospital, where he passed away early the next morning. He was 41 years old, and in the final indignity, Dave Tough's body was held unidentified in the Newark morgue for three days.[6] "Hospital authorities listed him under his proper name, but said the name meant nothing to them," the Associated Press reported.[7]

As word of his demise spread, Tough's Chester Street apartment in Newark was flooded with telegrams of remembrances and condolences from what a *Newark Star-Ledger* reporter described as "the top names of the music world." Dave left behind his wife, Marjorie Majors Tough, spuriously identified by the Associated Press as "a Negro." "The only drag," drummer Mel Lewis said, "was we didn't have him long enough. We never had a chance to see what he would have done in the '50s."[8]

Max Kaminsky would get over his own nightmares and plug away in various outfits. He reclaimed a place in New York City's nightclubs, and for a number of years he would play the society band circuit. It was an upper-crust world where, as Max told the story, a dowager once asked a bandleader if he was Jewish. Without missing a beat the bandleader answered, "Not necessarily, ma'am."[9] Max put together a basement club in Boston, a dive gussied up with abstract art and a fresh coat of paint. Its main virtue was that it gave Max a chance to play in his hometown. "For 25 years, I've worked for other men, and 25 is enough," Max said, "especially after sharing foxholes with the Guadalcanal rats."[10]

Max was tapped in 1957 for a seven-week overseas tour of Europe, and the next year he signed up for a four-month tour of Middle East and Asian countries that ended in Japan with performances before full houses in Nagoya, Osaka, and Hiroshima. At Hiroshima the American musicians were taken to a war memorial tablet commemorating the tens of thousands of Japanese civilians consumed in the August 6, 1945, dropping of the atomic bomb. "One of the Japanese officials said something about how terrible it was," Max wrote, "but I got sore and snapped, 'Next time, don't mess around.' There was a moment of coolness before the bland smiles took over again."[11]

Claude Thornhill recovered from the ailments that precipitated his navy discharge. Appearing at the Hotel Pennsylvania in late 1946 with a band that included his former navy colleagues Tak Takvorian on trombone and Joe Aglora on tenor saxophone, Claude was approvingly noted by *DownBeat* to have "improved enormously as a showman." The magazine reported that he was "working the crowd, making cracks at the mike and in general being much less retiring than he was four years ago."[12]

Even as *Look* magazine named his the "Band of 1948," Claude kept innovating. His work with the arranger Gil Evans helped set the foundation for the birth of what became known as cool jazz. Through the 1950s Claude's various orchestral configurations toured constantly, but it took a toll. He was drinking heavily. His recall of bandmembers' names came and went. He would say strange things at strange times, play odd practical jokes, abruptly recite a poem he'd written about some unnamed Pacific island. Word went around that Claude had undergone shock treatments.[13]

Eccentricities notwithstanding, through the late 1950s and early 1960s, Claude kept plugging away, leading ever-smaller bands on a backwater circuit of country clubs, school gyms, and American Legion halls. It was a living. On Thursday, July 1, 1965, he was off the road briefly at his home in Caldwell, New Jersey, in advance of a weekend appearance at the Steel Pier in Atlantic City. The first of two consecutive heart attacks flattened him; a second attack forty minutes later killed him. He was 56.

Claude's third wife, former actress Ruth Caldwell, called Artie. The two men hadn't spoken in ten years.[14] "She said Claude had told her that I was his best friend," Artie recounted to the *New Yorker*'s Whitney Balliett, adding that "later, I found out that Claude had been paying frequent visits to my mother." Thornhill, Artie learned, had made Artie's mom promise not to speak of the visits, and she never did.[15]


Sam Donahue's exemplary leadership of the post-Shaw navy band may well have been his career highlight, though he kept playing for many years. He carried on for decades through gigs that included a return to military service as an instructor at the Naval School of Music during the Korean War.

A tart February 11, 1947, *Variety* review of his latest recording said the saxophonist was "still floundering" and had produced a "rather dull" take on the song "Believe." The critics' disappointment continued in subsequent years, as if Sam had sold out his true talent. The prolific writer Leonard Feather summed up this school of thought when he lamented in 1964 that while Sam had always been a "capable and talented soloist," his more recent "gallery-courting gyrations" as part of the "packaged nostalgia" industry were "tasteless" and a sad comedown for a talented guy who could have gone the distance.[16] Donahue would end his playing days backing up Frank Sinatra Jr. and serving as musical director of John Ascuaga's Nugget in Sparks, Nevada, before dying of cancer in 1974.[17]

The other veterans of Navy Band 501, too, played out their hands.

Typical, in some way, was the postwar career of trombone player Tak Takvorian. After his navy discharge, the Massachusetts native went on to play in a succession of outfits as a consummate, reliable professional. He worked alongside Claude Thornhill for a time, and then in the mid-1950s he was with the Dorsey Brothers organization, an outfit formed when the long-feuding brothers Tommy and Jimmy patched up their differences. Tak began teaching trombone in Concord, Massachusetts, schools and picked up gigs where he could, playing in clubs, traveling ice shows, and the circus.[18]

Trumpet player Conrad Gozzo, one of the band members most rankled by Artie's leadership, kept playing as a reliable sideman until, in 1954, RCA Victor signed him to lead his own combo. Despite the high regard of his fellow musicians, he never took off commercially. Gozzo would spend years as an NBC staff musician; his gigs included playing in the orchestra for the Dinah Shore Show. But, like his old navy band mentor Dave Tough, Goz undermined himself. He drank and gambled, running up big debts. When he died on October 8, 1964, at the age of 44, the *Los Angeles Times* attributed the cause to "liver disease." With his widow and two teenage sons reportedly left with little to survive on, A-list talent including the likes of Frank Sinatra and Dinah Shore staged a benefit at the Palladium in Los Angeles that raised some $25,000 for the family of the man who, as *Variety* put it in its inimitable style, had been a "vet tooter."[19]

Staff orchestra spots put bread on the table for other Navy Band 501 veterans as well, like trumpet player Frank Beach, who joined the 20th Century Fox orchestra in 1950. Barney Spieler, the big, strapping bass player, took off for Paris after the war to study with the help of his GI Bill benefits while he played on the side with touring American musicians. In May 1949, looming large on stage above the rest of the players, Spieler joined the Miles Davis/Tadd Dameron Quintet to showcase some fresh bebop at the Paris International Festival of Jazz. Two years later Spieler secured a seat with Amsterdam's famed Concertgebouw Orchestra. He ascended to the first bass seat and seemed to flourish there before he died when he crashed the small Citroen that he bought with a pay raise.[20]

Some former Shaw's Rangers ventured beyond music. Trumpet player John Best, after playing in Benny Goodman's postwar band, moved to California and eventually owned an avocado orchard at the behest of his then wife. "She hated the music business," Best said. "It made nothing but enemies."[21]

Best fell from a ladder while pruning trees in 1982 and fractured his neck. Thereafter consigned to a wheelchair, Best nonetheless kept playing, including performances for the University of California at San Diego Hospital staff in the two months immediately following his catastrophic accident. He managed to revisit Australia in 1996, where his wife, Mary Lou, passed away. Back home, he practiced incessantly for years before passing away in 2003.[22]

Nostalgia put bread in the table for some. Alto saxophonist Ralph LaPolla was still playing the old favorites into the mid-1980s with his Swinging Years Big Band, an outfit that delivered just what the audience wanted: memories on a platter.[23] Pianist Ricky Collucio changed his name to the less ethnic sounding Rocky Cole and accompanied singer Patti Page from the mid-1950s and into the 1980s. The duo held extended runs in Las Vegas, where one reviewer in 1968 praised his "virile, aggressively masculine tones" as a complement to Page's "femininity."[24] Musical partners for thirty-five years, Rocky and Page also maintained a long-running affair on the side that finally buckled under the weight of divergent expectations. "He still hadn't given up thinking we were going to get married," Page recounted, "but I had tried to make him understand that I never saw our dating moving toward permanency."[25]

Some went on to teach, including Takvorian and tenor saxophonist Mack Pierce Pitt. A high school dropout, like a number of his fellow bandmembers, Mack was among the few to use his GI Bill benefits for college. He earned bachelor's and master's degrees in education from Wayne State University and spent much of his career in Detroit-area schools.[26] Trombone player Tasso Harris led two Colorado high school bands to state championships, and in 1963 his University of Denver jazz orchestra took first place in the original composition and band categories at the Notre Dame University Collegiate Jazz Festival.[27] The award-winning outfit was subsequently tapped by the State Department for a three-month overseas tour in 1965 that included Australia and New Zealand, as well as a number of Asian countries. Twenty years after his service in the all-out war against Japan, Tasso presented a letter of friendship from Denver's mayor to the mayor of Takayama, Denver's sister city.[28] Tasso also kept playing, including in backup groups for touring musicians that on one occasion included Elvis Presley. Harris offered his then teenage daughter a guest pass to meet the swivel-hipped singer and get his autograph. "A Beatles fan, she declined, a decision she later regretted," the *Denver Post* recounted.[29]

Harris's 2005 obituary in the *Denver Post* was festooned with the embellishments that accompanied much of the reporting on Artie Shaw's Navy Band. The trombone player, according to the paper, "saw action at Guadalcanal and then served aboard Atlantic destroyers targeting Nazi U-boat wolf-packs."[30]

Harris's fellow trombone player, Earle "Dick" LeFave, had played backup with both Donahue and Goodman after the war and then taught at what later became the Berklee College of Music. His July 14, 1998, obituary in the *Boston Globe* saluted his military service with the usual puffery, declaring that Shaw's navy band had "traveled throughout the Pacific war zones entertaining the troops in those areas too dangerous for USO groups."

Dick Jones, the arranger who was an unsung but important contributor to the band, was tapped by his friend Frank Sinatra in November 1951 to play the piano at the crooner's wedding to Artie's ex-wife, Ava Gardner.[31] Jones's fellow navy band arranger, David Rose, went on to work for Arthur Godfrey and as music director for *The Red Skelton Show* and won two Emmys for his TV show compositions.

Some kept playing until the end of their days. Max Kaminsky made a well-received swing through England in the 1950, recorded some New

Orleans–tinged pieces in the 1970s, and gigged at a New York City club called Ryan's in the 1980s. He passed away in 1994 following a stroke at the age of 85.

Harold Wax, the young accordion player whose mother had beseeched Artie to protect him so that he might return home safely, did make it back to port. He entered in 1946 into what would be a sixty-two-year-long marriage and played with the Lester Lanin Orchestra. This was a society band, known for hiring genuine jazz musicians to play at what one writer described as "lawn parties, nonstop cocktail fests in private apartments, divorce celebrations and comparable festivities."[32] After leaving the society band, he and his wife ran a retail clothing store. Late in life he formed his own band. In August 2008, at the age of 86, Harold Wax and his outfit played two valedictory gigs. A few days later, he passed away. At his funeral his last band played "When the Saints Go Marching In."[33]

# Epilogue

Artie's war was done, and so was he.

"I didn't want to get out of bed," he recalled decades later. "There was nothing to live for. When I saw the world as I saw it, and thought, [expletive redacted] it. I was over there in that [expletive deleted] war, being shot at, losing my left ear, and all this bullshit, for what? To come back to Beverly Hills, to the height of rarefied atmospheres, and listen to you people complain because you had to stand in line to get certain cuts of meat?"[1]

The bleakness was genuine, even if he exaggerated his "being shot at." Untold numbers of other veterans faced similar difficulties with reentering civilian life, a challenge poignantly portrayed in William Wyler's 1946 classic *The Best Years of Our Lives.* The wrenching postwar transitions of the guilt-ridden former bombardier, alcoholic former infantryman, and mutilated former sailor in that movie hinted at Artie's own sense of alienation, to which were added the burdens and opportunities created by his celebrity status. The spotlight was not conducive to healing, though it did lead him to the Beverly Hills office of Dr. May Romm, analyst to the stars.

Artie was always looking in the mirror, examining himself, his motives, and his actions. He found himself fascinating, a worthy object of study, and he had no problem seeking the help of a professional guide. About the time he had split for Mexico in 1939, he had been seeing two New York City psychiatrists.[2] With Romm he would embark on an extended course of self-examination.

Romm was in her early 50s, about twenty years older than Artie. Newspaper columnist Robert Ruark described her as "little dark lady,"[3] while another newspaperman wrote that she was a "spry little woman" who was graying slightly.[4] Romm had been a general practitioner before training at the New York Psychoanalytic Institutes. She had become a go-to analyst for Hollywood's leading lights since her arrival in California in 1938. It was a case of mutual attraction. Hollywood folk liked talking about themselves, while Romm liked to listen to them. She was, some thought, quite starstruck.

Producer David O. Selznick had been one of Romm's prominent movie industry clients. As recounted by his wife Irene Mayer Selznick, in her score-settling memoir *A Private View*, the producer of *Gone with the Wind* had sought help for his mood swings when he was directed to see Romm. At the time she was one of the relatively few analysts around the Hollywood community. Irene subsequently described Romm as a "wise little motherly lady" whose sessions seemed to do her manic, Benzedrine-popping husband a world of good.[5] Working with Selznick gave Romm an in to the Hollywood colony. Alfred Hitchcock named her technical adviser to a film that was released in 1945 as *Spellbound*. She welcomed as clients the actors Robert Taylor and Edward G. Robinson, and, like any Hollywood player, she fed items to the powerful columnist Hedda Hopper. "Dr. May Romm, psychoanalyst, was telling me she'll soon have a busman's holiday in New York to learn more of the psychoid methods used to treat returning soldiers," Hopper dished in April of 1945.[6]

Artie settled on to Romm's couch for an eighteen-month course of self-study that at times included five hourly sessions a week.[7] "That's a long time to spend talking about yourself," Artie allowed. "By the time a fellow is through putting in that much time discussing it, he ought to have learned at least a few interesting things about the way he ticks. . . . I certainly did."[8]

Artie and Romm had a lot of material to work with, the gist of which navy doctors had already outlined following their own assessments. "According to the man's own statement, he was fearful and shy as a child because of violent family quarrels which culminated in his father leaving home," navy doctors had reported in January 1944. "He had night terrors and fear of contracting disease."[9] He had a specific, inexplicable fear of contracting leprosy. Artie had, the doctors noted, "always been excitable, restless, impulsive and insecure." This unstable foundation had been further shaken by the nomadic life of a professional musician, the unrelenting stress of bandleader competition, the distorting glare of the celebrity spotlight, the chronic fatigue from his months in the Pacific, and the acute frights from the Guadalcanal air raids.

Romm could have helped Artie honestly confront each and every one of his travails. For public consumption, though, his complicated navy experience was packaged into a simplified narrative. One draft press release asserted that "a long hitch in the Navy did Shaw a lot of good," and that he had "had little time for his own thoughts and problems [and] he saw then how much music meant to the men in combat." The experience, the press agents wrote, "made Artie realize that there were many, many things that could be done with music. He is now making full use of that experience."[10]

The postwar searching that led Artie to Dr. Romm's office also led him to a brush with Hollywood's political fringes. In 1945 he joined the executive board of the Independent Citizens Committee of the Arts, Sciences and Professions, a progressive-minded organization with a reassuringly estimable roster that included Rita Hayworth and Orson Welles. Red hunters in both Sacramento and Washington, DC, though, considered it to be a Communist front, one of a number operating in and around the entertainment industry. Questioned about this affiliation and others, an emotional Shaw told the House Un-American Activities Committee on May 4, 1953, that he was "duped" into lending his name to several such groups. As mitigation, he summoned memories of his wartime navy stint as evidence of his undying patriotism. "This country has been very kind to me," he told the HUAC panel. "I started out as a minority member of a poor family, and I have come a long way for a guy like me, and I have found on the roads

I am met with a lot of love and affection, and when I was serving in the service that same thing happened."[11]

Enigmatically, Artie added that "I think one of the members of the committee here could bear that out." He was referring to Rep. Donald Jackson, a California Republican who had served in the South Pacific as an officer in the Second Marine Division. Elements of the division had been entertained by Shaw's Rangers while recuperating and training in New Zealand in 1943.

Shaw survived the 1953 HUAC grilling, though his abject demeanor drew mockery from those accustomed to his chilly arrogance. Jazz historian Michael Zirpolo, in his blog *Swing & Beyond*, noted that "many in the Hollywood film community thought that his performance before the HUAC needlessly kicked people who were already down and hurting simply because they had exercised their First Amendment free speech rights."[12]

During the postwar years, Artie formed and reformed different orchestras. He was like a man twirling the combination of a safe, trying to find his way back inside the treasure trove. He had formed in later 1944 what music industry reporters called another "million-dollar band" but then dismantled it. Artie explained, rather quaintly, that "I don't want to leave my wife," who at that time was Ava Gardner. He said he had no plans and was "just going to take it easy."[13]

Taking it easy, though, was never really Artie's style.

His October 1945 marriage to Gardner had, predictably, gone off the rails. A self-made intellectual, adamant as only an autodidact can be, Artie had insisted on trying to mold Ava's mind. He assigned her reading, with the likes of *The Brothers Karamazov* and *The Magic Mountain* replacing the lighter fare she might have preferred. Ava would gamely comply, but she could never meet the master's standards. She submitted herself to analysis by Dr. Romm, but even the sessions could not cure the marriage. In October 1946 Artie divorced Ava and married author Kathleen Winsor, famous for her steamy and long-winded 1944 bestseller *Forever Amber*.

Artie and Kathleen managed to stay together until April 1948. Winsor alleged in her subsequent divorce filing that Artie had subjected her to extreme mental cruelty. "He told me what books to read, and I read them,"

Winsor stated in a court filing. "He told me what clothes to wear, and I wore them. He told me what I must think on every subject conceivable, and would tolerate no difference of opinion."[14] But Winsor, a University of California graduate whose most famous book spanned some 970 pages, could also give it right back to Artie in a way that Ava, Lana, and Elizabeth could not. "When Artie met Kathleen Winsor, he hadn't read her book 'Forever Amber,'" columnist Leonard Lyons wrote. "Then he bought a copy and told her, 'Of course, it's too long.' She bristled: "So's Tolstoy's War and Peace.'"[15]

Once again single, Artie in early 1949 signed with Columbia Records to put out an album of classical music. He brought a symphony-sized orchestra and a classical repertoire of material from the likes of Debussy and Prokofiev to a newly opened New York City jazz club called Bop City, where the gutsy performance was widely panned.[16] There followed over the next few years a succession of bands and recording sessions, interrupted by the publication in 1952 of his eccentric autobiography *The Trouble with Cinderella: A Problem of Identity*. The book was serialized over many issues in *DownBeat* and received some respectful reviews. It was also a hot mess, congested with various musings but lacking essential facts, coherent chronology, clear narrative, and an index, among other shortcomings. Critic Max Harrison laceratingly said of it that Artie's book "confirms Talleyrand's idea that words were given men to conceal their thoughts."[17]

Remarkably, in a nearly four-hundred-page book, Artie devoted only about three wispy pages to his World War II navy experience. His failure, or refusal, to illuminate his unique wartime service is all the more frustrating because he knew how to spin a yarn. His short story "A Nice Little Post-War Business" offered some fine-grained observations in the account of a weary navy musician. "The deck was hard," Artie wrote in the short story. "So was the life preserver I sat on. Actually, we weren't supposed to sit on the life preservers, but after the second day out everybody did it anyway."[18]

Artie's eagle eye would have captured many such moments during his navy service. Instead, he kept most of them to himself. Trumpet player Max Kaminsky came closer to delivering the goods with his own autobiography, written with the help of V. E. Hughes and published in 1963 under the title

*My Life in Jazz*. Kaminsky devoted some 30 anecdote-rich pages of the 296-page book to his World War II experiences. The wartime yarns accompany what the *New Yorker* described as "shoulder to shoulder vignettes" of his fellow musicians and "monotonously hard" criticisms of music promoters, nightclub owners, jazz critics, and bebop players. The magazine's anonymous reviewer clinically described Max as a "trumpeter of the second rank," but as a reservoir of anecdotes Max was first-rate so long as factual accuracy was of secondary concern.[19]

In 1953, hounded by the IRS over some $82,000 in back taxes, Artie went on the road again. By September of that year, he was leading an innovative revival of a small group he called the Gramercy Five, whimsically named for a Manhattan telephone exchange. His head shaved, his focus intense, Artie led piano player Hank Jones, guitarist Tal Farlow, and the others toward some new frontiers. Reviewers applauded, with *Time* observing how the famously impatient bandleader's "glum face relaxed into smiles, and the crowed began to hear the new Artie Shaw."[20]

Artie's innovative Gramercy Five outfit went into a Hollywood recording studio in June 1954 and undertook a residency at the Sahara Hotel in Las Vegas. A sardonic *Melody Maker* writer described in a July 3, 1954, article how he came upon Artie's small group playing "in the Sahara Hotel, there behind the slot machines behind the gaming tables behind the lounge behind the bar behind a huge cash register." Behind the cash register was right. The Las Vegas gig paid well. Artie earned as much as $8,000 weekly for the shows.[21]

About the time of Artie's Sahara Hotel run, a pair of US-born, Australia-residing promoters concocted the idea of luring America's big-name entertainers Down Under. Benn Reyes was a fast-talking, gimmick-loving flack of the old school. Dressed as if straight from central casting, Reyes was described by one reporter as sporting "a monogrammed shirt, cameo cuff links set in pearls, an outsized gold watch and a ring with a stoner about as big as a pullet's egg."[22] Reyes had previously boosted the likes of fan dancer Sally Rand and the Folies Bergère. His partner Lee Gordon was a 31-year-old Michigan native and University of Miami alumni with an ambiguous past that reportedly included time booking acts into Havana's Tropicana nightclub.[23]

For the first of what would become a years-long series dubbed the Big Show, Reyes and Gordon in July 1954 brought together Artie, singer Ella Fitzgerald, drummer Buddy Rich, and comedian Jerry Colonna. The promoters dangled fat paychecks to reel in the performers, with Shaw and Fitzgerald each reportedly getting $10,000. This happened to be the maximum amount that Australia's tax law allowed to be transferred out of the country. The goggle-eyed jokester Colonna was reportedly paid $6,000 and Rich got $2,000.[24]

Artie would not be innovating in his return to Australia. He would confine himself to his familiar repertoire, the same songs he had played Down Under while leading his navy band a decade before. He would not even be bringing his own band. Instead, he would front a pickup orchestra borrowed from the 35-year-old Australian bandleader Wally Norman, a former accountant-turned-trombonist. The idea seemed more efficient than forming his own US outfit and hauling it across the Pacific, but leading unfamiliar musicians through stock arrangements would tax Artie and the Australians in other ways.

On Monday, July 19, one day after Rich and Colonna landed, Artie arrived at Sydney's airport. A large crowd estimated to be somewhere between five hundred and two thousand people had showed up the day before expecting Artie, but on Monday there was only a small contingent of gum-chewing teenage girls, a few members of Norman's band, and a pack of reporters to see Artie as he was the first to exit from the plane. Artie told the reporters that he had missed the prior flight from Hawaii after running into someone he called "an old Navy friend." He did not elaborate. He said that once the brief Australian tour was done, he would return to his New York state farm. The reporters pressed him on everything from his appearance a year earlier before the House Un-American Activities Committee to his many marriages. For the most part, the reporters received polite but shallow responses. "Smile Artie, for Heaven's sake, smile," one newspaper photographer told him.

"Say something funny," Artie retorted.[25]

As banter, this was not bad, but Artie's sharp comeback also foreshadowed what would be a testy relationship with some of Australia's prominent journalists who, when treated brusquely, would bite back in print.

Artie set about rehearsing his dozen inherited musicians from Wally Norman's group. It did not go well. A correspondent for Sydney's *The Sun* newspaper sat in for several hours of an all-day rehearsal Wednesday, July 21, and described Artie's growing frustration as the pickup band stumbled through his theme song "Nightmare." Norman's outfit was a local favorite, whose theme song was Tommy Dorsey's favorite "I'm Getting Sentimental over You," and it played in a variety of styles, but with Artie it struggled to make the grade. Thirty times or more, the newspaperman reported, Artie stopped the music in the middle of a song. Over and over he would imitate how each instrument should sound, but even with the insistent tutoring, the Australians could never finish the piece before Artie cut them short. "No, no, no, you fellas, no!" Artie exclaimed. "It's gotta' go like machinery. Get me? Pa, pa. Pa, pa."[26]

The rehearsal went on late into the night, giving Artie an excuse to skip out on an autograph session scheduled for the next day at noon, another slap in the face to disappointed teenagers. The next day, Friday, July 23, some ten thousand fans gathered at Sydney's sports stadium. They were clapping and yelling during the opening number, "What Is This Thing Called Love?" when Artie abruptly snapped the music to a halt. The musicians he had known for less than a week had failed to meet his high standards, and Artie could not compromise. "The boys have tried really hard for the last three days," Artie told the bewildered audience members, "but they can't be expected to do three months' work in that time." He added that he thought the audience would rather that he interrupt the music than "gloss over mistakes," although it's more likely that the mistakes were audible to him alone. The interruption stung Norman, who had been leading his band for years, and it humiliated his musicians. The best that could be said about it was that it showed the Australian audience several of Artie Shaw's many facets, his quest for perfection and his hair-triggered readiness to call it quits.[27]

Once the band resumed, Artie sought to make up for his slap in the face by graciously summoning the musicians to their feet and declaring that by the end of the tour they would be comparable to any outfit in the United States. As the tour went on, Artie did his part to promote the Australian shows, chatting on a radio show one evening and sitting down with 35-year-old columnist

Charles Buttrose for an in-depth morning conversation. With a background as both music critic and war correspondent, Buttrose had the self-confidence to judge Artie following a thirty-minute interview as a "disturbingly earnest middle aged-man, 44 and balding, interested in many things but humanity in particular—a man who has framed his own strict code and strives to live up to it."[28]

By the time Artie's pickup orchestra arrived in Melbourne for an outdoors July 26 show, a combination of cold weather and high prices kept the crowd under three thousand. Some thought Ella Fitzgerald, described by one Australian reporter as "14 stone of personality" and another as a "dark coloured buxom crooner" stole the show when she appeared after about ninety minutes to perform "That Old Black Magic," "Lady Be Good," and "St. Louis Blues." Artie, as in his wartime tour through Australia, shouldered multiple responsibilities on and off the stage. During nine hours in Brisbane on July 29, Artie marched through an airport reception, a press conference, a civic welcome, and two shows, at 6:00 p.m. and 9:00 p.m. The fans responded warmly to the familiar old hits, but Artie felt like he was going through the motions. His mind drifted, and he sought other distractions. Along with promoter Benn Reyes, he started exploring the idea of hiring a mining geologist to search for uranium. "I guess music isn't fun anymore," Artie told reporters in Brisbane. "It's just a way to make a living."[29]

A show Friday night, July 30, at Sydney's sports stadium was described as a partial benefit, with some of the proceeds promised to the NSW Institution for Deaf, Dumb and Blind Children. A *Daily Mirror* photo of Artie with two young boys was headlined "Artie Shaw Is Fatherly," an assertion that might have surprised his own two sons. Show promoters subsequently clashed with institution representatives over what was due, with Reyes pronouncing himself "all het up" over suggestions that he and Gordon were welching on a commitment. Ella Fitzgerald, meanwhile, was threatening to sue Pan American Airways for allegedly discriminating against her in failing to provide a first-class seat on her flight from Hawaii to Australia.[30]

On those sour notes, Artie was done with his Australian tour. When an airline official at Sydney airport subsequently called his name for boarding the return flight to Honolulu, Artie wasn't around to answer. He was, according to news accounts, believed to be fishing "somewhere in New South Wales."[31] The lingering disputes from the Australian tour would take years to resolve. The Institution for Deaf, Dumb and Blind Children eventually got its cut, while Fitzgerald made good her threat and sued in December 1954; the suit was settled in 1956. As for Artie, when he returned from Australia, he put his away his clarinet and walked away from musical performance, this time for good.

Artie would live to the age of 94. During the decades between his abrupt musical retirement in 1954 and his death on December 30, 2004, he would explore new ventures with his characteristic energy. He picked up target shooting as a hobby in 1949. By 1963 Artie placed second in the Pennsylvania state benchrest shooting contest. *Guns* magazine put him on the cover of the February 1964 issue, making note of his having once placed five precision shots in one hole. Artie, being Artie, wanted more. He wanted to surpass himself. "Now," Artie told the *Guns* writer, "I want to make that hole smaller."[32]

Though he stayed off of the bandstand, save for a brief late-in-life resurrection, he was not a recluse. He would periodically appear on television, including a 1950 spot on *What's My Line?* that was followed by a repeat performance on the show several decades later. The first blindfolded panel member to question him on his second appearance asked whether he was in the music business. "No, señora," Artie replied, with his customary panache.

Artie would sit, as well, for assorted press interviews, spurning questions about his multiple marriages as menial gossip but going into detail about his music. He would serve up, if asked, a few familiar navy anecdotes. Visitors to his house, late in his life, would take note of a few wartime mementos, including a Japanese battle flag and a model of a P-38 fighter plane that a Seabee had fashioned for him from shell casings. A painting done by a *Life* magazine artist fancifully depicted Artie mid-solo on a South Pacific island, troops listening closely in the background. Mostly, though, Artie seemed intent on leaving World War II behind him.

Not long, apparently, after he was discharged from the service in 1944, Artie visited the home of his longtime attorney Andrew Weinberger. Weinberger had three sons. One of them, Tony, was about 6 years old at the time of Artie's visit. In a 2022 interview, Tony Weinberger recalled that Artie was carrying his chief petty officer's uniform. The bandleader, once again a civilian, gave the discarded uniform to Tony's father, the attorney, for safekeeping or perhaps just to get it out of his hair. The moment, however ambiguous, made an impression. Some eight decades later, Tony Weinberger recalled immediately the name and location of Rogers Peet and Company, the bespoke New York City tailors that had fashioned Artie's uniform. Tony further recalled how the uniform was put aside in one of the Weinberger family's closets. And he remembered one final thing:

After Artie cast off his navy garb, he never came calling for it again.

But that is, perhaps, ending on a false note.

In 2001, when he was 91 years old, Artie helped put together a CD box set of his remarkable life's work. The package included extensive liner notes in a fifty-page booklet, in which he reflected on his life and times. "At some point, probably while I was in the navy, as a result of seeing the way those men reacted to our music, it began to dawn on me that, whether I realized it or not, I'd created a good-sized chunk of Americana," Artie Shaw wrote. "Something lasting."

# Acknowledgments

I start by saluting the late Harold S. Kaye. A deeply informed jazz aficionado and dogged researcher, Kaye was a serious music historian in addition to his full-time job as a microbiologist with the federal government. His persistent work on a planned biography of drummer Dave Tough in particular led to the publication of an indispensable account of Navy Band 501 in the late, great magazine Storyville. Kaye also did considerable work on the background of trumpet player Conrad Gozzo, among a number of other related topics, and any study of Artie Shaw's navy service necessarily stands on Kaye's shoulders.

Kaye's stepson, Danny Levin, is both a swinging Austin, Texas–based musician in his own right and a diligent keeper of Kaye's few remaining research materials. Danny's willingness to share documents and photographs enhanced this book. One of my lifelong friends, Cornell Hurd—yet another Austin musician—became, through one of the happy coincidences that shaped this work, the guide who connected me with Danny. Kaye's daughter, Miranda Rehm, was helpful, as was the staff of the National Jazz Archive in Essex, England.

Mike Zirpolo, a deeply informed big band aficionado and author of the wonderful *Swing & Beyond* blog, found at swingandbeyond.com, was more than generous in giving a draft version of the manuscript a good scrubbing. Mike went above and beyond the call of duty with his attention to detail and he saved me from myriad flubs; any that remain, and there surely are some, are entirely of my own making.

Dennis Spragg and Reinhard Scheer-Hennings generously provided guidance and encouragement early on; their own acutely detailed accounts of the various Shaw bands published online by the American Music Research Center at the University of Colorado are essential works. Also at a crucial early stage, Russ Girsberger, the librarian at the US Naval School of Music, steered me in some good directions, as did retired Navy Master

Chief Musician Michael Bayes. Dennis and Russ subsequently read the completed draft manuscript and provided numerous, invaluable critiques and suggestions.

Managing Editor Amy Maddox at the University of North Texas Press saw the potential in this endeavor, and she has been a joy to work with, as has her entire team. Mapmaker Rhys Davies did a great job in capturing the look we were striving for.

Researcher Ann Trevor used her considerable expertise to locate navy documents stored deep within the National Archives. A dogged investigator, Ann also offered much-appreciated advice and words of encouragement at several crucial stages. In Los Angeles, researcher Diane Hellmer was persistent in tracking down elusive court documents from the 1940s. Shelley Finke opened up some illuminating articles in the International Association of Jazz Collectors' *IAJC Journal*, itself an invaluable resource in tracking jazz history.

One of the pleasures of research is coming upon new (to me) deep wells of information. Peter Dunn, author of the incredibly detailed Australia@ War website, and Marc Myers, author of the endlessly entertaining *JazzWax* website, deserve special mention. Seth Washburne, the dogged historian of the 13th Troop Carrier Squadron, has done a remarkable job in tracking down documents and family members and was very helpful with his incisive comments on the text.

I've said it before and I'll say it again: All hail the librarians! The staff members of the Institute of Jazz Studies at the Rutgers University–Newark campus were very helpful; certainly, the institute's holdings are a national treasure. Kathleen Feeney and the rest of the staff at the University of Chicago Library's Hanna Holborn Gray Special Collections Research Center moved with dispatch and good cheer in the search for old photographs. Morgan Davjs, music reference specialist at the Library of Congress, patiently got me started on nifty databases. Speaking of which, the people behind the Internet Archive and HathiTrust digital libraries deserve special thanks. The Trove database of Australian newspapers maintained by the National Library of Australia and the Papers Past collection maintained by the National Library of New Zealand were both essential and highly entertaining.

*DownBeat*'s remarkably thorough and entertaining coverage of the jazz scene over many decades makes this work possible. As the saying goes, its reporters, along with those from *Variety* and *Metronome*, wrote the first draft of this history.

Joe Hooper, a writer, friend, and colleague of many years standing has been an invaluable sounding board and collaborator. He helped polish the manuscript, contributing both his wit and his jazz expertise.

I reached some of the children of Tasso Harris, Artie Shaw, and Tak Takvorian, and I thank them for their time.

And my wife, Beth—well, she's my partner in this and in everything.

# Endnotes

## Notes for Introduction

1. Max Harrison, "Swing Era Big Bands and Jazz Composing and Arranging," in *The Oxford Companion to Jazz*, ed. Bill Kirchner (Oxford: Oxford University Press, 2005), 287.
2. Artie Shaw, "Artie Shaw's Own Exposure of the Amazing American Dance Music Business," *Melody Maker*, January 13, 1940, 3.
3. Dave Dexter Jr., "Artie's Should Be Greatest Dance Combo Ever Assembled," *DownBeat*, September 1, 1941, 1.
4. Geoffrey C. Ward and Ken Burns, *Jazz: A History of America's Music* (New York: Alfred A. Knopf, 2000), 284.
5. Artie Shaw, interview by Joe Smith, "Off the Record," July 1, 1986, https://www.loc.gov/item/jsmith000014/.
6. Shaw, interview by Smith, "Off the Record."
7. Undated press release, General Artists Corporation, Artie Shaw clippings file, Institute of Jazz Studies, Rutgers University Library, New Brunswick, NJ (hereafter cited as Institute of Jazz Studies).
8. Charles Buttrose, "Artie Shaw: Philosopher of the Clarinet," *Sydney Daily Telegraph*, January 24, 1954, 19.
9. Steve Voce, "Artie Shaw," *The Independent*, January 1, 2005, https://www.independent.co.uk/news/obituaries/artie-shaw-26697.html.
10. "Tough Luck Story: How Musicians in Shaw Band Almost Got Jap Sub," *Capitol News from Hollywood*, February 1944, 5.
11. Artie Shaw, interview by Freddie Johnson, KPCC Radio, March 9, 1994, https://www.youtube.com/watch?v=TxcxSdMDjkk.
12. Medical history, January 3, 1944, Artie Shaw medical file (hereafter cited as Shaw medical file), National Personnel Records Center, St. Louis, MO (hereafter cited as NPRC).
13. "Benny Goodman, Glenn Miller Voted Champs!," *DownBeat*, January 1, 1942, 1, 21.
14. Hugh N. Brown, "Famous Navy Swing Band Makes GIs Rave," *Washington* (DC) *Evening Star*, June 10, 1945, 40.
15. "Musician 2/C," *New Yorker*, December 25, 1943, 14.
16. Mike Daniels, "Musician of the Year," *Metronome*, January 1944, 18.

17. Samuel Eliot Morrison, *The Struggle for Guadalcanal*, vol. 5, *History of United States Naval Operations in World War II* (Boston: Little, Brown, 1950), 272.
18. "Beat Editors Eat the Word Amazing," *DownBeat*, April 15, 1944, 10.
19. Tom Nolan, *Artie Shaw, King of the Clarinet: His Life and Times* (New York: W. W. Norton, 2011), 181.
20. Statement of Mark Gerstle Jr., Shaw medical file.
21. Artie Shaw, interview with Bruce Talbot, *Smithsonian Jazz Masters*, October 7–8, 1992, https://www.si.edu/media/NMAH/NMAH-AC0808_Shaw_Artie_Transcript.pdf.


# Notes for Chapter 1


1. Nolan, *Artie Shaw*, 1.
2. Report of physical examination, April 27, 1942, Shaw medical file.
3. Medical history, December 28, 1943, Shaw medical file.
4. Artie Shaw, *The Trouble with Cinderella: An Outline of Identity* (New York: Farrar, Straus and Young, 1952), 86.
5. Shaw, *Trouble with Cinderella*, 142.
6. Shaw, *Trouble with Cinderella*, 45.
7. Sammy Cahn, *I Should Care: The Sammy Cahn Story* (New York: Arbor House, 1974), 247.
8. Walter McCarty, "Promoter Sues Artie Shaw," *DownBeat*, October 1, 1939, 1.
9. Gunther Schuller, *The Swing Era: The Development of Jazz, 1930–1945* (Oxford: Oxford University Press, 1989), 694.
10. Report of medical survey, January 17, 1944, Shaw medical file.
11. Shaw, *Trouble with Cinderella*, 251.
12. Louis Sobel, "New York Cavalcade," *Detroit Evening Times*, September 13, 1942, 62.
13. "Palace, Cleve," *Variety*, October 8, 1941, 46.
14. "'Hot Lip' Page Here Saturday," *Black Dispatch*, October 18, 1941, 9.
15. Artie Shaw, interview by Terry Gross, "Fresh Air," *National Public Radio*, December 24, 1985, https://www.npr.org/transcripts/126972706?ft=nprml&f=17085176.
16. John Warburton, ed., *Artie Shaw: The Quest for Perfection* (UK: BBC, 2003).
17. Shaw, interview by Gross.

# Notes for Chapter 2

1. Shaw, *Trouble with Cinderella*, 23.
2. Shaw, *Trouble with Cinderella*, 24.
3. Shaw, *Trouble with Cinderella*, 55.
4. Shaw, *Trouble with Cinderella*, 56.
5. Nolan, *Artie Shaw*, 9.
6. Nolan, *Artie Shaw*, 10.
7. Shaw, *Trouble with Cinderella*, 91.
8. Jack Sher, "He Wanted to Know," *South Bend Tribune*, November 23, 1938, 47.
9. "Popularity Won by Austin Wylie at Castle Farm," *The Enquirer*, November 29, 1929, 70.
10. Shaw, *Trouble with Cinderella*, 118.
11. Whitney Balliett, "Jazz: Claude Thornhill," *New Yorker*, April 18, 1988, 122.
12. Ian Crosbie, "Claude Thornhill," *Coda*, October 1975, 2.
13. "Profiling the Players: Claude Thornhill and his Orchestra," *DownBeat*, September 15, 1942, 19.
14. Shaw, *Trouble with Cinderella*, 148.
15. "Judges Select Air Song Title," *Indianapolis Star*, August 29, 1929, 9.
16. Shaw, *Trouble with Cinderella*, 131.
17. Vladimir Simosko, *Artie Shaw: A Musical Biography and Discography* (London: Rowman and Littlefield, 2000), 23.
18. Shaw, *Trouble with Cinderella*, 141.
19. Shaw, *Trouble with Cinderella*, 210.

# Notes for Chapter 3

1. Shaw, *Trouble with Cinderella*, 166.
2. "Car Kills Man, Pair Held," *New York Times*, October 16, 1930, 24.
3. "Car Kills Man."
4. "Couple Held in Hit-and-Run Death of L.I. Victim," *Brooklyn Daily Eagle*, October 16, 1930, 3.
5. "Kills This Iron Shark," *Baltimore Sun*, April 17, 1918, 4.
6. Shaw, *Trouble with Cinderella*, 215.
7. Gene Lees, "The Anchorite," *Jazzletter*, June 2004, 3.
8. Kristine McKenna, "Altered Chords," *LA Weekly*, November 10, 1999.

9.  Jonathan Shaw, *Scab Vendor: Confessions of a Tattoo Artist* (Nashville: Turner Publishing, 2017), 221.

10.  Shaw, *Trouble with Cinderella*, 215.

11.  Ashtabula County, Ohio marriage records, accessed October 3, 2024, https://www.ancestry.com/discoveryui-content/view/903090562:61378.

12.  Shaw, *Trouble with Cinderella*, 216.

13.  Nolan, *Artie Shaw*, 33.

14.  Artie Shaw, "Snow White in Harlem, 1930," in *The Best of Intentions and Other Stories* (Santa Barbara: John Daniel, 1989), 9.

15.  Jacob Womack, *Luckey Roberts, Willie "the Lion" Smith, Fats Waller and James P. Johnson: An Analysis of Historical, Cultural and Performance Aspects of Stride Piano from 1910 to 1940* (doctor of musical arts diss., West Virginia University, 2013), 48.

16.  Quoted in Nolan, *Artie Shaw*, 35.

17.  Simosko, *Artie Shaw*, 39.

18.  George Simon, "Dance Band Reviews," *Metronome*, October 1936, 22.

19.  Artie Shaw, interview by Rod Soar, *Jazz Journal International*, November 1987.

20.  Shaw, *Trouble with Cinderella*, 305.

21.  Shaw, *Trouble with Cinderella*, 333.

22.  Miles Kastendieck, "Music of the Day," *Brooklyn Daily Eagle*, January 17, 1938, 3.

23.  Nolan, *Artie Shaw*, 74.

24.  Reinhard Scheer-Hennings and Dennis M. Spragg, *Artie Shaw, 1938–1939*, Glenn Miller Collections (Boulder: University of Colorado American Music Research Center, 2022), 5, https://www.dennismspragg.com/wp-content/uploads/2022/05/Artie-Shaw-1938-1939.pdf.

25.  Shaw, interview by Gross.

26.  Bernie Woods, "Battle of the Killer Dillers in N'wrk All This Week: Goodman vs. Shaw," *Variety*, February 22, 1939, 1.

27.  *Variety*, March 8, 1939.

28.  Karl Krug, "Pittsburgh by Night," *Pittsburgh Sun-Telegraph*, April 19, 1939, 29.

29.  David W. Stowe, *Swing Changes: Big-Band Jazz in New Deal America* (Cambridge, MA: Harvard University Press, 1994), 6.

30.  Scheer-Hennings and Spragg, *Artie Shaw*, 165.

31.  "Artie Shaw's Own Exposure of the Amazing American Dance Music Business," *Melody Maker*, January 13, 1940, 2.

32.  Nolan, *Artie Shaw*, 124.

33. Dave Dexter Jr., "Artie Shaw Fed Up with the Music Racket," *DownBeat*, October 15, 1939, 1.

34. "Admen Chide Artie Shaw's Behavior," *Variety*, October 4, 1939, 4.

35. "Artie Shaw's Walkout Irks Beach Throng," *Buffalo Courier Express*, September 5, 1939, 22.

36. "Loves Morons," *Variety*, October 25, 1939, 1.

37. Schuller, *Swing Era*, 702.

38. Cahn, *I Should Care*, 252.

39. B. R. Crisler, "News and Comment in a Quiet Week," *New York Times*, November 26, 1939, 134.

# Notes for Chapter 4

1. USS Arizona Mall Memorial, *Facebook*, December 1, 2021, https:// www.facebook.com/USSArizonaMallMemorial/posts/wendell-ray-hurley-was-born-sept-12-1919-at-north-grove-indiana-his-father-raymo/1825705870958557/.

2. Patrick Michael Jones, "A History of the Armed Forces School of Music" (PhD diss., Pennsylvania State University, 1992), 181.

3. "Four Navy Groups to Vie Tonight in Battle of Bands," *Honolulu Star-Bulletin*, October 11, 1941, 7.

4. Lew Shaw, "The Saga of Navy Band 22," *Syncopated Times*, October 27, 2023, https://syncopatedtimes.com/the-saga-of-navy-band-22/.

5. "Battling Bandsmen," *All Hands*, August 1969, 12

6. "Battling Bandsmen," 13.

7. Jones, "History of the Armed Forces School of Music," 87.

8. "Frank Emond," interview, *American Veterans Center*, June 22, 2018, https://www.americanveteranscenter.org/2018/06/frank-emond/.

9. Terrence S. Tickle, "Saxie Dowell: Saxophonist, Bandleader, War Hero," *Southern Culture*, Fall 2010, 147.

10. "Musicians Heroes of Franklin Saga," *DownBeat*, June 1, 1945, 1.

11. "Battling Bandsmen," 12.

12. "150 Bands to Play for Shows at Camps," *Buffalo News*, December 24, 1941, 8.

13. "Says We Need 5 CT Song," *New York Times*, January 29, 1942, 21.

14. "With Truesdell in Hollywood," *Cincinnati Enquirer*, December 9, 1941, 17.

15. Kathleen E. R. Smith, *God Bless America: Tin Pan Alley Goes to War* (Lexington: University Press of Kentucky, 2003), 28.

16. Robert Leckie, *A Helmet for My Pillow* (New York: Random House, 1957), 22.
17. *Time*, May 11, 1942.
18. Annegret Fauser, *Sounds of War: Music in the United States during World War II* (Oxford: Oxford University Press, 2013), 103.
19. Joint Army/Navy Subcommittee on Music, March 14, 1942, Music Division, Joint Army and Navy Committee on Welfare, Subcommittee on Music (hereafter cited as "Music Division"), Library of Congress, Washington, DC.
20. "First Division Band in on Three Invasions," *DownBeat*, April 15, 1945, 2.

# Notes for Chapter 5

1. "Artie Shaw's Testimony before the House Un-American Activities Committee," May 4, 1953, *Swing and Beyond*, https://swingandbeyond. com/wp-content/uploads/2020/05/Shaw-testimony.pdf.
2. "6,000 Rug-cutters See New Year in Dance at Hall," *Cleveland Plain Dealer*, January 1, 1942, 13.
3. "Artie Shaw Slowdown," *Variety*, January 21, 1942, 37.
4. "Artie Shaw Ill," *Greenville* (SC) *News*, January 21, 1942, 2.
5. Nolan, *Artie Shaw*, 21.
6. "Shaw into Hospital; May Be Drafted When He Leaves," *DownBeat*, February 1, 1942, 1.
7. "Artie Shaw's Contract is Peddled for 15 G's!," *DownBeat*, February 15, 1942, 1.
8. Ward and Burns, *Jazz*, 296.
9. Peter J. Levinson, *Tommy Dorsey: Livin' in a Great Big Way* (Boston: Da Capo Press, 2005), 160.
10. "This Is No Fancy Pants Job, Says Artie Shaw," *DownBeat*, May 15, 1942, 2.
11. "Artie Shaw Returns Via Morris Agency," *Variety*, February 4, 1942, 37.
12. "The Theater: Extra Army Rations," *Time*, August 6, 1945.
13. "Extra Army Rations."
14. "Composer's Daughter Weds Band Leader," *New York Daily News*, March 4, 1942, 196.
15. *Variety*, April 8, 1942.
16. "Past Presidents," *American Bandmasters Association*, accessed September 10, 2024, http://www.americanbandmasters.org/past-presidents/.

17. Howard C. Bronson, "Wartime Music Services," *Music Educators Journal* 29, no. 1 (Sept.–Oct. 1942): 56.

18. Joint Army/Navy Subcommittee on Music, Minutes, Music Division, September 1942, Library of Congress.

19. A Freedom of Information Act request for an FBI file on Artie Shaw produced only partial results.

20. *Music and Rhythm*, June 1942.

21. "Lana Turner and Artie Shaw Together," *Philadelphia Inquirer*, September 26, 1940, 15.

22. "Shaw, O. Tucker Will Join Navy, Others Called," *DownBeat*, May 15, 1942, 1.

23. "Say Aroff Rushed Martin's Papers," *New York Times*, August 1, 1942, 9.

24. Kathleen Ellen Rahtz Smith, "Goodbye Mama, I'm off to Yokohama: The Office of War Information and Tin Pan Alley in World War II" (PhD diss., Louisiana State University and Agricultural and Mechanical College, 1996), 10.

25. Louis Sobel, "New York Broadway Cavalcade," *Santa Rosa* (CA) *Press-Democrat*, June 22, 1942, 12.

26. Walter H. Waggoner, "Andrew D. Weinberger, Lawyer," *New York Times*, May 16, 1984, D-26.

27. Max Kaminsky, *My Life in Jazz* (Boston: Da Capo Press, 1981), 152.

28. "Army Enlistments Hit Record; 1,600 in One Day," *New York Herald Tribune*, December 16, 1941, 4.

29. "53 Ratings Open to Sound Sailors," *Mamaroneck* (NY) *Daily Times*, April 9, 1942, 10.

30. "Men in Service Give Own Show at Metropolitan," *New York Herald Tribune*, April 28, 1942, 17.

31. "Men in Service," 17.

32. Robert Taylor, "Middle-Aged Man without a Horn," *New Yorker*, May 11, 1962, 86.

33. "Artie Shaw's New Hobby," *Radio and Television Mirror*, July 1942, 61.

## Notes for Chapter 6

1. Report of physical examination, June 19, 1942, Shaw medical file.

2. Lenny Bruce, *How to Talk Dirty and Influence People* (Chicago: Playboy Press, 1963), 20.

3. *Stars and Stripes*, July 25, 1942.

4. Shaw, interview with Gross.

5.  Mike Daniels, "Musician of the Year," *Metronome*, January 1944, 18.

6.  *Corpus Christi Caller-Times*, June 17, 1945, C-2.

7.  Robert Lewis Taylor, "Middle-Aged Man without a Horn," *New Yorker*, May 11, 1962, 86.

8.  Joint Army/Navy Subcommittee on Music, Feb. 27, 1942.

9.  Report of medical survey, January 17, 1944, Shaw medical file.

10.  Medical history, Lt. R. Kelley, October 2, 1942, Shaw medical file.

11.  Medical history, H. S. Bray, October 2, 1942, Shaw medical file.

12.  Artie Shaw file, Harold Kaye Folder, Institute of Jazz Studies.

13.  John Truesdell, "In Hollywood," *Des Moines Register*, November 5, 1942, 12.

14.  Louella Parsons, "Lana Turner Will Play Role of Dizzy Movie Star in Musical," *Sacramento Bee*, November 21, 1942, 17.

15.  "Forrestal Named a Roosevelt Aide," *New York Times*, June 23, 1940, 16.

16.  Shaw, interview with Gross.

17.  "Appointments and Phone Calls," January 1–June 30, 1942; series 1, subseries 1B, James V. Forrestal Papers, Department of Special Collections, Princeton University Library, Princeton, NJ.

18.  Robert Greenleigh Albion and Robert Howe Connery, *Forrestal and the Navy* (New York: Columbia University Press, 1962), 34.

19.  Shaw, interview with Talbot.

20.  Shaw, interview with Talbot.

21.  Albion and Connery, *Forrestal and the Navy*, 16.

22.  Albion and Connery, *Forrestal and the Navy*, 16.

23.  Taylor, "Middle-Aged Man without a Horn," 86.

24.  Hedda Hopper, "Hedda Hopper's Looking at Hollywood," *Harrisburg (PA) Telegraph*, November 7, 1942, 10.

## Notes for Chapter 7

1.  Whitney Balliett, "Dave Tough," in *American Musicians: 56 Portraits in Jazz* (New York: Oxford University Press, 1986), 126.

2.  Balliett, "Jazz: Little Davy Tough," *New Yorker*, November 18, 1985, 160.

3.  Kenneth Rexroth, *Kenneth Rexroth: An Autobiographical Novel* (New York: Doubleday, 1966), 163.

4.  "Swing Stuff," *Variety*, February 26, 1936, 57.

5.  Harold S. Kaye, "Dave Tough with the New Yorkers in Europe, 1927–1929," undated manuscript, 53, Harold S. Kaye Collection.

6.  Burt Korall, "Jazz Drumming," in Kirchner, *Oxford Companion to Jazz*, 687.

7.  Kaye, "Dave Tough with the New Yorkers in Europe," 6.

8.  Kaminsky, *My Life in Jazz*, 161.

9.  Leonard Feather, "The Dave Tough Story," *DownBeat*, July 1, 1953, 21.

10. Kaye, "Dave Tough with the Artie Shaw Navy Band in World War II," in *Storyville, 2000–2001*, edited by Laurie Wright (Chigwell, Essex, England: L. Wright, 2001), 27.

11. Balliett, "Little Davy Tough," 123.

12. Steven A. Cerra, "Dave Tough: 1908–1948," *Jazz Profiles*, May 8, 2009, https://jazzprofiles.blogspot.com/2009/05/davy-tough-1908-1948.html.

13. Simosko, *Artie Shaw*, 194.

14. Shaw, *Trouble with Cinderella*, 148.

15. Whitney Balliett, "Bright Unison Clarinets," in *American Musicians II: Seventy-One Portraits in Jazz* (Jackson: University Press of Mississippi, 1986), 475.

16. Balliett, "Bright Unison Clarinets," 474.

17. Leo Walker, *The Big Band Almanac* (New York City: Da Capo Press, 1989), 318.

18. Stowe, *Swing Changes*, 94.

19. Christopher Popa, "Claude Thornhill: 'The Sound Hung Like a Cloud,'" *Big Band Library*, December 2006, http://www.bigbandlibrary.com/claudethornhill.html.

20. "Thornhill's New Troupe Good Hotel Prospects," *Metronome*, February 1940, 12.

21. "New War Tune on Air Again," *Los Angeles Times*, March 24, 1942, 38.

22. Popa, "Claude Thornhill."

23. *Music and Rhythm*, June 1942.

24. "Thornhill Wants Action; Into Navy," *DownBeat*, October 12, 1942, 1.

25. "Salary Takes a Tail Spin But Musician Is Happy," *Honolulu Star-Bulletin*, January 23, 1943, 1.

26. John Skelton, "Navy Hot," *Metronome*, March 1945, 16.

27. Kaminsky, *My Life in Jazz*, 73.

28. Leonard Feather, "Maxie Speaks Up," *Metronome*, September 1944, 14.

29. Kaminsky, *My Life in Jazz*, 13.

30. Kaminsky, *My Life in Jazz*, 112.

31. Kaminsky, *My Life in Jazz*, 113.

32. "Musician 2/C," *New Yorker*, 14.

33. Kaminsky, *My Life in Jazz*, 158.

34. Kaminsky, *My Life in Jazz*, 158.

35. George T. Simon, "Kenton Blames Momism for Sugary Jazz," *Minne-apolis Sunday Tribune*, October 22, 1961, 75.
36. "Profiling the Players," *DownBeat*, October 1, 1942, 14.
37. "Wife Divorces Band Leader Sam Donahue," *Los Angeles Times*, December 23, 1954, 2.
38. "Sam Donahue," *DownBeat*, October 15, 1942, 9.
39. Warren Vache, "Best on the Bandstand," *Mississippi Rag*, February 1989, 1.
40. John Best, oral history interview by Monk Rowe, February 15, 1998, *Fillius Jazz Archive at Hamilton College*, https://www.youtube.com/watch?v=HQWk99bSpWQ.
41. Vache, "Best on the Bandstand," 3.
42. Vache, "Best on the Bandstand," 3.
43. Vache, "Best on the Bandstand," 4.
44. Best, oral history interview by Rowe.
45. Harold S. Kaye, "The Great 'Goz': The Conrad Gozzo Story," pt. 5, *IAJRC Journal* 26, no. 2 (Spring 1993), 54.
46. Kaye, "Great 'Goz,'" pt. 1, *IAJRC Journal* 25, no 2 (Spring 1992): 2.
47. Kaye, "Great 'Goz,'" pt. 1, p. 2.
48. "Bandsman Going Up," *Hartford Courant*, February 15, 1942, 40.

## Notes for Chapter 8

1. "Profiling the Players," *DownBeat*, December 1, 1943, 15.
2. Kaye, "Dave Tough," 49.
3. "Charles Wade," *Santa Fe New Mexican*, November 23, 1988, 4.
4. Jeanne May, "Mack Pitt: Veteran Musician, Teacher," *Detroit Free Press*, March 6, 2002, B-5.
5. "LaPolla Salute to Big Bands Slated," *Desert Sun* (Palm Springs, CA), February 23, 1985, F-12.
6. Kaye, "Dave Tough," 20.
7. "Wilson Leetch," *Moline* (IL) *Dispatch*, July 16, 2006, 4.
8. "Profiling the Players," *DownBeat*, December 1, 1943, 15.
9. *Ogden* (UT) *Standard-Examiner*, October 4, 1942.
10. "Profiling the Players," *DownBeat*, October 1, 1942, 14.
11. Richard Vacca, "Tak Takvorian Part 1: Navy Trombonist," Richard Vacca.com, January 26, 2020, https://www.richardvacca.com/tak-takvorian-part-1-navy-trombonist/.
12. *Variety*, December 9, 1942.
13. "Profiling the Players, *DownBeat*, September 15, 1942, 19.

14. Leslie Gerber, "Barney Spieler, The Falstaffian Bassist," LeslieGerber. net, May 2012, http://www.lesliegerber.net/2012/05/barney-spieler-the-falstaffian-bassist/.

15. Kaye, "Dave Tough," 22.

16. Kaye, "Dave Tough," 19.

17. Kaye, "Dave Tough," 19.

18. Kaye, "Dave Tough," 84.

19. Kaye, "Dave Tough," 30.

20. "Miller Band Breaks Entirely," *DownBeat*, October 1, 1942, 1.

21. Schuller, *Swing Era*, 667.

22. Dennis M. Spragg, *Glenn Miller Declassified* (Lincoln: Potomac Books, an imprint of the University of Nebraska Press, 2017).

23. "Men All Scatter as Miller Joins," *DownBeat*, October 1, 1942, 4.

24. "Batoneers Rate 4-F After Exam," *DownBeat*, March 1, 1944, 1.

25. Kaye, "Dave Tough," 29.

26. Vache, "Best on the Bandstand," *Mississippi Rag*, February 1989, 4.

27. Kaminsky, *My Life in Jazz*, 161.

28. "Artie Shaw Ork Off for Secret Destination," *DownBeat*, December 15, 1942, 2.

29. Kaye, "Dave Tough," 33.

## Notes for Chapter 9

1. "Banddom Bits," *Buffalo News*, December 19, 1942, 60.

2. "Marine Patrols Mop Up in Jungle Fighting," *Atlanta Constitution*, December 3, 1942, 19

3. "Oh, Minnie!," *DownBeat*, December 1, 1942, 1.

4. Dick Raichelson, "Artie Shaw & His Orchestra, Part 5: Dr. Ian Crosbie's Sidemen Correspondence," *IAJRC Journal* 49, no. 2 (Summer 2016): 69.

5. Shaw, *Trouble with Cinderella*, 339.

6. Shaw, *Trouble with Cinderella*, 304.

7. Michael P. Zirpolo, "Shavian Matters Revisited," *IAJRC Journal* 43, no. 4 (December 2010): 39.

8. *Our Navy*, February 1, 1943.

9. *Our Navy*, February 1, 1943.

10. "Artie Shaw will Lead Band Tonight," *San Francisco Examiner*, December 15, 1942, 18.

11. Vache, "Best on the Bandstand," *Mississippi Rag*, February 1989, 4.

12. Harold S. Kaye, "Jazz in Hawaii, 1935–1941," 5.

13. "Allies Must Kill Japs to Win, Halsey Says," *Honolulu Advertiser*, December 25, 1942, 4.

14. "Allies Must Kill Japs to Win, Halsey Says."

15. *Pearl Harbor Bulletin* 2, no. 11 (1943).

16. Bob Dye, ed., *Hawaii Chronicles III: World War Two in Hawaii, from the pages of* Paradise of the Pacific (Honolulu: University of Hawai'i Press, 2000), 41.

17. Shaw, interview with Talbot.

18. Kaye, "Dave Tough," 39.

19. Kaye, "Dave Tough," 40.

20. Betty MacDonald, "Crossroads Comment," *Honolulu Star-Bulletin*, January 12, 1943, 6.

21. Kaye, "Dave Tough," 40.

22. Shaw, interview with Talbot.


## Notes for Chapter 10


1. Charles M. Hatcher, "Playtime for Jack Tar," *Honolulu Star-Bulletin*, December 6, 1941, 45.

2. Joe James Custer, "Navy Spirit and Morale are of Highest Order," *Hilo* (HI) *Tribune-Herald*, January 13, 1942, 4.

3. "You'll Get the Best Ice Cream at The Breakers," *Honolulu Star-Advertiser*, December 2, 1942, 3.

4. Betty MacDonald, "4,000 Turn Out to Hear Artie and his Band," *Honolulu Star-Bulletin*, January 11, 1943, 2.

5. "High Drama and Comedy of the OSS Gaily Told in 'Undercover Girl,'" *Honolulu Star-Bulletin*, October 27, 1947, 2.

6. Betty MacDonald, "Sam's Desire Is to Blow Saxophone in Tokyo," *Honolulu Star-Bulletin*, February 11, 1943, 3.

7. Helen Berkey, "Service Sketches," *Honolulu Star-Bulletin*, March 27, 1943, 16.

8. "Artie Shaw Hopes to Lead Parade to Hirohito's Palace," *Atlanta Journal*, January 23, 1943, 21.

9. Management Planning and Review Department, *Command History Pearl Harbor Navy Shipyard*, July 1959, accessed September 23, 2024, https://issuu.com/pearlharbornavalshipyard/docs/nsy_pearl_harbor__command_history__.

10. "Shaw Sends 'Em," *Pearl Harbor Bulletin*, January 1943, 3.

11. "Shaw Sends 'Em."

12. "More Calls for Artie Shaw," *Honolulu Star-Bulletin*, January 26, 1943, 4.

13. "US Naval Base, Pearl Harbor, Operations Building, Ford Island, Enterprise Street near Intrepid Boulevard, Pearl City, Honolulu County, HI," photo collection, Historic American Buildings Survey, Library of Congress, https://www.loc.gov/item/hi0229/.

14. Nolan, *Artie Shaw*, 108.

15. Kaye, "Great 'Goz,'" pt. 3, *IAJRC Journal* 25, no. 4 (Fall 1992): 78.

16. Kaye, "Dave Tough," 49.

17. Charles Hatcher, "Recreational Development at Pearl Harbor," *US Naval Institute Proceedings* 69, no. 488 (October 1943): 1348.

18. "Workers at PH Win New Honors," *Honolulu Star-Bulletin*, April 19, 1943, 6.

19. "Communique," *Metronome*, July 1943, 34.

20. "Shaw Is Hoping to Play Music in Jap Palace," *Enid* (OK) *Daily Eagle*, January 23, 1943.

21. "First Birthday of The Breakers Observed Today," *Hawaii Star-Bulletin*, December 2, 1943, 12.

22. Dye, *Hawaii Chronicles III*, 112.

23. "Kokinski Reports on Honolulu Leave," *Hopewell* (VA) *News*, March 12, 1943, 5.

24. "Georgia Camp Has Mood For, But No Band," *DownBeat*, April 1, 1943, 20.

25. Shaw, interview with Talbot.

26. "USO Hospitality Notes for Nurses," *Honolulu Star-Bulletin*, March 29, 1943, 12.

27. Kaye, "Dave Tough," 53.

28. Shaw, interview with Talbot.

29. Kaminsky, *My Life in Jazz*, 163.

30. Kaye, "Great 'Goz,'" pt. 3, p. 79.

31. Kaye, "Dave Tough," 50.

32. Kaminsky, *My Life in Jazz*, 164.

33. Kristine McKenna, "Altered Chords," *LA Weekly*, November 10, 1999.

34. Ward and Burns, *Jazz*, 250.

35. Balliett, "Little Davy Tough," 60.

36. Balliett, "Little Davy Tough," 60.

37. Kaye, "Dave Tough," 56.

38. Kaye, "Dave Tough," 51.

39. Chris Wray, *The Big Bands Go to War* (London: Mainstream, 1991), 266.

40. Brigitte Berman, dir., *Artie Shaw: Time Is All You've Got* (Canada: Bridge Film Productions, 1985).

# Notes for Chapter 11


1. Claude Thornhill personnel file, NPRC (hereafter cited as "Thornhill personnel file").
2. "Salary Takes a Tail Spin But Musician Is Happy," *Honolulu Star-Bulletin*, January 23, 1943, 1.
3. Ian Crosbie, "Claude Thornhill," *Coda*, October 1975, 8.
4. Nolan, *Artie Shaw*, 177.
5. Whitney Balliett, "Claude Thornhill," *New Yorker*, April 18, 1988, 122.
6. Shaw, *Trouble with Cinderella*, 150.
7. "War Workers' Sunset Dance Huge Success," *Banner* (Honolulu), May 28, 1943, 1.
8. Morrison, *Struggle for Guadalcanal*, 133.
9. Fats Baker, "Gentleman of Jazz," in *Selections from the Gutter: Jazz Portraits from the Jazz Record*, ed. Art Hodes and Chadwick Hansen (Berkeley: University of California Press, 1977), 192.
10. Baker, "Gentleman of Jazz," 192.
11. Deck logs, USS *North Carolina*, May 9–17, 1943, Record Group 24, Box 6688, National Archives at College Park, MD (hereafter cited as NACP).
12. Artie Shaw, "A Nice Little Post-War Business," in *Best of Intentions*, 31.
13. Shaw, "Nice Little Post-War Business," 29.
14. Kaminsky, *My Life in Jazz*, 168.
15. Deb Mulvey, Clancy Strock, and Mike Beno, eds., *We Pulled Together— and Won!* (Greendale, WI: Reminisce Books, 1993), 133.
16. "Swingin' and Refuelin' in the South Pacific," *Wall Street Journal*, March 7, 2003.
17. Stowe, *Swing Changes*, 106.
18. Shaw, interview with Talbot.
19. Shaw, interview with Talbot.
20. Simosko, *Artie Shaw*, 100.
21. Gene E. Salecker, "Cultural Clash in New Caledonia," *Warfare History Network*, February 2018, https://warfarehistorynetwork.com/article/cultural-clash-in-new-caledonia/.
22. Morrison, *Struggle for Guadalcanal*, 186.
23. Vern Haugland, "French Assail U.S. Soldiers' Caledonia Acts," *Atlanta Journal*, December 24, 1943, 19.
24. Cited in Kim Munholland, "Yankee Farewell: The Americans Leave New Caledonia, 1945," *Proceedings of the Meeting of the French Colonial Historical Society*, vol. 16 (1992): 186.

25. Joseph Driscoll, "Jeeps Awaken Sleepy Natives in Picturesque Caledonia," *Buffalo Evening News*, April 14, 1943, 19.

26. Special Service Division, Services of Supply, United States Army, *Pocket Guide to New Caledonia* (Washington, DC: War and Navy Departments, 1944), 9

27. Haugland, "French Assail U.S. Soldiers," 19.

28. *Southern Economist*, March 21, 1943.

29. Kaye, "Dave Tough," 62.

30. Morrison, *Struggle for Guadalcanal*, 186.

31. "Tall Free French Girls Impress Iowa Sailor," *Cedar Rapids Gazette*, May 5, 1943, 9.

32. Vern Haugland, "Misconduct Charged to American Troops," *Charlotte Observer*, December 24, 1943, 3.

33. Special Service Division, US Army, *Pocket Guide to New Caledonia*, 17.

34. Kaminsky, *My Life in Jazz*, 169.

35. "Armed Services Urge Recreation as Morale Builder," *Cincinnati Post*, September 29, 1942, 19.

36. B. J. Richards, ed., *Sara: The Story of the USS Saratoga*, 14, at https://www.navysite.de/cruisebooks/cv3-45/014.htm.

37. "Armed Services Urge Recreation as Morale Builder," *Cincinnati Post*, September 29, 1942, 19.

38. Deck logs, USS *Saratoga*, May 17–18, 1943, Record Group 24, Box 8555, NACP.

39. War Diary, USS *Saratoga*, May 1–31, 1943, Record Group 38, NACP.

40. Kaminsky, *My Life in Jazz*, 170.

41. Berman, *Time Is All You've Got*.

42. Spragg, *Glenn Miller Declassified*, 43.

43. Taylor, "Middle-aged Man without a Horn," 91.

44. Department of the Navy, *Building the Navy's Bases in World War II: History of the Bureau of Yards and Docks and Civil Engineering Corps, 1940–46*, (Washington, DC: Government Printing Office, 1947), https://www.ibiblio.org/hyperwar/USN/Building_Bases/bases-24.html.

45. Kramer J. Rohfleisch, "The Thirteenth Air Force," in *The Army Air Forces in World War II*, vol. 4, *The Pacific: Guadalcanal to Saipan, August 1942 to July 1944*, ed. W. P. Craven and J. L. Cate (Chicago: University of Chicago Press, 1951), 78, https://www.ibiblio.org/hyperwar/AAF/IV/AAF-IV-3.html.

46. Kaye, "Dave Tough," 63.

47. "Whitney (AD-4)," *Naval History and Heritage Command*, accessed October 5, 2024, https://www.history.navy.mil/research/histories/ship-histories/danfs/w/whitney.html.

48. "*San Juan* II (CL-54), *Naval History and Heritage Command*, accessed October 5, 2024, https://www.history.navy.mil/research/histories/ship-histories/danfs/s/san-juan-ii.html.

49. "USS *San Diego* (CL-53)," *Naval History and Heritage Command*, accessed October 5, 2024, https://www.history.navy.mil/browse-by-topic/ships/modern-ships/uss-san-diego.html.

50. "Oral History of Charles T. Henry," Library of Congress American Folklife Center, Veteran's History Project, accessed October 5, 2024, https://memory.loc.gov/diglib/vhp/story/loc.natlib.afc2001001.21001/.

51. Kaye, "Dave Tough," 65.

# Notes for Chapter 12

1. Deck log, USS *Gamble*, June 23, 1943, Record Group 24, NACP.

2. Kaye, "Dave Tough," 66.

3. *Building the Navy's Bases in World War II*, vol. 2, *History of the Bureau of Yards and Docks and Civil Engineering Corps, 1940–46* (Washington, DC: United States Government Printing Office, 1947), 205, https://www.ibiblio.org/hyperwar/USN/Building_Bases/bases-24.html.

4. "Sailor Describes Experiences at Sea," *Vermont Standard* (Woodstock), October 28, 1943, 7.

5. Lena Gelott, "Veteran's Testimony: Lena R. Gelott," *WW2 Medical Research Centre*, excerpted from Gelott, "World War II Memories South Pacific" pamphlet, 2002, https://www.med-dept.com/veterans-testimonies/veterans-testimony-lena-r-gelott/.

6. "Ravings at Reveille," *DownBeat*, July 15, 1943, 18.

7. "*Preble* IV (Destroyer No. 35)," *Naval History and Heritage Command*, accessed October 14, 2024, https://www.history.navy.mil/research/histories/ship-histories/danfs/p/preble-iv.html.

8. James Michener, *Tales of the South Pacific* (New York: Random House, 1947), 11.

9. Lamont Lindstrom, "The Vanuatu Labor Corps Experience," chap. 5 in *The Pacific Theater: Island Representations of World War II*, ed. Geoffrey M. White and Lamont Lindstrom (Honolulu: University of Hawaii Press, 1989), https://scholarspace.manoa.Hawaii.edu/bitstream/10125/15553/1/OP36-47-57.pdf.

10. B. J. McQuaid, "Initiative Ours, Knox Says," *St. Louis Globe-Democrat*, February 1, 1943, 1.

11. Taylor, "Middle-Aged Man without a Horn," 91.

12. Kaminsky, *My Life in Jazz*, 172.

13. Leonard Lyons, "The Lyons Den," *Montgomery* (AL) *Advertiser*, September 30, 1943, 4.

14. Peg McCartney, "Swing King Artie Shaw Here to Play for Troops," *Australian Women's Weekly*, October 16, 1943, 9.

15. War Diary, Marine Fighter Squadron 122, July 3, 1943, Marine Corps Archives, Quantico, VA.

16. Jim Lucas, "Artie Shaw Can Still Swing It," *Leatherneck*, October 1943, 63.

17. *Billboard*, June 5, 1943.

18. "Ravings at Reveille," *DownBeat*, August 15, 1943, 13.

19. "Jim G. Lucas, a Pulitzer Prize Winner for Korean War Coverage, Dies," *New York Times*, July 22, 1970, 40.

# Notes for Chapter 13

1. Mary Ellen Condon-Rall and Albert E. Cowdrey, *The Medical Department: Medical Service in the War against Japan*, (Washington, DC: Center of Military History, 1998) 73.

2. Condon-Rall and Cowdrey, *Medical Department*, 117.

3. Roy A. Burgess, ed., *63rd Naval Construction Battalion Cruise Book* (New York: Robert W. Kelly Publishing, n.d.), 59, https://www.history.navy.mil/content/dam/museums/Seabee/Cruisebooks/wwiicruisebooks/ncb-cruisebooks/63rd%20%20NCB.pdf.

4. Burgess, *63rd Naval Construction Battalion Cruise Book*, 14.

5. Davis B. Webb, ed., *Sea Foam: 61st Naval Construction Battalion Cruise Book* (Baton Rouge, LA: Army & Navy Pictorial Publishers, 1945), https://www.history.navy.mil/content/dam/museums/Seabee/Cruisebooks/wwiicruisebooks/ncb-cruisebooks/61st%20NCB%201942-1944.pdf.

6. TBF Operations Guadalcanal, Intelligence Report, July 25, 1943, Record Group 137, Box 10, NACP.

7. Kaye, "Great 'Goz,'" pt. 3, 81.

8. Burgess, *63rd Naval Construction Battalion Cruise Book*, 15.

9. Morrison, *Struggle for Guadalcanal*, 68.

10. Mark Jordan, ed., *Saga of the Sixth: 6th Naval Construction Battalion Cruisebook*, https://www.history.navy.mil/content/dam/museums/Seabee/Cruisebooks/wwiicruisebooks/ncb-cruisebooks/6%20%20NCB%201942-45.pdf.

11. "Local Man in Band on Guadalcanal," *Burlington* (VT) *Daily News*, June 16, 1943, 7.

12. Webb, *Sea Foam*, 14.

13. Kaye, "Dave Tough," 71.

14. McCartney, "Swing King Artie Shaw Here to Play for Troops," *Australian Women's Weekly*, October 16, 1943, 9.

15. Burgess, *63rd Naval Construction Battalion Cruise Book*, 64.

16. Leckie, *Helmet for My Pillow*, 51.

17. Leckie, *Helmet for My Pillow*, 12.

18. War Diary, Marine Fighter Squadron VMF 221, July 12, 1943, Box 532, Folder 6210, Marine Corps Archives.

19. Burgess, *63rd Naval Construction Battalion Cruise Book*, 16.

20. Webb, *Sea Foam*, 13.

21. War Diary, VMF 221, July 12, 1943, Marine Corps Archives.

22. Lowell Limpus, "Night Fighter School Dooms Nazi, Jap Pilots," *New York Daily News*, September 19, 1943, M-3.

23. Peg McCartney, "Swing King Artie Shaw Here to Play for Troops," *Australian Women's Weekly*, October 16, 1943, 9.

24. Kaminsky, *My Life in Jazz*, 174.

25. Bernie Woods, "Artie Shaw's Naval Band Back in U.S.," *Variety*, December 8, 1943, 35.

26. Morrison, *Struggle for Guadalcanal*, 181.

27. Condon-Rall and Rowley, *Medical Department*, 125.

28. Kaminsky, *My Life in Jazz*, 173.

29. "D.C. Man Says South Pacific Strains Men to the Limit," *Washington Evening Star*, October 8, 1943, B-4.

30. Woods, "Artie Shaw's Naval Band Back in U.S.," 36.

31. Charles Davis Jr., "Benefit to Aid Widow of Famous Trumpeter," *Los Angeles Times*, November 15, 1964, F-1.


## Notes for Chapter 14


1. Best, oral history interview with Rowe.

2. Best, oral history interview with Rowe.

3. Sprague, *Glenn Miller Declassified*, 52.

4. "Amazing Saga of Shaw Band in War Area," *DownBeat*, December 15, 1943, 29.

5. Mike Daniels, "Musician of the Year," *Metronome*, January 1944, 20.

6. Leonard Lyons, "The Lyon's Den," *Montgomery Advertiser*, October 9, 1943, 4.

7. Kaye, "Great 'Goz,'" pt. 3, 81.

8. Kaminsky, *My Life in Jazz*, 174.

9. "Otto Keith Williams Oral History," November 21, 2002, National Museum of the Pacific War / Admiral Nimitz Foundation, University of North Texas Libraries, *Portal to Texas History*, https://texashistory.unt.edu/ark:/67531/metapth1604270/.

10. Morrison, *Struggle for Guadalcanal*, 124.

11. Kaye, "Dave Tough," 70.

12. Nolan, *Artie Shaw*, 181.

13. Joseph LaLonde, diary entry, July 17, 1943, courtesy of Seth Washburne.

14. Kaminsky, *My Life in Jazz*, 175.

15. Quoted in *Thirsty Thirteenth Newsletter*, June 2020, 9, accessed October 11, 2024, https://thirsty13th.com/Images/Thirsty13thUpdate202006.pdf.

16. John Henry, "Artie Shaw, Band Visit Guadalcanal," *Pasadena* (CA) *Post*, August 31, 1943, 7

17. Henry, "Artie Shaw, Band Visit Guadalcanal," 7.

## Notes for Chapter 15

1. Kaye, "Dave Tough," 76.

2. Kaye, "Dave Tough," 76.

3. Kaye, "Dave Tough," 77.

4. Shaw, *Trouble with Cinderella*, 373.

5. Shaw, *Trouble with Cinderella*, 373.

6. "Report of Action," SS *Mormacport*, July 30, 1943, Records of the Office of Chief of Naval Operations, Armed Guard Files, Record Group 48, Box 481, NACP.

7. Mike Daniels, "Musician of the Year," *Metronome*, January 1944, 18.

8. Kaye, "Great 'Goz,'" pt. 3, 82.

9. "US Forces in New Zealand: Arrival," *New Zealand History*, updated May 10, 2021, https://nzhistory.govt.nz/war/us-forces-in-new-zealand/arrival.

10. Chris Bourke, *Blue Smoke: The Lost Dawn of New Zealand Popular Music, 1918–1964*, (Auckland: Auckland University Press, 2010), 17.

11. Ward and Burns, *Jazz*, 254.

12. Bourke, *Blue Smoke*, 20.

13. "Modern Dances Castigated by Dr. P. C. Fenwick," *Manawatu* (NZ) *Times*, August 30, 1922, 5.

14. Bourke, *Blue Smoke*, 32.

15. Bourke, *Blue Smoke*, 69.

16. Bourke, *Blue Smoke*, 67.

17. "Over the Air," *Waikato* (NZ) *Times*, August 1, 1943, 1.

18. "U.S. Army Band Says Farewell to Whangerai," *Northern Advocate* (Whangārei, NZ), November 16, 1942, 5.

19. Aleisha Ward, "American Bands in New Zealand During WW2," *NZJazz*, August 14, 2013, https://nzjazz.wordpress.com/2013/08/14/american-bands-in-new-zealand-during-ww2/.

20. Bourke, *Blue Smoke*, 125.

21. Bourke, *Blue Smoke*, 129.

22. Quoted in Aleisha Ward, "Any Rags, Any Jazz, Any Boppers Today? Jazz in New Zealand, 1920–1955" (PhD diss., University of Auckland, 2012), 207.

23. Dennis O. Huggard, "Artie Shaw in New Zealand, 1943," New Zealand Series, no. 15 (Auckland: self-published, 2007), unpaginated.

24. Shaw, *Trouble with Cinderella*, 226.

25. Nolan, *Artie Shaw*, 80.

26. Chris Bourke, "Esme Stephens," *AudioCulture*, March 25, 2014, https://www.audioculture.co.nz/profile/esme-stephens

27. Bourke, *Blue Smoke*, 129.

28. *New Zealand Observer*, August 4, 1943.

29. Sahiban Hyde, "Service of Taradale, 100-Year-Old Who Was an Army Nurse in WW II, Recognized by RSA," *Hawkes Bay Today* (Hastings, NZ), April 23, 2019.

30. Huggard, "Artie Shaw in New Zealand."

31. "Second World War Overview: Counting the Cost," *New Zealand History*, updated May 17, 2017, https://nzhistory.govt.nz/war/second-world-war/counting-the-cost.

32. Nancy M. Taylor, *The New Zealand People at War: The Home Front, Vol. 1*, Official History of New Zealand in the Second World War, 1939–45 (Wellington, NZ: V. R. Ward, Government Printer, 1989), 644, https://nzetc.victoria.ac.nz/tm/scholarly/tei-WH2-1Hom-c14.html#fn3-644.

33. Chris Bioletti, *The Yanks Are Coming: The American Invasion of New Zealand, 1942–1944* (Auckland: Random House New Zealand, 1989), 152.

34. Ward, *Any Rags, Any Jazz, Any Boppers Today?*, 189.

35.  "U.S. Dance for Furlough Men," *Auckland Star*, August 3, 1943, 4.

36.  "From the National Stations," *Wireless Weekly*, July 29, 1938, 32.

37.  "Po Atarau / Haere Ra / Now is the Hour," *New Zealand Folk Song*, accessed October 5, 2024, https://folksong.org.nz/poatarau/index.html.

# Notes for Chapter 16

1.   "Air Force Band," *Ashburton* (NZ) *Guardian*, August 27, 1943, 4.

2.   "Local and General," *Ashburton Guardian*, August 31, 1943, 2.

3.   "Swing Music," *Ashburton Guardian*, September 2, 1943, 2.

4.   "Letter to Editor: Swing Music," *Ashburton Guardian*, September 1, 1943, 2.

5.   Bourke, *Blue Smoke*, 119.

6.   Ward, *Any Rags, Any Jazz, Any Boppers?*, 129.

7.   "Ace Dance Band," *Bay of Plenty Beacon* (Whakatane, NZ), April 24, 1945, 6.

8.   Huggard, "Artie Shaw in New Zealand."

9.   Bourke, *Blue Smoke*, 130.

10.  "American Dance," *Wellington Evening Post*, August 14, 1943, 10.

11.  Huggard, "Artie Shaw in New Zealand 1943."

12.  Bourke, *Blue Smoke*, 257

13.  Ward, *Any Rags, Any Jazz, Any Boppers Today?*, 196.

14.  Huggard, "Artie Shaw in New Zealand 1943."

15.  "A Crowded House," *Wellington Evening Post*, August 16, 1943, 3.

16.  Bourke, *Blue Smoke*, 356.

17.  Bourke, *Blue Smoke*, 130.

18.  Kaye, "Dave Tough," 80.

19.  Huggard, "Artie Shaw in New Zealand 1943."

20.  "Returned Men, A Welcome Ball," *Wellington Evening Post*, August 23, 1943, 3.

21.  "City Entertains Its Fighting Men," *Dominion* (Wellington), August 23, 1943, 6.

22.  "My Day, by Eleanor Roosevelt," September 2, 1943, Eleanor Roosevelt Papers, George Washington University, Washington, DC, https://www2.gwu.edu/~erpapers/myday/displaydoc.cfm?_y=1943&_f=md056584.

23.  "Call at Dance," *New Zealand Herald* (Auckland), September 2, 1943, 2.

24.  Eleanor Roosevelt, "My Day," *Nevada State Journal*, September 3, 1943, 4.

25.  Kaye, "Dave Tough," 82.

## Notes for Chapter 17


1.  Leckie, *Helmet For My Pillow*, 73.
2.  Kaye, "Dave Tough," 82.
3.  Kaye, "Dave Tough," 82.
4.  "Soldier Charged Over City Riot," *Brisbane Telegraph*, January 12, 1943, 4.
5.  "A Brawl," *Warwick Daily News* (Australia), November 5, 1942, 5.
6.  "Benny's Band Brother," *ABC Weekly*, May 5, 1940, 23.
7.  "Swing Maestro Says; Jitterbugs are Intelligent," *Pix*, March 30, 1940, 4.
8.  Peg McCartney, "Swing King Artie Shaw Arrives to Play for Troops," *Australian Women's Weekly*, October 16, 1943, 9.
9.  "Big Queues for Swing," *Courier Mail* (Brisbane), September 10, 1943, 9.
10. "Big Queues for Swing."
11. Graeme Bell, *Australian Jazzman* (Sydney: Child & Associates, 1989), 49.
12. Bell, *Australian Jazzman*, 49.
13. Russell Davies, writer, *Artie Shaw: The Quest for Perfection* (UK: BBC, 2003), part 4.
14. Office of the Chief Engineer, General Headquarters, Army Forces Pacific, *Engineers of the Southwest Pacific: Airfield and Base Development* (Washington, DC: Government Printing Office, 1951), 22.
15. Bradley L. Garrett et al., "The World War II Landscape of Townsville, Queensland," *Bulletin of the Australasian Institute for Maritime Archaeology* 30 (2006): 77.
16. "U.S. Senators in Queensland," *Barrier Daily Truth* (Broken Hill, New South Wales, Australia), September 11, 1943, 1.
17. Garrett et al., "World War II Landscape of Townsville," 80.
18. Kaye, "Great 'Goz,'" pt. 3, 82.
19. Department of the Army, *Army Battle Casualties and Nonbattle Deaths in World War II* (Washington, DC: Office of the Comptroller of the Army, 1946), https://apps.dtic.mil/sti/pdfs/ADA438106.pdf.
20. McCartney, "Swing King Artie Shaw Arrives to Play for Troops," 9.
21. Lester Lee and Frank Manners, "Pennsylvania Polka" (New York: Shapiro, Bernstein, 1942).


## Notes for Chapter 18


1.  Kaminsky, *My Life in Jazz*, 180.
2.  Kaye, "Dave Tough," 90.
3.  "Death of Sammy Lee," *Canberra Times*, July 23, 1975, 3.
4.  "Sammy Lee on Baccarat," *Daily Telegraph* (Sydney), July 4, 1952, 5.

5. Gerard Oakes, "Samuel (Sammy) Lee (1912–1975)," *Australian Dictionary of Biography*, accessed October 6, 2024, https://adb.anu.edu.au/biography/lee-samuel-sammy-10805.

6. Kaminsky, *My Life in Jazz*, 179.

7. "Artie Shaw Is Not Coming to Perth?" *Sunday Times* (Perth), October 10, 1943, 11.

8. "Shaw and Clarinet Stop Dance," *Sydney Sun*, October 3, 1943, 3.

9. "Artie Shaw in Sydney," *Sydney Morning Herald*, October 2, 1943, 11.

10. Peter A. Thompson and Robert Macklin, *The Battle of Brisbane: America and Australia at War* (Brisbane: ABC Books, 2000).

11. "Gave Swing But No Autographs," *Sydney Daily Telegraph*, October 4, 1943, 8.

12. "Terpsichorean Artie," *Sydney Sun*, October 4, 1943.

13. "Colored Idea, a Popular One," *Melbourne Herald*, February 21, 1928, 13.

14. Chris Dixon, *African Americans and the Pacific War, 1941 to 1945: Race, Nationality, and the Fight for Freedom* (Cambridge: Cambridge University Press, 2018), 41.

15. Kay Saunders and Helen Taylor, "The Reception of Black American Servicemen in Australia during World War II: The Resilience of 'White Australia,'" *Journal of Black Studies* 25, no. 3 (January 1995): 343.

16. Dixon, *African Americans in the Pacific War*, 155.

17. "Band Leader 'Muzzy' in the Head," *Sydney Daily Telegraph*, October 1, 1943, 7.

18. Kaminsky, *My Life in Jazz*, 182.

19. Kaye, "Dave Tough," 91.

20. Shaw, "A Nice Little Post-War Business," in *Best of Intentions*, 29.

21. Application for Adjusted Compensation, Gerstle Navy Personnel File, NPRC.

22. *U.S. Naval Medical Bulletin*, January 1945, 895.

23. "Dr. Gerstle Is Sued by Wife, Alimony Asked," *San Francisco Examiner*, July 29, 1930, 3.

24. "Wealthy S.F. Psychiatrist Sues for Divorce," *Oakland Tribune*, July 30, 1937, 1.

25. Mark Gerstle, *The Doctor Answers Your Questions* (San Francisco: J. W. Stacey, 1929).

26. Mark Gerstle Jr., Robert Lowell Wagner, and Townsend Lodge, "The Inapt Naval Recruit," *U.S. Naval Medical Bulletin*, no. 41 (January 1943): 488.

27. Gerstle, Wagner, and Lodge, "Inapt Naval Recruit," 490.

28. "From Mark Gerstle, Jr., Lt. Cmdr., MC, U.S.N.R.," *California and Western Medicine* 58, no. 4 (April 1943): 241.

29. Statement of Mark L. Gerstle Jr., Shaw medical file.

30. Shaw, *Trouble with Cinderella*, 265.

31. Nolan, *Artie Shaw*, 181.

32. Taylor, "Middle-Aged Man without a Horn," 92.

33. Kaye, "Dave Tough," 70.

34. Shaw, interview with Talbot.

35. "Artie Shaw's Testimony before the House Un-American Activities Committee," May 4, 1953, *Swing and Beyond*, https://swingandbeyond. com/wp-content/uploads/2020/05/Shaw-testimony.pdf.

36. Kaye, "Dave Tough," 92.

37. Kaye, "Dave Tough," 93.

38. Bell, *Australian Jazzman*, 50.

39. "Roy Goedeke Oral History," October 23, 2007, National Museum of the Pacific War / Admiral Nimitz Foundation, *Portal to Texas History*, https://texashistory.unt.edu/ark:/67531/metapth1609112/?q= Goedeke.

40. Kaminsky, *My Life in Jazz*, 181.

41. *Capitol News from Hollywood*, February 1944.

## Notes for Chapter 19

1. "Deaths in the News," *Orlando Evening Star*, September 27, 1963, 9.

2. Medical History, November 18, 1943, Shaw medical file.

3. Medical History, November 18, 1943, Shaw medical file.

4. Dave Dexter, "Dave Dexter's Surface Noise," *Capitol News from Hollywood*, January 1944, 2.

5. "Amazing Saga of Shaw Band!," *DownBeat*, December 15, 1943, 1.

6. "Amazing Saga of Shaw Band!," 1.

7. "Beat Editors Eat the Word 'Amazing,'" *DownBeat*, April 15, 1944, 10.

8. "Beat Editors Eat the Word 'Amazing,'" 10.

9. "Beat Editors Eat the Word 'Amazing,'" 10.

10. Mike Daniels, "Musician of the Year," *Metronome*, January 1944, 20.

11. Daniels, "Musician of the Year," 18.

12. Daniels, "Musician of the Year," 20.

13. Daniels, "Musician of the Year," 20.

14. *International Jazz Journal*, November 1987.

15. "Sidekick Hinted Rehearsing Ork for Artie Shaw," *DownBeat*, March 1, 1943, 1.

16. Davis, *Artie Shaw*, part 4.

17. Medical History, Lt. Cmdr. T. P. Richards, December 28, 1943, Shaw medical file.

18. Department of the Navy, *Environmental Impact Statement: The Disposal and Reuse of Naval Medical Center Oakland* (Oakland: US Department of the Navy, December 1996), I-5.

19. "Senator Hart's Son Dies on West Coast," *Meriden* (CT) *Monitor*, June 18, 1945, 7.

20. "Mrs. Roosevelt Visits Oak Knoll Hospital," *Oakland Post Enquirer*, April 7, 1943, 1.

21. Shaw, *Trouble with Cinderella*, 373.

22. Medical History, T. P. Rogers, December 28, 1943, Shaw medical file.

23. Nolan, *Artie Shaw*, 183.

24. Report of Medical Survey, January 17, 1944, Shaw medical file.

25. "Artie Shaw's Testimony before the House Un-American Activities Committee," May 4, 1953, *Swing and Beyond*, https://swingandbeyond. com/wp-content/uploads/2020/05/Shaw-testimony.pdf.

26. Kaminsky, *My Life in Jazz*, 182.

27. Kaminsky, *My Life in Jazz*, 195.

28. Kaye, "Dave Tough," 96.

## Notes for Chapter 20

1. "Composer's Daughter Divorces Artie Shaw," *Los Angeles Times*, September 29, 1944, 6.

2. "4th Sheds Artie Shaw," *New York Daily News*, September 29, 1944.

3. "Lucille Ball Sues Sgt. Desi Arnaz for Divorce," *Los Angeles Times*, September 8, 1944, 13

4. "Complaint for Divorce," Shaw vs. Shaw, Case D265250, August 22, 1944, Los Angeles Superior Court.

5. Declaration, Swarts and Tannenbaum, September 8, 1944, Shaw vs. Shaw, Los Angeles County Superior Court.

6. "Artie Shaw Divorced," *Daily Variety*, September 29, 1944, 8.

7. Joyce Wadler, "Bold Face Names: Artie Shaw, without Music," *New York Times*, January 5, 2005, B-2.

8. Barry Ulanov, "Shaw in '44," *Metronome*, September 1944, 18.

9. "Shaw Band Stringless," *Metronome*, September 1944, 9.

10. "Artie Shaw Having Difficulty Rounding Up Sidemen for New Band," *Variety*, November 1, 1944, 35.

11. Quoted in Simosko, *Artie Shaw*, 107.

12. "Tale of 'Dying Duck'; Artie Shaw Pops Off Again," *Daily Variety*, February 25, 1945, 1.
13. Lee Server, *Ava Gardner: Love Is Nothing* (New York: St. Martin's Press, 2006), 102.
14. "Artie Shaw Weds Actress at Home of Judge Mosk," *Los Angeles Times*, October 18, 1943, 13.

## Notes for Chapter 21

1. "Shaw, Band Split, Donahue New Boss," *Metronome*, February 1944, 7.
2. Best, oral history interview with Rowe.
3. Wray, *Big Bands go to War*, 163.
4. Craig L. Symonds, "The Unloved, Unlovely, Yet Indispensable LST," *Navy Times*, June 6, 2019.
5. Richard Vacca, "Tak Takvorian Part 1: Navy Trombonist," Richard Vacca.com, January 26, 2020, https://www.richardvacca.com/tak-takvorian-part-1-navy-trombonist.
6. "Donahue Band Found GIs Were Jive-Hungry," *DownBeat*, June 1, 1945, 1.
7. "Importance of Music to Life Discussed at Los Angeles Institute," *Pittsburgh Press*, September 10, 1944, 27.
8. FBI memo, December 15, 1948, 100-HQ-355889, Serial 1, NACP.
9. "Forgotten Jazz Orchestras: Sam Donahue's Navy Band," *Art Music Lounge*, July 17, 2017, https://artmusiclounge.wordpress.com/2017/07/17/forgotten-jazz-orchestras-sam-donahues-navy-band/.
10. Don Gold, "Everything Is Jake: With Studio Man Don Jacoby," *DownBeat*, January 23, 1958, 12.
11. Spragg, *Glenn Miller Declassified*, 54.
12. David Bittan, "Miller over There," *Metronome*, September 1944, 27.
13. Spragg, *Glenn Miller Declassified*, 130.
14. David Bittan, "Hot Navy," *Metronome*, March 1945, 17.
15. Quoted in Wray, *Big Bands at War*, 67.
16. Quoted in Wray, *Big Bands at War*, 67.
17. Johnny Gunn, "'Big Band Is Not Dead but One-Nighters Are Changed' – Sam Donahue," *Nevada State Journal* (Reno), April 23, 1971, 42.
18. Quoted in Wray, *Big Bands at War*, 68.
19. Wray, *Big Bands at War*, 68.
20. Spragg, *Glenn Miller Declassified*, 131.
21. Vache, "Best on the Bandstand," *Mississippi Rag*, February 1989, 44.
22. Spragg, *Glenn Miller Declassified*, 1.
23. Spragg, *Glenn Miller Declassified*, 284.

24. Shaw, interview with Talbot.

25. Charles Garrod and Bill Korst, *Sam Donahue and His Orchestra* (Zephyrhills, FL: Joyce Record Club, 1992), 3.

26. Wray, *Big Bands at War*, 67.

27. "Donahue Builds New Service Band," *DownBeat*, November 1, 1945, 7.

28. "Donahue Band Found GIs Were Jive Hungry," *DownBeat*, June 1, 1945. 1.

29. Commanding Officer, Service Force Administration, First Endorsement, 24 July 1944, Thornhill personnel file.

30. Commander service force to chief of naval personnel, July 27, 1943, Thornhill personnel file.

31. Chief of naval personnel to commander service force, Pacific Fleet, August 26, 1944, Thornhill personnel file.

32. Cmdr. H. H. Henderson, Memo, February 11, 1944, Thornhill personnel file.

33. "Lei Day Dance," *Honolulu Star-Bulletin*, April 26, 1944, 2.

34. "In the Same Boat," *Variety*, May 30, 1945, 41.

35. "Thornhill Lays Plans for Post-War Band," *DownBeat*, February 15, 1945, 15.

36. Dick Murray, "3 Decades: Earle Parchman's Talent on Local Display Since '33," *Lansing* (MI) *State Journal*, May 13, 1967, B-2.

37. Commander service squadron ten, memo, June 2, 1944, Thornhill personnel file.

38. Samuel Eliot Morrison, *Aleutians, Gilberts and Marshalls, June 1942–April 1944*, vol 7. of *History of United States Naval Operations in World War II* (Annapolis: Naval Institute Press, 2011), 228.

39. Morrison, *Aleutians, Gilberts and Marshalls*, 250.

40. Commander, US Naval Repair Base to Claude Thornhill, September 19, 1944, Thornhill personnel file.

41. "Jack Benny's Stooge in Navy," *Boston Globe*, March 24, 1944, 13.

42. Jackie Cooper with Dick Kleiner, *Please Don't Shoot My Dog: The Autobiography of Jackie Cooper* (New York: Berkley Books, 1982), 147.

43. "Thornhill Lays Plans for New Post-War Band," *DownBeat*, February 15, 1945, 15.

44. Harry J. Lambeth, "Thornhill Dreams of Writing Music in Confines of Little Grass Shack," *Honolulu Star-Bulletin*, December 2, 1944, 1.

45. Brig. Gen. Ogden Ross to commander, US Service Force, Pacific Fleet, February 15, 1945, Thornhill personnel file.

46. Cooper, *Please Don't Shoot My Dog*, 151.

47. Ian Crosbie, "Claude Thornhill," *Coda*, October 1975, 8.

48. Memo, Headquarters Island Command, May 23, 1945, Thornhill personnel file.

49. "Thornhill Impresses," *DownBeat*, June 1, 1945, 10.

50. Atoll Commander Tarawa to Commander Service Force, March 5, 1945, Thornhill personnel file.

51. Cooper, *Please Don't Shoot My Dog*, 148.

52. Ward, *Any Rags, Any Jazz, any Boppers Today?*, 208.

53. "Thornhill Lays Plans for New Post-War Band," 15.

54. Report of medical survey, September 18, 1945, Thornhill personnel file.

55. Noble Johnson to Navy Bureau of Enlisted Personnel, September 4, 1945, Thornhill personnel file.

## Notes for Chapter 22

1. Woody Herman and Stuart Troup, *The Woodchoppers Ball: The Autobiography of Woody Herman* (New York: Limelight Editions, 1994), 48.

2. Wild Bill Davison, "Wild Bill Calls Tough 'Little Bludgeon Foot,' Defends Old Jazzmen, *DownBeat*, March 26, 1947, 11.

3. "Chicago Band Briefs," *DownBeat*, March 24, 1948, 4.

4. Harold S. Kaye, "The Death of Dave Tough: A Tragedy of Errors," unpublished manuscript, 6, Harold S. Kaye Collection.

5. Kaye, "Death of Dave Tough," 5.

6. "Dave Tough, Drummer, Dies of Fractured Skull," *Evansville* (IN) *Press*, December 11, 1948, 12.

7. "Man Killed in Fall in Street Identified as Noted Drummer," *Washington Evening Star*, December 13, 1948, 3.

8. HanksJazz, "The History of Jazz Drums, episode 10: Dave Tough & Sid Catlett," 1989, https://www.youtube.com/watch?v=mo4sr9pJdxM.

9. Kaminsky, *My Life in Jazz*, 229.

10. Baker, "Gentleman of Jazz," 193.

11. Kaminsky, *My Life in Jazz*, 288.

12. "Claude Thornhill: Band of Year?" *DownBeat*, October 21, 1946. 2.

13. Whitney Balliett, "Jazz: Claude Thornhill," *New Yorker*, April 18, 1988, 125.

14. "Band Tops in Nation," *Kansas City Star*, July 2, 1965, 9.

15. Balliett, "Bright Unison Clarinets," 480.

16. Leonard Feather, "Sam Donahue and the Pursuit of Nostalgia," *DownBeat*, January 16, 1964, 5.

17. "Donahue's Life Touched Many," *Nevada State Journal*, March 28, 1974, 4.

18. Richard Vacca, "Tak Takvorian Part 1: Navy Trombonist," RichardVacca.com, January 26, 2020, https://www.richardvacca.com/tak-takvorian-part-1-navy-trombonist.

19. "H'wood Showfolk Prep Nov. 8 Benefit for Vet Tooter Gozzo's Widow," *Variety*, October 28, 1964, 43.

20. Leslie Gerber, "Barney Spieler, The Falstaffian Bassist," LeslieGerber.net, May 2012, http://www.lesliegerber.net/2012/05/barney-spieler-the-falstaffian-bassist/.

21. Best, oral history interview with Rowe.

22. Jack Williams, "Johnny Best, 89, Among Greatest Big Band Trumpeters," *San Diego Union Tribune*, September 28, 2003, B-6.

23. "Outdoor Shows," *Los Angeles Times*, June 19, 1984, 62.

24. "Nitery Reviews," *Variety*, March 25, 1968, 14.

25. Patti Page with Skip Press, *This Is My Song: A Memoir* (Bath, NH: Kathdan Books, 2009), 216.

26. "Requiem: Mack Pierce Pitt," Allegro 102, no. 6 (June 2002), https://www.local802afm.org/allegro/articles/requiem-9/.

27. "Bruce Warren to Far East," *Sutherland* (IA) *Courier*, November 12, 1965, 1.

28. "DU Band Starts Far East Tour," *Fort Collins Coloradan*, January 3, 1965, 4.

29. Claire Martin, "Musician, Jazz-band Leader Harris," *Denver Post*, May 26, 2005.

30. Martin, "Musician, Jazz-band Leader Harris."

31. "Sinatra Weds Ava as Police Bar Reporters," *Chicago Daily Tribune*, November 8, 1951, F-2.

32. "The Hot Box," *DownBeat*, July 7, 1960, 44.

33. "The Harold Wax Memorial Fund," *Sweet Relief Musicians Fund*, accessed October 11, 2024, https://www.sweetrelief.org/the-harold-wax-memorial-fund.html.

## Notes for Epilogue

1. Shaw, interview with Talbot.

2. Report of medical survey, January 17, 1943, Shaw medical file.

3. Robert C. Ruark, "How's Your Neuroses? Maybe You Need a Personality Checkup," *El Paso Herald-Post*, May 8, 1946, 5.

4. Ray Coll Jr., "No One Should Retire, Psychiatrist Declares," *Honolulu Advertiser*, August 18, 1948, 4.

5. Irene Mayer Selznick, *A Private View* (New York: Alfred A. Knopf, 1983).

6. Hedda Hopper, "Hedda's Hollywood," *Passaic* (NJ) *Herald News*, April 7, 1945, 13.

7. "Dr. May E. Romm, Pioneer in the Field of Psychiatry," *New York Times*, October 19, 1977, B-2.

8.  Shaw, *Trouble with Cinderella*, 374.

9.  Report of medical survey, January 17, 1944, Shaw medical file.

10.  General Amusement Corp., undated, Artie Shaw clipping file, Institute of Jazz Studies.

11.  "Artie Shaw's Testimony before the House Un-American Activities Committee," May 4, 1953, *Swing and Beyond*, https://swingandbeyond.com/wp-content/uploads/2020/05/Shaw-testimony.pdf.

12.  Michael Zirpolo, "'Innuendo' (1949) Artie Shaw and Johnny Mandel," *Swing & Beyond*, May 14, 2020, https://swingandbeyond.com/2020/05/14/innuendo-1949-artie-shaw-and-johnny-mandel/.

13.  "Artie Shaw Will Retire Again to Take It Easy," *DownBeat*, November 15, 1945, 1.

14.  "Artie Shaw's Wife Tells of Rages at Refusal to Join Communism," *Bridgeport Post*, August 10, 1948, 1.

15.  Leonard Lyons, "The Lyons Den," *Buffalo News*, October 3, 1957, 31.

16.  Simosko, *Artie Shaw*, 117.

17.  Harrison, "Swing Era Big Bands," 286.

18.  Shaw, "Nice Little Post-War Business," 30.

19.  "My Life in Jazz by Max Kaminsky," *New Yorker*, August 10, 1963, 91.

20.  Quoted in Simisko, *Artie Shaw*, 133.

21.  Nolan, *Artie Shaw*, 290.

22.  "He Thinks of the Craziest Things," *Sydney Daily Telegraph*, November 7, 1954, 15.

23.  Michael Sturma, "Lee Lazar Gordon (1923–1963)," *Australian Dictionary of Biography*, https://adb.anu.edu.au/biography/gordon-lee-lazer-10332.

24.  "Big Money for 'Big Names': The U.S. Star Invasion," *Sydney Morning Herald*, September 28, 1954, 2.

25.  "Much Married Artie Shaw Is Charming but Brusque, *Australian Women's Weekly*, July 28, 1954, 18.

26.  J. H. Adams, "The Artie Mr. Shaw," *Sydney Sun*, July 22, 1954, 9.

27.  "Stop the Music, Said Artie Shaw," *Melbourne Argus*, July 24, 1954, 3.

28.  Charles Buttrose, "Artie Shaw: Philosopher of the Clarinet," *Daily Telegraph* (Sydney), July 24, 1954, 19.

29.  "Artie Says His Music Now Is Just a Living," *Brisbane Courier-Mail*, July 30, 1954, 3.

30.  "U.S. Show Man 'All Het Up,'" *Sydney Daily Mirror*, August 4, 1954, 16.

31.  "Artie Shaw Misses Aircraft," *Perth Daily News*, August 3, 1954, 2.

32.  "Artie Shaw: Bandstand to Benchrest," *Guns*, February 1964, 23.

# Bibliography

## Newspapers and Periodicals


*ABC Weekly*
*All Hands*
*Armidale Express*
*Ashburton* (NZ) *Guardian*
*Atlanta Constitution*
*Atlanta Journal*
*Auckland Star*
*Australian Women's Weekly*
*Baltimore Sun*
*Banner* (Honolulu)
*Barrier Daily Truth* (Broken Hill, New South Wales, Australia)
*Bay of Plenty Beacon* (Whakatane, NZ)
*Bay of Plenty Times* (NZ)
*The Billboard*
*The Black Dispatch*
*Bridgeport Post*
*Brisbane Courier-Mail*
*Brisbane Telegraph*
*Brooklyn Daily Eagle*
*Buffalo Courier Express*
*Buffalo Evening News*
*Buffalo News*
*Burlington* (VT) *Daily News*
*California and Western Medical News*
*Canberra Times*
*Capitol News from Hollywood*
*Cedar Rapids Gazette*
*Charlotte Observer*
*Chicago Daily Tribune*
*Chicago Defender*
*Cincinnati Enquirer*
*Cincinnati Post*

*Cleveland Plain Dealer*
*Coda*
*Corpus Christi Caller-Times*
*Courier Mail* (Brisbane, Australia)
*Daily Sun*
*Daily Telegraph* (Sydney)
*Denver Post*
*Desert Sun* (Palm Springs, CA)
*Des Moines Register*
*Detroit Evening Times*
*Detroit Free Press*
*Dominion* (Wellington)
*DownBeat*
*El Paso Herald-Post*
*Enid* (OK) *Daily Eaglet*
*The Enquirer*
*Evansville* (IN) *Press*
*Fort Collins Coloradan*
*Greenville* (SC) *News*
*Harrisburg* (PA) *Telegraph*
*Hartford Courant*
*Hawkes Bay Today* (Hastings, NZ)
*Hilo* (HI) *Tribune-Herald*
*Honolulu Advertiser*
*Honolulu Star-Advertiser*
*Honolulu Star-Bulletin*
*Hopewell* (VA) *News*
*The Independent*
*Indianapolis Star*
*Jazz Journal International*
*Jazzletter*
*Lansing* (MI) *State Journal*
*LA Weekly*
*Leatherneck*
*Los Angeles Times*
*Mamaroneck* (NY) *Daily Times*
*Manawatu* (NZ) *Times*
*Melbourne Argus*
*Melbourne Herald*
*Melody Maker*

*Meriden* (CT) *Monitor*
*Metronome*
*Minneapolis Sunday Tribune*
*Mississippi Rag*
*Moline* (IL) *Dispatch*
*Montgomery* (AL) *Advertiser*
*Music Educators Journal*
*Music and Rhythm*
*Navy Times*
*Nevada State Journal* (Reno)
*New York Daily News*
*New York Herald Tribune*
*New York Post*
*New York Times*
*New Yorker*
*New Zealand Herald* (Auckland)
*Northern Advocate* (Whangārei, NZ)
*Oakland Post Enquirer*
*Oakland Tribune*
*Ogden* (UT) *Standard-Examiner*
*Orlando Evening Star*
*Our Navy*
*Pasadena* (CA) *Post*
*Passaic* (NJ) *Herald News*
*Pearl Harbor Bulletin*
*Perth Daily News*
*Philadelphia Inquirer*
*Pittsburgh Press*
*Pittsburgh Sun-Telegraph*
*Pix*
*Radio and Television Mirror*
*Sacramento Bee*
*San Francisco Chronicle*
*San Francisco Examiner*
*Santa Fe New Mexican*
*Santa Rosa* (CA) *Press Democrat*
*South Bend Tribune*
*Southern Culture*
*Southern Economist*
*Stars and Stripes*

*St. Louis Globe-Democrat*
*Sunday Times* (Perth)
*Sutherland* (IA) *Courier*
*Sydney Daily Telegraph*
*Sydney Morning Herald*
*Sydney Sun*
*Sutherland Courier*
*Tweed Daily*
*Variety*
*Vermont Standard* (Woodstock)
*Waikato* (NZ) *Times*
*Wall Street Journal*
*Warwick Daily News* (Australia)
*Washington* (DC) *Evening Star*
*Wellington Evening Post*
*Wireless Weekly*

## Archives and Collections

American Music Research Center, University of Colorado, Boulder.
    Glenn Miller Collections
Hanna Holborn Gray Special Collections Research Center. University of
    Chicago Library, Chicago, IL.
Harold S. Kaye Collection.
Library of Congress, Washington, DC.
    Performing Arts Reading Room
    William P. Gottlieb Collection
Marine Corps Archives, Quantico, VA
National Archives at College Park, College Park, MD.
National Personnel Records Center, St. Louis, MO.
Naval School of Music Library, Virginia Beach, VA.
Princeton University Library, Princeton, NJ.
    Department of Special Collections
Rutgers University Library, New Brunswick, NJ.
    Institute of Jazz Studies

## Other Sources

Albion, Robert Greenleigh, and Robert Howe Connery. *Forrestal and the
    Navy*. New York: Columbia University Press, 1962.

Army Information Branch. *Pocket Guide to New Caledonia*. Washington, DC: War and Navy Departments, 1944.

Baker, Fats. "Gentleman of Jazz." In Hodes and Hansen, *Selections from the Gutter*, 190–92.

Balliett, Whitney. *American Musicians: 56 Portraits in Jazz*. New York: Oxford University Press, 1986.

Balliett, Whitney. "Bright Unison Clarinets." In *American Musicians II: Seventy-One Portraits in Jazz*. Jackson: University Press of Mississippi, 1986.

Barnard, Loretta. "The Trocadero: A Glimpse into the Glamor of a Bygone Time." *Australia Explained*. April 20, 2020. https://australia-explained. com.au/music/the-trocadero-a-glimpse-into-the-glamour-of-a-bygone-time.

Bell, Graeme. *Australian Jazzman*. Sydney: Child & Associates, 1989.

Berman, Brigitte, dir. *Artie Shaw: Time Is All You've Got*. Canada: Bridge Film Productions, 1985.

Bindas, Kenneth J. *Swing, That Modern Sound*. Jackson: University Press of Mississippi, 2001.

Bioletti, Harry. *The Yanks Are Coming: The American Invasion of New Zealand, 1942–1944*. Auckland: Random House New Zealand, 1989.

Bourke, Chris. *Blue Smoke: The Lost Dawn of New Zealand Music, 1918–1964*. Auckland: Auckland University Press, 2010.

Bronson, Howard C. "Wartime Music Services." *Music Educators Journal* 29, no. 1 (Sept.–Oct. 1942): 45, 56–57.

Bruce, Lenny. *How to Talk Dirty and Influence People*. Chicago: Playboy Press, 1963.

*Building the Navy's Bases in World War II*. Vol. 2, *History of the Bureau of Yards and Docks and Civil Engineering Corps, 1940–46*. Washington, DC: United States Government Printing Office, 1947.

Burgess, Roy A., ed. *63rd Naval Construction Battalion Cruise Book*. New York: Robert W. Kelly Publishing, n.d.

Cahn, Sammy. *I Should Care: The Sammy Cahn Story*. New York: Arbor House, 1974.

Condon-Rall, Mary Ellen, and Albert E. Cowdry. *The Medical Department: Medical Service in the War against Japan*. Washington, DC: Center of Military History, 1998.

Cooper, Jackie, with Dick Kleiner. *Please Don't Shoot My Dog: The Autobiography of Jackie Cooper*. New York: Berkley Books, 1982.

Cooper, Page. *Navy Nurse*. New York: McGraw-Hill, 1946.

Davies, Russell, writer. *Artie Shaw: The Quest for Perfection*. UK: BBC, 2003.

Department of the Army. *Army Battle Casualties and Nonbattle Deaths in World War II*. Washington, DC: Office of the Comptroller of the Army, 1946.

Department of the Navy. *Building the Navy's Bases in World War II: History of the Bureau of Yards and Docks and Civil Engineering Corps, 1940–46*. Washington, DC: Government Printing Office, 1947.

Department of the Navy. *Environmental Impact Statement: The Disposal and Reuse of Naval Medical Center Oakland*. Oakland: US Department of the Navy, December 1996.

Dixon, Chris. *African Americans and the Pacific War, 1941 to 1945: Race, Nationality, and the Fight for Freedom*. Cambridge: Cambridge University Press, 2018.

Doyle, William. *PT 109: An American Epic of War, Survival, and the Destiny of John F. Kennedy*. New York: William Morrow, 2015.

Dye, Bob, ed. *Hawai'i Chronicles III: World War Two in Hawai'i, from the pages of* Paradise of the Pacific. Honolulu: University of Hawai'i Press, 2000.

Fauser, Annegret. *Sounds of War: Music in the United States During World War II*. Oxford: Oxford University Press, 2013.

Firestone, Ross. *Swing, Swing, Swing: The Life & Times of Benny Goodman*. New York: W. W. Norton, 1993.

Garrett, Bradley L., Erika Stein, Nikolas Bigourdan, and Bill Jeffery. "The World War II Landscape of Townsville, Queenland." *Bulletin of the Australasian Institute of Archaeology* 30 (2006): 76–84.

Garrod, Charles, and Bill Korst. *Sam Donahue and His Orchestra*. Zephyrhills, FL: Joyce Record Club, 1992.

Gerstle, Mark. *The Doctor Answers Your Questions*. San Francisco: J. W. Stacey, 1929.

Gerstle, Mark. "From Mark Gerstle, Jr., Lt. Cmdr., MC, U.S.N.R.." *California and Western Medicine* 58, no. 4 (April 1943): 241.

Gerstle, Mark, Robert Lowell Wagner, and Townsend Lodge. "The Inapt Naval Recruit." *U.S. Naval Medical Bulletin*, no. 41 (January 1943), 480–92.

Harrison, Max. "Swing Era Big Bands and Jazz Composing and Arranging." In Kirchner, *Oxford Companion to Jazz*, 277–91.

Hatcher, Charles. "Recreational Development at Pearl Harbor." *US Naval Institute Proceedings* 69, no. 488 (October 1943): 1348–58.

Herman, Woody, and Stuart Troup. *The Woodchopper's Ball: The Autobiography of Woody Herman*. New York: Limelight Editions, 1994.

Hodes, Art, and Chadwick Hanson, eds. *Selections from the Gutter: Jazz Portraits from The Jazz Record*. Berkeley: University of California Press, 1977.

Hoffman, Jon T. *Silk Chutes and Hard Fighting: U.S. Marine Corps Parachute Units in World War II*. Washington, DC: History and Museums Division, US Marine Corps, 1999.

Huggard, Dennis O. "Artie Shaw in New Zealand, 1943." *New Zealand Series*, no. 15. Auckland: self-published, 2007.

Jones, Patrick Michael. "A History of the Armed Forces School of Music." PhD diss., Pennsylvania State University, 1992.

Kaminsky, Max. *My Life in Jazz*. Boston: Da Capo Press, 1981.

Kaye, Harold S. "Dave Tough with the Artie Shaw Navy Band in World War II." In *Storyville, 2000–2001*, edited by Laurie Wright, 12–105. Chigwell, Essex, England: L. Wright, 2001. https://nationaljazzarchive.org.uk/explore/journals/storyville/storyville-2000-2001/1265035?q=jazz%20news.

Kaye, Harold S. "The Great 'Goz': The Conrad Gozzo Story." Pts. 1–5. *International Association of Jazz Collectors Journal* 25, no 2 (Spring 1992): 1–5; 25, no. 3 (Summer 1992): 14–20; 25, no. 4 (Fall 1992): 76–83; 26, no. 1 (Winter 1993): 29–36; 26, no. 2 (Spring 1993): 54–62.

Kirchner, Bill, ed. *The Oxford Companion to Jazz*. Oxford: Oxford University Press, 2005.

Korall, Burt. "Jazz Drumming." In Kirchner, *Oxford Companion to Jazz*, 681–95.

Leckie, Robert. *A Helmet for My Pillow*. New York: Random House, 1957.

Lee, Lester, and Frank Manners. "Pennsylvania Polka." New York: Shapiro, Bernstein, 1942.

Leff, Leonard J. *Hitchcock and Selznick: The Rich and Strange Collaboration of Alfred Hitchcock and David O. Selznick in Hollywood*. Berkeley: University of California Press, 1987.

Levinson, Peter J. *Tommy Dorsey: Livin' in a Great Big Way*. Boston: Da Capo Press, 2005.

Lindstrom, Lamont. "The Vanuatu Labor Corps Experience." Chapter 5 in *The Pacific Theater: Island Representations of World War II*, ed. Geoffrey M. White and Lamont Lindstrom. Honolulu: University of Hawaii Press, 1989.

McCuen, Joseph Molina. *A History of Bands in the United States Navy*. Master's thesis, University of Maryland, 1967.

Michener, James. *Tales of the South Pacific*. New York: Random House, 1947.

Morrison, Samuel Eliot. *Aleutians, Gilberts and Marshalls, June 1942–April 1944*. Vol. 7 of *History of United States Naval Operations in World War II*. Annapolis: Naval Institute Press, 2011.

Morrison, Samuel Eliot. *The Struggle for Guadalcanal, August 1942–February 1943*. Vol. 5 of *History of United States Naval Operations in World War II*. Boston: Little, Brown, 1950.

Mulvey, Deb, Clancy Strock, and Mike Beno, eds. *We Pulled Together—and Won!* Greendale, WI: Reminisce Books, 1993.

Munholland, Kim. "Yankee Farewell: The Americans Leave New Caledonia, 1945." *Proceedings of the Meeting of the French Colonial Historical Society*, vol. 16 (1992): 181–94.

Nolan, Tom. *Artie Shaw, King of the Clarinet: His Life and Times*. New York: W. W. Norton, 2010.

Office of the Chief Engineer, General Headquarters, Army Forces Pacific. *Engineers of the Southwest Pacific: Airfield and Base Development*. Washington, DC: Government Printing Office, 1951.

Page, Patti, with Skip Press. *This Is My Song: A Memoir*. Bath, NH: Kathdan Books, 2009.

Raichelson, Dick. "Artie Shaw & His Orchestra, Part 5: Dr. Ian Crosbie's Sidemen Correspondence." *IAJRC Journal* 49, no. 2 (Summer 2016): 67–70.

Rexroth, Kenneth. *Kenneth Rexroth: An Autobiographical Novel*. New York: Doubleday, 1966.

Rohfleisch, Kramer J. "The Thirteenth Air Force." In *The Army Air Forces in World War II*, vol. 4, *The Pacific: Guadalcanal to Saipan, August 1942 to July 1944*, ed. W. P. Craven and J. L. Cate, 61–91. Chicago: University of Chicago Press, 1951.

Saunders, Kay, and Helen Taylor. "The Reception of Black American Servicemen in Australia during World War II: The Resilience of 'White Australia.'" *Journal of Black Studies* 25, no. 3 (January 1995): 331–48.

Scheer-Hennings, Reinhard, and Dennis Spragg. *Artie Shaw, 1938–1939*. Boulder: University of Colorado American Music Research Center, 2022. https://www.dennismspragg.com/wp-content/uploads/2022/05/Artie-Shaw-1938-1939.pdf.

Scheer-Hennings, Reinhard, and Dennis Spragg. *Artie Shaw: January 1940 to March 1941*. Boulder: University of Colorado American Music

Research Center, 2022. https://www.dennismspragg.com/wp-content/uploads/2022/05/Artie-Shaw-1940-1941.pdf.

Scheer-Hennings, Reinhard, and Dennis Spragg. *Artie Shaw: June 1941 to January 1942*. Boulder: University of Colorado American Music Research Center, 2022. https://www.dennismspragg.com/wp-content/uploads/2022/05/Artie-Shaw-1941-1942.pdf.

Schoenberg, Loren. *The NPR Curious Listener's Guide to Jazz*. New York: Grand Central Press, 2002.

Schuller, Gunther. *The Swing Era: The Development of Jazz, 1930–1945*. Oxford: Oxford University Press, 1989.

Selznick, Irene Mayer. *A Private View*. New York: Alfred A. Knopf, 1983.

Server, Lee. *Ava Gardner: Love Is Nothing*. New York: St. Martin's Press, 2006.

Shaw, Artie. *The Best of Intentions and Other Stories*. Santa Barbara, CA: John Daniel, 1989.

Shaw, Artie. Interview with Bruce Talbot. *Smithsonian Jazz Masters*, October 7–8, 1992. https://www.si.edu/media/NMAH/NMAH-AC0808_Shaw_Artie_Transcript.pdf.

Shaw, Artie. *The Trouble with Cinderella: An Outline of Identity*. New York: Farrar, Straus and Young, 1952.

Shaw, Jonathan. *Scab Vendor: Confessions of a Tattoo Artist*. Nashville: Turner Publishing, 2017.

Simosko, Vladimir. *Artie Shaw: A Musical Biography and Discography*. London: Rowman and Littlefield, 2000.

Smith, Kathleen E. R. *God Bless America: Tin Pan Alley Goes to War*. Lexington: University Press of Kentucky, 2003.

Smith, Kathleen Ellen Rahtz. "Goodbye Mama, I'm off to Yokohama: The Office of War Information and Tin Pan Alley in World War II." PhD diss., Louisiana State University and Agricultural and Mechanical College, 1996.

Special Service Division, Services of Supply, United States Army. *Pocket Guide to New Caledonia*. Washington, DC: War and Navy Departments, 1944.

Spragg, Dennis M. *Glenn Miller Declassified*. Lincoln: Potomac Books, an imprint of the University of Nebraska Press, 2017.

Stowe, David. W. *Swing Changes: Big-Band Jazz in New Deal America*. Cambridge, MA: Harvard University Press, 1994.

Taylor, Nancy M. *The New Zealand People at War: The Home Front*. Vol. 1, *Official History of New Zealand in the Second World War, 1939–45*. Wellington, NZ: V. R. Ward, Government Printer, 1989.

Taylor, Robert Lewis. "Middle-Aged Man without a Horn." *New Yorker*, May 11, 1962.

Thompson, Peter A., and Robert Macklin. *The Battle of Brisbane: America and Australia at War*. Brisbane: ABC Books, 2000.

Turner, Lana. *Lana; The Lady, the Legend, the Truth*. New York: Dutton, 1982.

Walker, Leo. *The Big Band Almanac*. New York: Da Capo Press, 1989.

Warburton, John, ed. *Artie Shaw: The Quest for Perfection*. UK: BBC, 2003.

Ward, Aleisha. "Any Rags, Any Jazz, Any Boppers Today? Jazz in New Zealand, 1920–1955." PhD diss., University of Auckland, 2012.

Ward, Aleisha. "Artie Shaw in New Zealand." *Current Research in Jazz* 5 (2013).

Ward, Geoffrey C., and Ken Burns. *Jazz: A History of American Music*. New York: Alfred A Knopf, 2000.

Washburne, Seth. *The Thirsty Thirteenth: The U.A. Army Air Forces 13th Troop Carrier Squadron, 1940–1945*. N.p.: Thirsty Thirteenth, LLC, 2011.

Webb, Davis B., ed. *Sea Foam: 61st Naval Construction Battalion Cruise Book*. Baton Rouge, LA: Army & Navy Pictorial Publishers, 1945.

Womack, Jacob. *Luckey Roberts, Willie "the Lion" Smith, Fats Waller and James P. Johnson: An Analysis of Historical, Cultural and Performance Aspects of Stride Piano from 1910 to 1940*. Doctor of musical arts diss., West Virginia University, 2013.

Wray, Chris. *The Big Bands Go to War*. London: Mainstream, 1991.

Young, William H., and Nancy K. *Music of the World War II Era*. Westport, CT: Greenwood Press, 2008.

Zirpolo, Michael P. "Shavian Matters Revisited." *IAJRC Journal* 43, no. 4 (December 2010): 34–47.

# Index